Political Science, Electoral Rules, *and* Democratic Governance

Report of the Task Force on
Electoral Rules and Democratic Governance

Edited by Mala Htun and G. Bingham Powell, Jr.

SEPTEMBER 2013

AMERICAN POLITICAL SCIENCE ASSOCIATION
1527 New Hampshire Avenue, NW
Washington, DC 20036-1206

I0118614

Task Force on Electoral Rules and Democratic Governance

Task Force Members

Mala Htun, *University of New Mexico, Chair*

G. Bingham Powell, Jr., *University of Rochester*;
President, APSA, 2011–12

John Carey, *Dartmouth College*

Karen E. Ferree, *University of California, San Diego*

Simon Hix, *London School of Economics*

Mona Lena Krook, *Rutgers University*

Robert G. Moser, *University of Texas, Austin*

Shaheen Mozaffar, *Bridgewater State University*

Andrew Rehfeld, *Washington University in St. Louis*

Andrew Reynolds, *University of North Carolina, Chapel Hill*

Ethan Scheiner, *University of California, Davis*

Melissa Schwartzberg, *Columbia University*

Matthew S. Shugart, *University of California, Davis*

Table of Contents

TASK FORCE MEMBERS ii

LIST OF TABLES AND FIGURES v

ACKNOWLEDGEMENTS vi

EXECUTIVE SUMMARY vii

LIST OF ACRONYMS ix

1. BETWEEN SCIENCE AND ENGINEERING: POLITICAL SCIENCE, ELECTORAL
   RULES, AND DEMOCRATIC GOVERNANCE 1
   Mala Htun and G. Bingham Powell, Jr.

2. HOW CONTEXT SHAPES THE EFFECTS OF ELECTORAL RULES 14
   Karen E. Ferree, G. Bingham Powell, Jr., and Ethan Scheiner

3. ELECTORAL RULES AND POLITICAL INCLUSION 31
   Mona Lena Krook and Robert G. Moser

4. WHY BALLOT STRUCTURE MATTERS 38
   Matthew S. Shugart

5. POLICY CONSEQUENCES OF ELECTORAL RULES 46
   John Carey and Simon Hix

6. DESIGNING ELECTORAL SYSTEMS: NORMATIVE TRADEOFFS
   AND INSTITUTIONAL INNOVATIONS 56
   Andrew Rehfeld and Melissa Schwartzberg

7. REPORT FROM THE FIELD: TWO SURVEYS OF POLITICAL SCIENTISTS 62
   John Carey, Simon Hix, Shaheen Mozaffar, and Andrew Reynolds

REFERENCES 74

APPENDIX A: INTERVIEW WITH ANDREW REYNOLDS 84
   Mala Htun and Betsy Super

APPENDIX B: INTERVIEW WITH PIPPA NORRIS 90
    Betsy Super and Mala Htun

APPENDIX C: CASE STUDIES: POLITICAL SCIENTISTS AS ELECTORAL
ENGINEERS 97
    Compiled by Andrew Reynolds

APPENDIX D: GLOSSARY OF ELECTORAL SYSTEMS TERMINOLOGY 105

APPENDIX E: APSA-WIDE SURVEY 113

APPENDIX F: INVITATION LETTER TO CONSULTANTS' SURVEY 117

NOTES 123

List of Tables and Figures

TABLES

Table 4.1: Two Dimensions of Ballot Structure 38

Table 7.1: Relationship between Representational Goals and Evaluation of
Different Electoral Systems 65

FIGURES

2.1: Mechanical, Behavioral, and Contextual Effects 16

2.2: Disproportionality 17

2.3: Number of Electoral Parties 18

2.4: Governance in Parlimentary Systems 23

2.5: Governance in Presidential Systems 24

2.6: Representation—Ideological Congruence of Voters and the Government 27

3.1: Electoral Systems and Descriptive Representation 32

3.2: Context, Electoral Systems, and the Election of Women 34

3.3: Electoral Systems and the Election of Ethnic Minorities 35

4.1: The Differential Effect of District Magnitude on the Intraparty Dimension 41

7.1: Mean Value Assigned to Electoral System Goals 63

7.2: Mean Rating Assigned to Electoral Systems 64

7.3: Year of Consulting Mission (or first year, if multiyear) 67

7.4: Consultant Prior Knowledge of Country 68

7.5: Time Spent in Country 68

7.6: Points of Contact 69

7.7: Content of Consultant's Advice 70

7.8: Consulting Agenda 70

7.9: Relative Weight Given by Local Actors to Various Potential Reform Priorities 71

7.10: Reaction by Political Actors to Consultant's Advice 72

7.11: How Much of Consultant's Advice Implemented? 72

Acknowledgements

Betsy Super, APSA task force liaison, was crucial to the success of this project. Pippa Norris, Bernard Grofman, David Farrell, and Jørgen Elklit offered constructive comments. Ulrike Theuerkauf helped with research assistance, and the Bridgewater State University Center for Legislative Studies provided support. The Committee on the Protection of Human Subjects of Dartmouth College reviewed and approved our survey of APSA members. We are grateful to Michael Brintnall, Jennifer Segal Diascro, Betsy Schroeder, and APSA for administering the survey, supporting our workshop, and publishing this report.

Executive Summary

Electoral rules are one of the important forces that make democracy work. Small variations in them can influence the type of democracy that develops. Political science is essential to the study of why and how this happens: hundreds of political scientists develop and test theories about the consequences of electoral rules and regulations for party systems, representation, governance, and other aspects of democratic politics. In addition, political scientists have worked as electoral system engineers, educating and advising policy makers around the world by authoring reports, delivering presentations at global and regional meetings, traveling on consulting missions, and training democracy promotion officers. By sharing scientific knowledge about the consequences of electoral rules and global trends in electoral reform, political scientists make their work relevant to the world.

The report shows how political scientists have contributed to the world of electoral systems as *scientists* and as *engineers*. Its separate essays and appendices take stock of their work. Its principal findings include the following.

- A great deal of recent scientific research concerns the ways that contextual factors intervene to modify the theoretically anticipated effects of electoral rules. Arguing that context matters in *specific* and *systematic* ways, we propose a fresh conceptual framework that distinguishes between the mechanical and behavioral effects of electoral rules and highlights the importance of the length of the causal chain that separates rules from outcomes.

- Electoral rules shape the political inclusion of women and minorities in different—and surprising—ways. Far more research is needed on how mechanisms to promote different types of excluded groups relate to one another and how they affect intersectionally marginalized groups, such as minority women.

- Ballot structure exerts a crucial influence on the degree to which political competition occurs *between* or *within* parties. It also shapes the degree to which legislative behavior is oriented toward nourishing the personal reputations of individual politicians or the collective good of political parties.

- Serving as levers for the advancement of "narrow" interests over "broad" ones, electoral rules are correlated with distinct patterns of redistribution and regulation, particularly in advanced democracies. Who benefits from which types of rules, however, depends largely on whether scholars conceive of narrowness and breadth in terms of social class, economic sector, geography, access to rents, or other characteristics.

- History shows that creative institutional schemes born from the minds of philosophers have produced lasting political improvements. Existing electoral systems could also benefit from institutional innovations. Alternative constituency designs and nonelectoral mechanisms to promote accountability, such as the Ancient Greek practice of *euthynai* (public rendering of accounts), could help promote political equality.

- Events of the Arab Spring and regime changes in the Middle East and Central Asia have created a "boom" in demand for electoral advising. Our multimethod research project, which consists of surveys, case studies, and personal interviews, reveals the diverse ways that political scientists share and apply their scientific knowledge.

This report reveals the varied ways that the scientific and engineering dimensions of the relationship between political scientists and electoral systems are mutually reinforcing. Successful electoral engineering depends on the successful development of political science scholarship, while good scholarship is stimulated by the impetus and evidence brought to the field by political science engineers.

List of Acronyms

ANC   African National Congress

AV   Alternative Vote

CL-PR   Closed-list Proportional Representation

FDI   Foreign direct investment

FPTP   First-past-the-post

FUSADE   Foundation for Economic Development

GATT   General Agreement on Tariffs and Trade

IDEA   International Institute for Democracy and Electoral Assistance

IFES   International Foundation for Electoral Systems

MM   Mixed-member

MM-C   Mixed-member Compensatory

MM-P   Mixed-member Parallel

NDI   National Democratic Institute

OECD   Organisation for Economic Co-operation and Development

OL-PR   Open-list Proportional Representation

PR   Proportional Representation

SMD   Single-member District

SMD-AV   Single-member District–Alternative Vote/Instant Run-off

SMD-P   Single-member District–Plurality

SMD-TR   Single-member District–Two Round

SNTV   Single-nontransferable Vote

STV   Single-transferable Vote

USAID   US Agency for International Development

WTO   World Trade Organization

1

Between Science and Engineering: Political Science, Electoral Rules, and Democratic Governance

Mala Htun and G. Bingham Powell, Jr.

Introduction and Overview

Electoral institutions are not a sufficient condition for the consolidation of democratic rule, but they are necessary. Without electoral rules to govern the election of executive and legislative powers, representative democracy is not viable. The rules go a long way toward shaping the type of democracy that develops. They determine whether relevant perspectives are included in decision making, the nature of the government that emerges, and the ways in which the public can hold this government accountable. The spread and consolidation of sustainable democratic practices depend on the diffusion of knowledge about the institutions that promote inclusion and deliver legitimate outcomes. By developing, testing, and sharing theories about how different electoral designs shape politics, political scientists play an important role in this process.

In this report, the APSA Presidential Task Force on Electoral Rules and Democratic Governance examines the relationship between political science and electoral institutions. We show that political science interacts with the world of electoral rules in two ways. One way is through political science as science, developing and testing theories about the consequences of different election rules and regulations for electoral outcomes of general interest, such as vote-seat disproportionality and the number of political parties. Political scientists use such theories to explain patterns of politics within and across countries. Most political scientists spend most of their time conducting research and disseminating its results to other scholars and to the general public, especially through education.

The second way political science interacts with the world of electoral rules is through engineering. Scores of political scientists have worked as consultants for international, regional, and national organizations, helping to design institutions in aspiring democracies and reform rules in established ones. They have offered "crash courses" on electoral design to help policy makers and other stakeholders make informed decisions. By writing policy reports and lecturing at regional and international meetings, political scientists have educated policy makers, political parties, civic groups, and other stakeholders about general trends in electoral reform, the expected consequences of particular configurations of electoral rules and regulations, and the options available for institutional design.

The essays contained in this report analyze the scientific and engineering contributions of (mostly US-based) political scientists to the world of electoral systems. We do not review the extensive contributions to the study of how election rules shape the disproportionality between votes and seats, the number of parties, and governability. Rather, the report focuses on more recent research that attempts to account for irregularities and exceptions to traditional relationships (such as Duverger's Law), especially as these have been extended to newer democracies in different parts of the world. In addition, we analyze recent political science research about the effects of electoral rules on previously understudied political outcomes, such as the inclusion of women and minorities in representative institutions, the encouragement of individual accountability, and public policy configurations. More speculatively, we suggest that attention be given to largely untried institutions that might enhance political equality, individual accountability, and political deliberation in representative bodies.

To explore the role of political scientists as engineers, we adopted a multimethod approach consisting of surveys, case studies, and personal interviews. To capture the preferences of political scientists vis-à-vis electoral rules, we conducted a small survey of APSA members. We administered a second survey to political scientists and other experts who had served as advisers or consultants during instances of electoral reform. The case studies and interviews reveal the varied roles political scientists have played, such as presenting political parties and legislative commissions with a blueprint for a new election system, compiling lists of options for stakeholders at regional meetings, conducting shuttle diplomacy between government and opposition in the halls of the United Nations, training the staff of democracy promotion organizations, and planting the seeds of new ideas—such as alternative voting (AV)—in the minds of government officials.

This report shows that the scientific and engineering dimensions of the relationship between political scientists and electoral systems are mutually reinforcing. By the 1980s and 1990s, evolution of the scientific field had yielded solid theoretical generalizations concerning the consequences of single-member district- (SMD-) plurality systems versus multimember low-threshold proportional representation systems, among other variations. Around the same time, dozens of new democracies had emerged. As *engineers*, political scientists were involved in these transitions as policy makers sought their help designing new constitutions. The consequences of electoral rules in new democracies did not always match theoretical predictions, however.

To explain the anomalies, political scientists as *scientists* went back to the drawing board, developing fresh theories about how contextual factors intervene to shape electoral rule effects. As the essay by Karen E. Ferree, G. Bingham Powell, Jr., and Ethan Scheiner shows, these works incorporate the particularities of local contexts into the internal causal logics of general theories, revealing how context affects the mechanical conversion of votes into seats and affects the way electoral rules provide incentives for the behavior of elites and voters. Predictions about how and in what ways context matters placed additional tools at the disposal of engineering political scientists when advising democracy promotion organizations and policy makers in new democracies. Effective choice of election rules and regulations depends both on the salience of particular goals and the interaction of rules and local context.

Political scientists have responded to the challenges of the real world in other ways as well. The mobilization of women and minorities around demands for political inclusion prompted electoral reform in many established democracies and altered the processes of constitution-making in new ones. Political scientists studying these experiences developed a large body of theory about the consequences of different electoral rules and regulations for the political presence of women and minorities, as the essay by Mona Lena Krook and Robert G. Moser points out. Engineering political scientists shared this knowledge about global trends and experiences via written reports (commissioned by democracy promotion and other international organizations), presentations at global and regional conferences of stakeholders, and smaller meetings with government officials and civil society groups. As the interview with Pippa Norris (Appendix B) makes clear, political scientists' work spreading information about gender quotas has been an important contributing factor to the global diffusion of these policies.

At the same time, growing evidence about the ways elections are actually practiced in many new democracies (and some older ones)—often involving voter fraud, intimidation, and other irregularities—helped motivate the development of the scientific field of electoral integrity, while mobilizing many political scientists to help improve these processes as engineers.[1] As Ferree, Powell, and Scheiner point out in their essay, electoral rules may not have their intended effects in the context of coercion, including illegal acts on Election Day, such as ballot stuffing, tabulation fraud, and voter intimidation, as well as less visible acts earlier in the electoral cycle, such as the introduction of restrictive voter registration laws and partisan gerrymandering of districts.[2] In addition, variations in electoral integrity may shape the relationship between the electoral system and its operational goals: rules on ballot access, for example, determine the number of third party and independent candidates—even when endogenous effects are taken into account.[3]

Though this report focuses mostly on the design of electoral systems, we believe that the administration of elections is a crucial area for research and intervention. Many scholarly works have investigated the conditions under which violations of electoral integrity are more or less likely.[4] These conclusions will help political science engineers design institutions to help minimize fraud and malpractice. In these and myriad other ways, successful political engineering depends on the successful development of political science scholarship. And good scholarship is stimulated by the impetus and evidence brought to the field by political science engineers.

Goals and Priorities of Electoral Systems

To properly analyze the relationship between political science and electoral rules, we must first take note of what electoral systems are supposed to achieve and what governments and voters want them to achieve. In theory, elections are a polity's primary "instruments of democracy."[5] Binding government to the popular will, they aim to promote the common good and ideals of fairness, representation, and political equality. These first-order goals offer standards against which electoral rules can and should be judged, as the essay by Andrew Rehfeld and Melissa Schwartzberg points out.

In practice, electoral systems consist of mechanisms to translate the people's preferences into a collective choice about public decision makers.[6] They enable popular selection of the people's representatives, who in turn are induced to deliberate and make decisions that promote the common good. As Madison put it in *The Federalist #57*:

> The aim of every political constitution is, or ought to be, first to obtain for rulers men who possess most wisdom to discern, and most virtue to pursue, the common good of the society; and in the next place, to take the most effectual precautions for keeping them virtuous whilst they continue to hold their public trust.[7]

Global human rights instruments, rather than Western political philosophy, supply the normative foundation of election rules in many new democracies.[8] The International Institute for Democracy and Electoral Assistance's (IDEA) handbook on international electoral standards, for example, identifies the source of its recommendations as major United Nations (and some regional) conventions, such as the Universal Declaration of Human Rights.[9] When it comes to such issues as the representation of minorities, access to polling places, and election oversight, international human rights conventions authorize more proactive measures to promote political equality than do older sources such as the US Constitution and *The Federalist Papers*. As a result, electoral rules and administrative systems in new democracies often appear—at least on paper—to be more explicitly concerned with political equality than those in more established democracies such as the United States.

In practice, there is enough convergence in the broad normative goals of most election systems to identify a common list of their second-order, or operational, goals. These goals provide a metric by which the consequences of different election systems can be compared.[10] They include:

- **Number of political parties**: Does the system permit multiple political parties to gain access to elected office or only a few?

- **Proportionality**: Is there a perfect (or close) correspondence between the percentage of the popular vote received by parties and the percentage of legislative seats they hold?

- **Single-party government**: Is the executive branch of government controlled by a single party or a coalition of parties?

- **Stability**: Does the elected government hold office for long enough that it can execute policy and be held accountable by voters?

- **Accountability of government**: Are voters able to identify policy makers and remove them at election time if they fail to fulfill their mandates or achieve generally popular goals?

- **Accountability of individual politicians**: Are representatives responsive to the voters who elected them, and are these voters able to reward or punish individuals at election time?

- **Programmatic political parties**: Are parties and party leaders able to uphold coherent policy programs and motivate representatives to pursue these programs collectively once in office?

- **Women's inclusion**: Does the legislature include a critical mass of women or equal numbers of women and men?

- **Minority representation**: Are minority racial, ethnic, religious, and linguistic groups included relative to their share of the population?

- **Ideological congruence**: Does the median legislator or government have commitments that align with those of the median voter? Does the government produce policies preferred by the median voter?

- **Decisive outcomes**: Do elections produce clear winners?

- **All votes count equally**: Do votes cast by citizens in all areas of the country figure equally into the allocation of legislative seats to parties?

- **Deliberation**: Do rules encourage elected representatives to engage in rational and equitable deliberation over norms, interests, and policy decisions?

Few electoral systems are able to achieve all of these goals simultaneously. Even a principle like political equality has different elements that may be in tension with one another. As Rehfeld and Schwartzberg note in their essay, political equality can be interpreted as the equal chance to vote for a winning candidate (thus imply proportionality and inclusion), the equal chance to influence a policy maker (implying single-party government), or the responsiveness of elected representatives to voters' policy preferences (implying ideological congruence). Since some of these ends are incompatible with others, electoral choice requires clarifying priorities and accepting tradeoffs.

A classic tradeoff is between the inclusion of political and social diversity on the one hand and government accountability on the other. The conventional wisdom maintains that most electoral systems can produce either inclusive parliaments that reflect the diversity of public opinion or a decisive government that voters can identify and reward (or punish) at election time—but not both simultaneously.[11] By facilitating the representation of many different parties, proportional representation electoral systems tend to promote inclusion but often produce fractious coalition governments that are difficult for voters to hold accountable. SMD-plurality systems, by contrast, generate fewer parties and less broad-based representation, but produce single-party governments that are more durable and decisive.[12]

Most democratic polities tend to conform to one type or the other: they are oriented around either a majoritarian or proportional vision.[13] Citizens' priorities are therefore crucial in guiding the choice of an electoral system. What do they value more: inclusion of diversity or government accountability? Proportionality or decisiveness? As the essay by John Carey and Simon Hix shows, electoral systems are consequential not just for the dynamics of party competition and representation, but also for patterns of social and economic policy. On average, countries that conform to the proportional vision are far more likely to redistribute wealth from rich to poor via taxation, offer a greater range of social services, and have cooperative relations with labor and business than are majoritarian ones.[14]

Curious about the goals that political scientists prioritize, we administered an Internet-based survey to a random sample of APSA members, asking them to rank the importance of different electoral system goals and their opinions about different electoral systems. (For details, see the essay by Carey, Hix, Shaheen Mozaffar, and Andrew Reynolds.) Political scientists placed the highest value on the goal of accountability of individual legislators, closely followed by the goal of governmental stability. The least important goal was single-party government, with the other six options—proportionality, a decisive outcome, minority representation, policy correspondence with the median voter, party cohesion, and women's representation—clumped around the middle. With the exception of single-party government, all of these goals were rated, at the minimum and on average, to be "Important."

The goals valued by political scientists were correlated with their electoral system preferences. For example, people who valued proportionality more highly were more likely to rate list–proportional representation (PR), mixed-member compensatory (MM-C), and single-transferable vote (STV) electoral systems favorably. People preferring decisive electoral outcomes were more favorable toward SMD-plurality and two-round systems, as well as mixed-member parallel (MM-P) ones. These associations imply that political scientists are familiar and agree with the results of traditional research on electoral systems (more about this later). Yet their priorities differed: whereas some political scientists upheld proportional visions of democracy, others preferred the majoritarian vision.[15]

Political Science as Science: Core Concerns of Traditional Research

For decades, the core concerns of political scientists working on electoral systems centered on how to achieve the highly valued goals of governmental stability and proportionality. Since John Stuart Mill observed in 1861 that rules with single-member or winner-take-all electoral districts tended to advantage the largest parties, political scientists have known that different election systems produce different results.[16] In the late 19th century and early 20th century, the consequences of electoral systems for political representation became increasingly apparent. Rules were developed and applied in a number of European democracies to enhance greater proportionality.[17]

The modern study of the consequences of election rules dates from Maurice Duverger's *Political Parties,*[18] which articulated the "sociological law" that single-member district–plurality rules promoted two-party systems and also observed that proportional representation rules promoted multiparty systems and greater vote-seat proportionality. In his highly influential study, Duverger proposed that these relationships were sustained by both "mechanical" and "psychological," or behavioral, processes.[19]

Douglas Rae's *Political Consequences of Electoral Laws*[20] converted Duverger's qualitative observations into testable quantitative hypotheses and tested them with cross-national data. A host of empirical studies, stimulated by several specialized academic journals, explored these relationships in a variety of ways over the next 30 years. In 1994, Arend Lijphart and his colleagues integrated many of these in a replication of Rae's work that Matthew S. Shugart has called the "pinnacle of studies of the macro-dimension."[21] Independent of these studies, theoretical studies of the micro-dimension[22] were developing and were integrated with this work by GaryCox.[23] In 2005, Shugart would write of a "mature field" of electoral systems and party systems, with the "core concerns" of these being the number of parties and the proportionality (in relation to votes) of their relationships.[24]

This "mature field" involved study of the way electoral systems shaped the translation of party votes into the distribution of party seats in the legislature. Although a variety of features of electoral systems were explored, the most widely accepted generalizations distinguished the consequences of single-member district (or high-threshold, low-district) magnitude PR from the consequences of multimember, low-threshold, high-district magnitude PR. Political scientists linked the former type of electoral system with "two-party" systems, greater vote-seat disproportionality of legislative representation, and frequent single-party majority governments. They associated the latter type, in interaction with the number of cleavages, with more parties, less disproportionality, and the absence of single-party governments. The outcomes of the number of parties, proportionality, and governance were in turn associated with secondary outcomes of government stability, effectiveness, accountability, and representation.

Despite Shugart's and William Riker's confidence in the maturity of the field of electoral studies, the generalizations and processes that generated these studies remained somewhat controversial. Too frequently, the world produced "exceptions" to the generalizations of political scientists' theories. These exceptions were academically uncomfortable and a source of unease to those planning to advise constitution makers and other stakeholders in the real world. To apply political science research more effectively, political scientists needed to think about the ways that contextual conditions intervene to alter the outcomes anticipated by theories.

Context and Conditionality

This report proposes a way to think about how context shapes the effects of electoral rules. Arguing that context matters in "specific and systematic ways," it identifies those theoretically expected and justified contexts under which political scientists' generalizations about electoral rules will work differently. In their essay, Ferree, Powell, and Scheiner show how contextual features intervene in the causal chains that connect the features of electoral rules with such outcomes as legislative representation or governance. Defining context as "anything external to the electoral rule itself," they distinguish between *coercive* and *noncoercive* contextual features. Coercive contextual features involve "blatant political interference that prevents the rules from working as anticipated," such as violence, intimidation, and fraud. They may be pervasive in new democracies. Noncoercive contextual factors include political, economic, social, and cultural variables, such as the depth of partisan attachments, the institutionalization of the party system, rules governing the election of the executive power, poverty, the spread of the media, trust, and social diversity, among others.

Ferree, Powell, and Scheiner propose a conceptual model that distinguishes between the *length* of the causal chain that connects election rules to political outcomes and the *types* of causal linkages in that chain. Context will be more important when political outcomes—such as the number of national parties, government stability, and so forth—are a more distant effect of electoral rules than when they are a more proximate result. In addition, context matters more when the causal linkage is *behavioral (*involving human decision making) than when it is *mechanical* (human decision making is absent). In most cases, only coercive contextual factors get in the way of mechanical causal linkages.

Ferree, Powell, and Scheiner offer multiple examples of the ways that contextual elements condition the relationships between election rules and outcomes. Consider the number of parties in the party system, one of the core concerns of traditional research, and the initial stage in some of the causal chains to other outcomes, such as government stability and accountability. As Duverger proposed and more recent research supports, the connection between election rules and the number of parties depends on both mechanical processes of vote counting and conversion and behavioral processes in which citizens and elites defect from preferred parties expected to lose. The causal chain is long, consisting of the link between electoral rules and the number of parties at the district level and the link between the number of district-level parties and national parties.

The mechanical linkages between rules and outcomes may be altered by coercive and manipulative contextual conditions, such as the miscounting of votes, voter intimidation, and violation of the secrecy of the ballot. Under "normal" conditions and given a particular distribution of votes, the mechanical processes of representation will be unaffected by contextual variations. However, the behavioral process of defection from smaller parties, as Cox[25] points out, depends on common expectations and good information about party voting strength and other theoretically identified conditions, which may not hold true in new or noninstitutionalized party systems. Often, voters in plurality elections in new democracies tend to stick with weak candidates, sometimes due to intense attachments or animosities from a previous conflict, which generates a larger number of parties than Duverger's Law would have predicted.[26] Duverger's Law–type results also depend on nationalization of the party system, linking candidates in different districts, which is shaped by the centralization and perceived importance of the executive institutions, as well as the geographic distribution of preferences.

Krook and Moser's essay analyzes the ways that electoral rules and regulations, which the authors define as specific provisions designed to increase the representation of targeted groups, affect the political inclusion of women and minorities. Following the framework proposed by Ferree, Powell, and Scheiner, they argue that the longer the causal chain separating the rule from the outcome, the more likely contextual factors will intervene. Basic electoral rules governing the translation of votes into seats—such as PR versus SMD—shape the political presence of women and minorities by "increasing or decreasing incentives for elites to nominate female and minority candidates and for voters to support them." In PR contests in large districts, party elites are far more likely to place women and minorities on the ballot in order to present a "balanced ticket" to the electorate.[27] In SMD and other candidate-centered races, by contrast, parties are more likely to concentrate resources on "safe" candidates from the dominant social group.[28]

The causal chain is long, however: party responses to these incentives are mediated by the social status of women and minorities, public attitudes, social mobilization of underrepresented groups, and demography, such as the extent of minority geographic concentration, among other contextual factors. If the status of women is very low, for example, parties will see few advantages to their nomination, even in large PR districts.[29] In contexts in which the status of women is very high, they may not be as disadvantaged by candidate-centered systems. For their part, when ethnic minorities are geographically concentrated, parties are likely to field minority candidates in SMD elections. As this suggests, whether PR or SMD is "best" for women and minorities may vary from context to context.

When it comes to electoral regulations such as quotas and reserved seats, the causal chain connecting rule to outcome is shorter. The effects of quotas and reserved seats are less affected by context and more by the details of the regulation and its interaction with the electoral system. It is widely argued, for example, that candidate quotas tend to work best under closed-list PR with large districts and placement mandates. In open-list PR systems, in which party magnitude is small and/or when the quota fails to require that women be placed in high positions on party lists (placement mandates), the effects of quotas will be minimal, even in contexts in which the status of women is relatively high.[30] Unless electoral regulations are thwarted by coercive contextual factors (such as noncompliance or violence toward women candidates and elected officials), their effects can usually be predicted independently of contextual factors.

Shugart's essay on ballot structure identifies the specific ways that a more "open" or "closed" ballot affects party cohesion and the accountability of individual representatives. More open ballots—on which voters make choices below the party level, such as by voting for particular individuals or ranking them—mean that electoral competition occurs both *between* parties and *within* them. Intraparty competition tends to undermine the alignment between the individual interests of legislators in their election and the collective goals of the party in maximizing its share of seats, especially as district magnitude increases. At the same time, open ballots complicate accountability. Representatives who compete against others from the same party are motivated to cultivate a personal vote (which may involve many types of actions), but in a large multimember district, voters may have a hard time giving credit or apportioning blame for services rendered.

Yet as Shugart points out, "ballot structure is not destiny." Contextual factors shape the degree to which ballot structure matters. In parliamentary systems, for example, in which parties organize to place their own members in executive positions, intraparty incentives tend to be more aligned with collective goals regardless of ballot structure. Similarly, some disciplinary tactics (restricting access to choice committee seats and executive posts) and candidate selection rules may enable party leaders to exert greater control over their members than the structure of the ballot would lead one to expect.

In their analysis of policy outcomes, Carey and Hix take stock of recent research that demonstrates a close connection between types of election systems and patterns of socioeconomic redistribution and regulation. On the one hand, PR systems are associated with higher taxes and more expansive public services, whereas SMD systems tend to have lower taxes and fewer public services (and lower public deficits). Yet party competition for the median voter in SMD systems creates an incentive for parties to support policies that lead to lower consumer prices, such as lower import tariffs, fewer regulations, and greater competition, whereas in PR systems, parties are more obligated to small groups of producers who prefer policies that result in higher consumer prices. Whether PR or SMD better promotes redistribution from "narrow" to "broad" economic interests thus depends on how these terms are conceived. Do electoral rules grant more leverage to the poor to force redistribution on the rich via taxation? Or do electoral rules enable consumers to extract lower price levels from producers via less favorable regulatory policies?

Based largely on research on Organisation for Economic Co-operation and Development (OECD) countries, the association between electoral rules and redistribution may be contextually specific. There is little evidence that PR encourages greater redistribution in developing countries, for example.[31] Some features of developing countries—including presidential systems, less institutionalized party systems, and personalistic or clientelistic (as opposed to ideological) parties—may preclude the dynamics that connect PR to redistribution. In particular, PR may not encourage the formation of coalition governments between parties that promote lower- and middle-class interests, which tend to promote redistribution in Europe.

Even within OECD countries, contextual factors may shape politicians' incentives to promote narrow interests over broad ones, especially if "narrow" is defined by geography and not social class or economic sector. It is generally believed that SMD systems encourage politicians to favor geographically targeted benefits and spending projects. Yet the effects of SMD may be largely conditional on the geographical concentration of voters who share particular interests, such as subsidies for a particular industry, and on district-level competitiveness, since no one will waste resources on a "safe" district.

The longer the causal chain connecting election rules to policy outcomes, the more likely it is that contextual features will intervene to modify the effects of the election rules, according to the model proposed by Ferree, Powell, and Scheiner. This may imply that context matters in specific, even predictable ways when it comes to the direct effects of electoral rules on politicians' incentives to favor specific groups, such as consumers or geographically concentrated economic interests. By contrast, context may matter in more complex ways when the hypothesized effects of electoral rules are more indirect; that is, when they are connected to policy outcomes via a longer causal chain that involves government formation and stability.

Rather than arguing that institutions matter absolutely, or denying that they matter at all, this report engages in the challenging but fruitful task of identifying how institutions and context work together to shape key political outcomes, including the number of parties, inclusion of women and minorities, personal vote seeking, and socioeconomic redistribution. Looking at institutions alone will not capture the entire story. As the essays in this report show, many of the effects of institutions are shaped by cross-country variations in the distribution of and relations between social groups, party systems, and levels of wealth. In turn, the effects of these contextual characteristics may be locked in and magnified—or conversely, reduced—by the incentives and constraints posed by electoral institutions.

Political Scientists as Engineers: How They Make a Difference

Political scientists[32] work as electoral engineers primarily by sharing knowledge about the consequences of different electoral rules and global trends in electoral reform. *How* and *where* this is done varies significantly. Some political scientists are intrepid travelers, visiting scores of countries to educate policy makers about electoral rules. Others work mostly at the global and regional levels, sharing information at seminars and conferences attended by stakeholders from multiple countries. Still others never need to leave home: they exert an impact by authoring policy briefs that influence discussions in national and international contexts.

Policy reports and briefs. Some of the most important work political scientists do involves writing policy reports and briefs that present typologies, explain theoretical findings, and summarize global and regional patterns. These reports may be very broad (such as Andrew Reynolds, Benjamin Reilly, and Andrew Ellis's handbook, *Electoral System Design*[33]) or very specific, containing information most relevant to specific issues or countries (such as Pippa Norris's report on options for women's reserved seats in Afghanistan[34] or Mala Htun's report on strategies to get more Afro-descendant women into elected office in Latin America[35]).

Presentations to global and regional audiences. Political scientists deliver presentations at global and regional meetings of policy makers, civic activists, and other stakeholders to inform them of cross-national patterns and present them with menus of options. At these meetings, political scientists supply frameworks and ideas that people can take back and put to use in their individual countries, often more successfully because they have a legitimate, academic backing. Recalling her participation in a UN Development Program–organized meeting in Mongolia, Pippa Norris notes, "Our report presented an analytical framework that could apply in any region and a list of six things they could do. We didn't say, 'You should do this, you should do that.' Rather, we asked, 'Which of these different options would be best for you given your own context?'"[36]

The global diffusion of gender quota policies is one area in which political scientists working at the global and regional levels have had a broad impact. By attending meetings organized by international organizations and development banks—in addition to contributing to policy briefs and handbooks (such as International IDEA's *Handbook on Women in Parliament*)—scholars have helped spread information about the countries with gender quotas, the details of the new laws surrounding these quotas, and their effect on getting women elected. This comparative knowledge has helped stakeholders understand why some quota laws work better than others and which aspects of poorly functioning laws need to be fixed.

Country missions. In greater numbers, political scientists are traveling to individual countries to offer information and guidance, usually in seminars and smaller meetings, about options and consequences of electoral reform. As Carey, Hix, Mozaffar, and Reynolds describe in their essay, events of the Arab Spring and regime changes in the Middle East and Central Asia have created a "boom" in demand for electoral advising. Most trips are arranged by democracy promotion organizations (such as the US Agency for International Development [USAID], International Foundation for Electoral Systems [IFES], and National Democratic Institute [NDI]) but may also occur at the behest of national governments.

Much of the work political scientists do on these trips involves educating policy makers, civil society advocates, journalists, and others about varieties of electoral systems, their anticipated consequences, and real-world experiences. John Carey recalls having conducted crash courses for members of parliament in Jordan and Yemen. As he reports of his 2011 trip to Jordan, "My job was not to advocate for a specific reform, but to provide them with a broad understanding of the various electoral system design options—that is, what the potential menu looks like—and to discuss the experiences of other countries with various methods of election."[37]

On the other hand, the survey and case studies reveal that many political scientists do offer specific recommendations for reform. Jørgen Elklit helped convince members of the Lesotho parliament to support the introduction of a mixed-member electoral system, for example. In many informal discussions stretching over a 20-year period, Arend Lijphart pressed South Africans to adopt a list-PR system. During multiple trips to Israel, Simon Hix initially proposed a mixed-member electoral system, and later, based on his scientific research with John Carey, a PR system with multimember districts of between four and 11 seats. In a briefing to the Reeve Commission (charged with recommending constitutional changes for Fiji), Donald Horowitz proposed that AV might be suitable, given the territorial intermixing of ethnic groups and the existence of more than one party per ethnic group. He reports that AV was subsequently adopted, with many exchanges of preference votes across ethnic lines in the 1999 elections. During conference presentations and meetings with policy makers in Chile (one of the few Latin American countries without a gender quota law), Mala Htun proposed that they eschew a women's quota and adopt a French-style gender parity law. Instead of granting women a right to representation as a particular social group, a parity law requires that candidates for elected office reflect the universal duality of the human condition as divided equally between men and women.[38] Htun believed that the philosophical rationale behind parity—based on universal and individualist principles, not group rights—as well as its practical application (50/50) was more suitable to Chile's political culture and two-member district electoral system than was a 30 or 40% quota policy.

Training staff of democracy promotion organizations. Political scientists are often invited to provide training in electoral systems design for the staff of democracy promotion organizations. Shaheen Mozaffar, for example, has conducted workshops for USAID Democracy Officers based in Washington, DC, and in country missions. Similar to the "crash courses" offered by political scientists abroad, these workshops introduced senior staff to key features of different electoral systems, their effects on political life, and the ways they can be adapted to different contexts. Since democracy officers in country missions are often nationals of those countries, the workshops helped to create a cadre of people with locally grounded knowledge of electoral systems.

On-the-spot policy advice. Some political scientists receive urgent requests to offer advice and information to policy makers. Andy Reynolds reports receiving a phone call from the United Nations asking him how big the Liberian parliament should be. In addition, Reynolds and John Carey authored a short paper for the National Security Council about Egypt's electoral rules, which helped raise awareness within the Obama administration about the implications of sticking with the majoritarian tendencies of the old Mubarak system.[39]

By drawing on their theoretical knowledge and experience with electoral rules in multiple contexts, political scientists broaden the perspective of policy makers and other stakeholders and expand the menu of options available to them. As Pippa Norris puts it,

> What Western political scientists can bring to the table is familiarity with broader comparisons and generalizations so that parallels can be drawn between, say, gender quotas in Afghanistan and Pakistan, or local government and conflict management in Nepal and India or constitution-building in Sudan and Sub-Saharan Africa. It is understanding the broader picture which is so vital for electoral engineering, by widening the range of policy options on the table and giving local stakeholders an awareness of more potential solutions which can be found in comparable societies.[40]

What did policy makers and other stakeholders do with the knowledge shared by political scientists? Were they merely enlightened by the presentation of global trends and theories, or did this work actually compel them to change their behavior? This report contains anecdotal evidence of the impact of political science ideas, including the adoption of AV in Fiji, PR in South Africa, and a mixed-member proportional (MMP) system in Lesotho, as well as the size of the Liberian parliament. We lack systematic evidence that political science knowledge compelled actors to choose courses of action they would not have taken otherwise. In fact, some of our evidence reveals the opposite: actors on the ground picked and chose among the scientific findings most useful to their purposes.

In their discussion of the results to our survey, Carey, Hix, Mozaffar, and Reynolds note that local actors were "motivated by partisan (or personal, sectarian, movement) concerns...[with a] proclivity to select results from academic research that could be used to bolster positions motivated by other factors." Reporting on the reaction to his proposals for electoral reform in Israel, Simon Hix describes how the opposition Likud Party and several smaller parties repeatedly blocked change. The schemes under consideration—including raising the threshold for representation and introducing smaller districts—would have helped larger parties gain more seats and stabilized coalition governments but would have harmed the smallest parties.[41] The very problem Hix and others were invited to try to correct—the inflated power of small parties over coalition formation and stability—prevented them from making any progress.

This example highlights a broader issue in social science research recognized by many of the authors of our essays: the difficulty of disentangling the effects of institutions from those of the conditions in which the institutions are operating.[42] As Carey, Hix, Mozaffar, and Reynolds note in their essay, electoral rules, though commonly analyzed as a cause of party systems, are also its effect.[43] Politicians want systems that preserve their positions and maximize their power. How and why they agree to change the rules is a question beyond the scope of our report. We show only that, in the event that agreements on change are possible, it is highly likely that a political scientist will be at the table with menus of options and ideas about their likely consequences.

Conclusion

The essays that comprise this report shed light on the current relationship between political science and the world of electoral institutions. We show that political scientists relate to electoral rules both as scientists and as engineers, developing a massive body of work about the consequences of different electoral configurations on political outcomes and then traveling the world applying this knowledge. Without compromising the integrity of the scientific research or the pragmatic considerations guiding policy interventions, it is important for political scientists to fulfill the APSA Presidential Task Forces' collective mission of promoting more sustained, evidence-based engagement with the world.

2

How Context Shapes the Effects of Electoral Rules

Karen E. Ferree, G. Bingham Powell, Jr., and Ethan Scheiner

As democracy emerges in previously authoritarian countries, policy makers confront decisions about what rules ought to be used to govern. Perhaps the most fundamental of these decisions relates to the choice of electoral rules. Many view the electoral system as one of the primary levers through which constitutional engineers shape emergent democratic polities. Yet most of what is known about the effects of electoral rules builds from the experience of well-established democracies. Should similar outcomes be expected when rules are placed in contexts that are new to free and fair elections?

The political, social, and economic contexts in many new democracies diverge significantly from those of most established democracies. In many new democracies, deep social divisions divide the polity; rule of law is only partially established; electoral fraud corrupts numerous aspects of the electoral process; violence and voter intimidation occur with regularity; the informational environment is undeveloped; voters lack education and experience evaluating parties and candidates; poverty creates incentives for politicians to buy votes rather than invest in public goods; and parties and party systems have shallow roots. A growing literature documents: 1) how these contextual factors mediate the effects of electoral rules and 2) how the mediating effects of context vary across different outcomes and environments. In some situations, electoral rules seem to shape outcomes regardless of context, but elsewhere context plays a strong role in mediating the effects of institutions.

In this essay, we concur with previous work that argues that differences in context are significant—electoral rules will not have the same effects in all cases.[1] Moreover, we push beyond the notion that "context matters" to argue that context shapes the effects of electoral rules in *specific and systematic ways*. We propose two hypotheses: First, the longer the causal chain connecting rules to an outcome, the more contextual factors should mediate the relationship. Second, contextual factors exert less impact when the causal linkage between an institution and the outcome is *mechanical* (involving no human discretion or decision making) versus *behavioral* (involving human discretion or decision making).

Our analysis implies that constitutional engineers should have the greatest success in influencing mechanical outcomes that flow directly from electoral institutions. When the intended effect of an institution is mediated by the discretionary actions of human beings, and/or that effect also requires many intermediate steps, outcomes may vary considerably across different contexts. Ultimately, most significant political outcomes that concern institutional engineers do not flow directly from the mechanical effects of electoral rules, thus providing numerous opportunities for context to shape outcomes.

What Are "Contextual" Factors?

We broadly and inclusively define context as anything external to the electoral rule itself, and we group contextual factors into two broad categories: coercive and noncoercive. Coercive contextual factors involve blatant political interference that prevents rules from working as anticipated; these factors shape the extent to which the formal institutions are the "real rules" of the game. Examples include the use of violence and intimidation to subvert outcomes, election fraud, and, more broadly, items from Andreas Schedler's "Menu of Manipulation."[2] While coercive contextual factors play a relatively small role in most established democracies, their influence can be extensive in places where democracy is new. Institutionalists often ignore coercive contextual factors, taking as their starting point the notion that *de jure* and *de facto* rules of the game coincide. In many countries with elections, however, the match is less than perfect, and *de facto* practices exert strong influence over how *de jure* rules shape outcomes.

We group noncoercive contextual factors into three categories: 1) political variables, 2) economic variables, and 3) cultural and social variables. Political variables include the intensity of partisanship, polarization of political preferences, age of the democracy, degree of party system institutionalization, and depth of partisanship—all variables that shape the ability and incentives of elites, voters, and candidates to engage in strategic electoral coordination. In this grouping, we also include other political institutions, such as presidential or parliamentary executive regime types. Economic variables include poverty, development, the spread of media, and macroeconomic conditions. These variables shape strategic behavior in elections and influence such outcomes as government stability and accountability. Our third category includes social and cultural factors, including trust within and across social groups, education and information levels, and social diversity.

How Does Context Shape the Effects of Electoral Rules?

We expect two features of the causal chain linking electoral institutions to outcomes to shape the mediating effects of contextual factors. First, we expect the *length* of the causal chain to be significant.[3] A particular outcome may flow immediately from an electoral rule or it may be distantly related. In the former (proximate) category are outcomes such as disproportionality and malapportionment. In the latter (distal) category are outcomes such as the size of the national party system, the stability of parliamentary governments, the accountability of governments to electorates, and the ideological representation of the electorate in government. Electoral rules do, to some extent, affect distal outcomes, but because there are many links in the chain, there are more opportunities for context to affect outcomes in these cases.

Second, we expect the *type* of causal linkages to be important. Following a tradition dating back to Maurice Duverger, we distinguish between "mechanical" and "behavioral" causal linkages.[4] Mechanical linkages flow directly from rules, independent of human decision making: given a set of inputs, the rules produce outputs by means of a mathematical algorithm. In contrast, behavioral mechanisms reflect discretionary human action. People interpret a rule and respond to it, filtering the rule through their perceptions, beliefs, and cost-benefit calculus (including anticipation of mechanical effects). Because people respond in ways shaped by context, we speculate that context will more systematically shape the outcomes of electoral rules when the link between the institution and the outcome involves human discretion.

In sum, the shorter the chain, and the more mechanical the linkages, the less context should matter. There is one clear exception to this expectation: Coercive contextual factors may interfere with both behavioral and mechanical linkages. For example, votes should mechanically translate into a distribution of seats, but electoral fraud may interfere with this process, awarding seats to candidates based on favoritism and corruption rather than actual voting outcomes.

Figure 2.1: **Mechanical, Behavioral, and Contextual Effects**

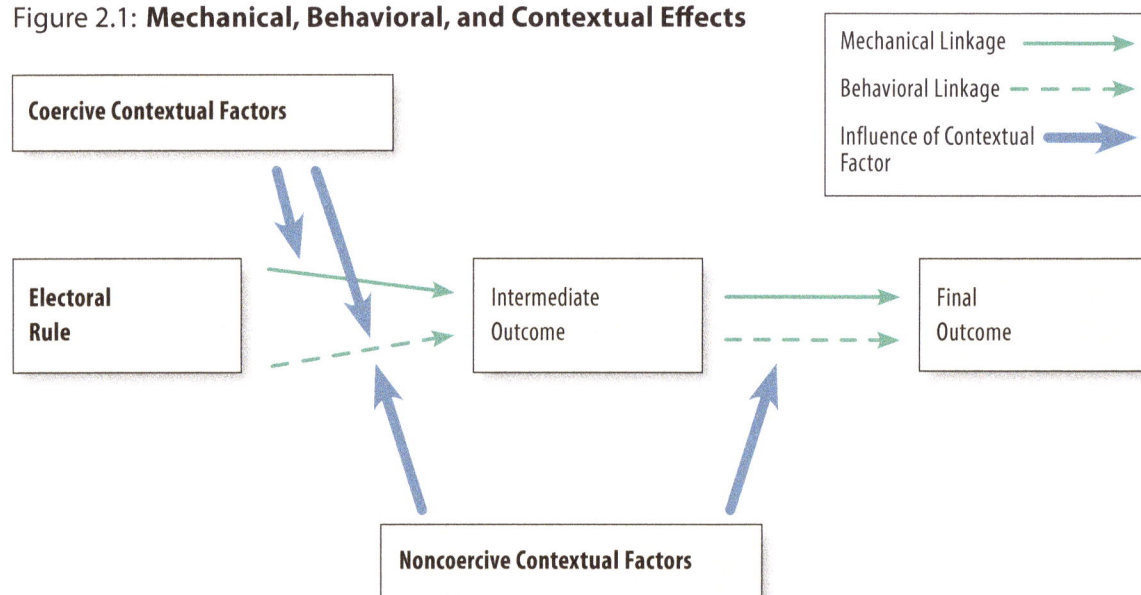

Source: Ferree, Powell and Scheiner, Task Force on Electoral Rules and Democratic Governance

Figure 2.1 illustrates both expectations in general form. Variables are in boxes. Causal mechanisms flowing from electoral rules are represented by thin, solid arrows for mechanical links and thin, dashed arrows for behavioral ones. We use thick, solid arrows to highlight where contextual variables affect the mechanical and behavioral causal links. Noncoercive contextual factors mediate behavioral mechanisms but not mechanical ones, whereas coercive contextual factors can mediate both kinds of mechanisms. For graphical clarity, we indicate the impact of coercive contextual factors on the mechanical and behavioral links between rules and intermediate outcomes only, but these factors can affect the causal mechanisms anywhere in the figure.

As the figure suggests, unless coercive factors intervene, outcomes linked mechanically and immediately to electoral rules will occur in a largely consistent fashion everywhere, without regard to context. However, the longer the causal chain, and the more behavioral linkages that comprise that chain, the more likely it is that noncoercive contextual factors will shape the outcomes of the rules, leading to significant variation across cases and no one-size-fits-all relationship between rules and outcomes.

In the following sections, we illustrate these general expectations through a discussion of specific outcomes, starting with party systems and then moving on to more distant outcomes—government stability and accountability, and representation—that are linked to electoral rules through the rules' effects on party systems.

Forming the National Legislature

A rich literature discusses how electoral institutions shape party systems.[5] Because electoral rules affect vote-seat disproportionality directly and mechanically, we expect contextual factors to exert relatively little influence on this relationship. In contrast, because the causal chain linking electoral rules to the national party system is long and involves many behavioral steps, contextual factors mediate that outcome to a much greater degree. We discuss each of these outcomes in turn in the following sections.

Disproportionality

Disproportionality is the degree to which the share of seats allocated to parties matches the share of votes they win—greater disproportionality exists when there are greater discrepancies between the share of votes and seats won. In first-past-the-post (FPTP) systems, whenever there is more than one contestant winning a significant number of votes, disproportionality at the district level is high. Disproportionality at the national level depends on the aggregation of district results and is usually reduced somewhat by victories by a party in one district being cancelled out by its losses in another.[6] Smaller parties may lose in most districts, however, unless their support is geographically concentrated. Thus, the net effect on national disproportionality depends on the degree of cancellation in the mechanical aggregation of the district results. In contrast, when there are many seats in a

Figure 2.2: **Disproportionality**

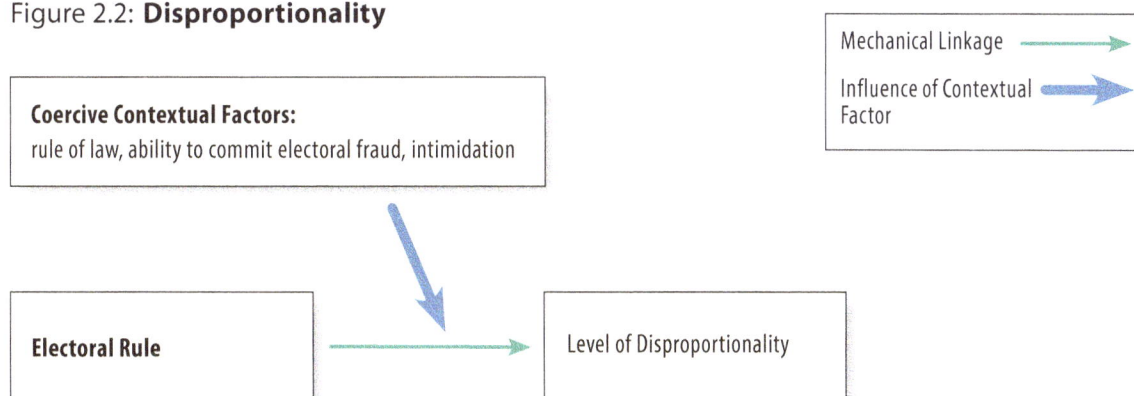

Source: Ferree, Powell and Scheiner, Task Force on Electoral Rules and Democratic Governance

district and there is no minimum number of votes needed for a party to gain seats, parties tend to win roughly the same share of votes and seats at the district level and both district and national disproportionality are low.

Ultimately, disproportionality is a formulaic and nondiscretionary application of a particular set of electoral rules to a particular distribution of votes.[7] Disproportionality therefore illustrates an outcome connected to an electoral rule through a short causal chain and largely mechanical linkage (see Figure 2.2). We consequently expect noncoercive contextual factors to have a limited mediating impact. Put another way, conditional on a particular distribution of votes and barring coercive efforts to manipulate outcomes, electoral rules should have the same effect on disproportionality everywhere.[8]

The Number of Parties in Elections to the National Legislature

In contrast, because there are many links in the causal chain, and several of these links involve human behavior, contextual factors should strongly mediate the effects of electoral rules on national party systems. There are two stages in the chain linking electoral rules to national party systems: from the electoral rule to the number of parties competing at the district level, and from the number of parties at the district level to the number of parties competing for seats in the national legislature[9] (see Figure 2.3).

Figure 2.3: **Number of Electoral Parties**

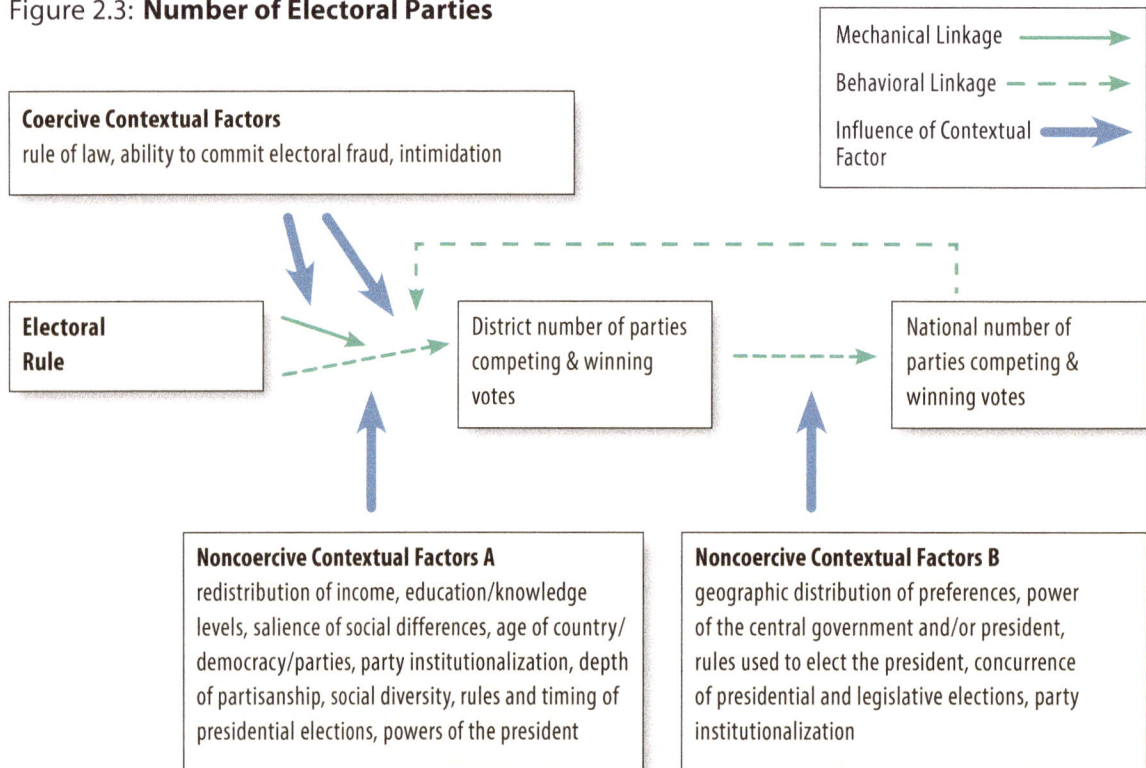

Source: Ferree, Powell and Scheiner, Task Force on Electoral Rules and Democratic Governance

Number of Parties at the District Level

The impact of electoral rules on the number of parties at the district level has been the focus of many waves of research in political science. As originally argued by Duverger,[10] there are both mechanical and behavioral mechanisms linking electoral rules to the district-level number of parties.

On the mechanical side: "Restrictive" rules—most notably, FPTP, which awards a single-member district seat to the top vote-winning candidate in a district—lead to high disproportionality, favoring large parties or parties with geographically concentrated support. In contrast, "permissive" rules—especially proportional representation with large numbers of seats per district—allow even small parties to win seats, and thereby minimize disproportionality.[11]

On the behavioral side: Anticipation of the mechanical effects shapes the behavior of voters and elites. Restrictive rules promote strategic behavior, in which voters and elites concentrate their support on truly competitive candidates.[12] Candidates anticipate these actions, and often choose not to run if they have no chance of victory. Put together, the behavior of voters, elites, and candidates reduces the number of candidates or parties winning votes in restrictive systems. In contrast, in permissive electoral systems, even parties that win relatively small numbers of votes can win seats. Voters and elites in such systems therefore worry less about wasting their support and can engage in more "sincere" behavior, backing their top choice in the election.

The expectation of Duverger's Law is, therefore, that FPTP rules lead to two viable candidates per district, whereas systems with permissive electoral rules tend to contain more than two viable candidates. Cox[13] synthesizes the logic underpinning these outcomes and identifies the common pattern across them: the $M+1$ rule, whereby the number of parties or candidates in a district is capped at the district magnitude (M) plus one. FPTP systems have a district magnitude of one, so they can, according to the theory, support, at most, two parties. Permissive systems with higher district magnitudes can support many more parties. Work by scholars such as Cox, Norris,[14] and Reed[15] provides empirical support for the $M+1$ rule.

The Effects of Context

Contextual factors can interact with electoral rules to shape the number of parties at the district level in several ways. They can winnow down the number of parties/candidates contesting seats below the $M+1$ ceiling. The $M+1$ rule places an upper boundary on the number of parties a system can support. For highly permissive systems, this is not particularly informative. For example, South Africa uses a national list proportional representation system, in which half of the 400 parliamentary seats are drawn from a single national list and the other half are drawn from nine provincial lists. Voters cast a single national vote, and votes are allocated to seats from a single national district of 400. Applying the $M+1$ rule to the national district implies that, at most, 401 parties will form. In practice, around seven parties win votes in most South African elections, with one party, the African National Congress (ANC), taking almost two-thirds of the vote. To explain this outcome, we need to look to context: the significance of race in shaping voting behavior after 40 years of apartheid and several centuries of segregation; the success of the ANC in becoming a focal point for anti-apartheid forces; the strategic use of resources by the ANC to prevent its opponents from making inroads into its constituency; and the ANC's success at cauterizing splinters within its coalition.[16]

Coercive contextual factors also may introduce mechanical distortions into the translation of votes into seats. For example, electoral authorities may fraudulently award seats to candidates who did not actually win enough votes to capture them legally. More broadly, if electoral rules exist on the books but are not followed in practice, election outcomes may bear little resemblance to the predictions of institutional theories.

Finally, noncoercive and coercive contextual factors may interfere with the strategic behavior of elites and voters that underlies the $M+1$ rule, producing a larger number of viable candidates or parties than predicted by the electoral rules. Put differently, contextual factors can cause the theoretical logic underpinning Duverger's Law and the $M+1$ rule to fail.

On the noncoercive side, Cox[17] highlights a number of conditions that shape the strategic coordination that underlies the $M+1$ rule. We give special attention to three here: First, when many voters see little difference between the competitive options, they will be less likely to strategically shift their votes away from their first-choice party (even if that party has little chance of winning), thus preventing the reduction in the number of parties necessary for the $M+1$ rule. A number of contexts may promote this situation. In post-conflict situations, in which parties form out of military or guerilla groups, intense animosities left over from the conflict may lead to strong electoral attachments, at least for a period of time. Ideological polarization may also increase the strength of partisan or candidate attachments or both and make strategic defections from probable losers less likely. In addition, salient social divisions (racial, ethnic, or religious) may breed intense partisan attachments, particularly if voters see the party as an extension of their group.[18] Indeed, perhaps for this reason, socially diverse countries appear to produce larger numbers of parties, even under FPTP rules.[19]

Second, the existence of a party or candidate that wins with near certainty will give voters little reason to strategically withdraw support from their preferred (even weak) party, since no amount of strategic behavior by voters would enable them to overcome the leader. This dynamic may explain fractured oppositions in various single-party dominant systems past (India, Mexico) and present (Uganda).

Third, widespread strategic behavior consistent with the $M+1$ rule will be unlikely when information is lacking about which candidates are in or out of the running. Indeed, in political systems with limited democratic experience, there may be significant uncertainty about likely political outcomes. Such countries lack a history of prior election results from which voters and elites can draw inferences about likely election outcomes.[20] They also may have rudimentary polling resources and limited media, especially if they are not only new at democracy but also lack economic resources, further constraining the ability of voters and elites to arrive at a common ranking of parties. The problems of forming common knowledge of the ranking of parties may be especially problematic in poorly institutionalized systems in which parties come and go, electoral volatility is high, and there are large numbers of independent candidates.[21] In fact, plurality races in new democracies, especially those with poorly institutionalized party systems, often involve relatively little strategic defection from weak candidates and, in turn, a large number of parties.[22] Finally, as Jeremy Horowitz and James Long[23] highlight, a lack of trust in the media in some contexts may lead voters to simply dismiss much of the information that is reported.

On the coercive side, most theoretical treatments of electoral rules implicitly assume a secret ballot, yet ballot secrecy is not guaranteed in many areas of the world. When there is a possibility of being punished for failing to vote in a particular way, voters may care less about strategic voting and avoiding "wasted votes." Intimidation of candidates and parties may also hamper strategic efforts, creating artificial pools of voters around parties that might not otherwise be viable.

Context can take the form of other political institutions within a polity. Most notably, presidentialism—or, more specifically, the number of parties contesting a presidential election—also shapes the district number of parties. Recent scholarship suggests that the presence of a concurrent presidential election may restrict the number of candidates running and winning votes in legislative elections under permissive legislative electoral rules yet raise the number when rules are restrictive. In other words, concurrent presidential elections moderate the $M+1$ logic. Voters and elites have incentives to behave sincerely under permissive electoral rules, but presidential elections may help push such voters and elites to behave strategically, leading to a concentration of support for candidates from parties with front-runners in the presidential race.[24]

Projection to the National Level

The district-level (Duvergerian) behavioral effect is but one step in the chain linking electoral rules to the number of parties at the national level (see Figure 2.3). In an additional step, voters and elites in each district decide—usually through the coordination of a nationally centralized organization—whether to join with voters and elites in other districts in support of a slate of candidates. When this coordination is successful, the district-level party systems become nationalized and the district-level number of parties "project" on to the national level. The number of parties represented in the national legislature is therefore a result of the extent to which the different district-level parties aggregate across the country.

This projection is founded on human discretion—that is, whether political actors in different districts coordinate with one another—thus adding another point at which any of a number of contextual factors can shape the outcome. Perhaps most obviously, the geographic distribution of preferences affects projection. In countries such as Canada, where a national minority group makes up a large percentage of the population in particular regions, the group can help a national third party win seats in those regions. Under FPTP rules, therefore, there may be two candidates per district (with the minority party as one of the two parties in certain regions), but more than two parties winning seats nationally.[25] Moreover, where parties do not have strong ties to voters—as ought to be common in cases of limited democratic experience and weak party institutionalization—it becomes markedly more difficult to coordinate political actors across many different districts, and is likely to lead to more than two national parties, even under FPTP systems.[26]

Nonlegislative institutions also shape projection. Rules that promote coordination across districts by tying presidential and legislative elections together or by increasing the significance of gaining control of either the presidency or the government in general often lead to greater matching of district-level and national outcomes. In this way, projection tends to be greater in systems in which there is a plurality elected president, legislative and presidential elections are held concurrently, or governmental power is centralized in the national government.[27]

In sum, in the causal chain linking electoral rules to the national party system, there are two discrete stages in which context can influence discretionary human decision making, thus creating significant opportunities for context to alter the expected effects of electoral rules.

Governance Outcomes

Thus far, the substantive focus of this report has been on the number of parties, but to many observers, outcomes related to governance are at least as important. As we demonstrate in this section, the effect of electoral rules on governance is mediated by many behavioral steps, providing significant opportunities for context to mediate the effects of electoral institutions on outcomes.

Executive regime type—that is, whether a system is presidential or parliamentary—is the very foundation of a system's governance structure. For this reason, we discuss presidential and parliamentary systems separately. We highlight how presidential systems generally involve a higher proportion of mechanical linkages than parliamentary systems, thus creating more opportunities for context to shape governance in parliamentary systems.

Government Formation in Parliamentary Systems

As Figure 2.4 illustrates, the effect of rules on governance simply continues the causal chain presented in Figure 2.3, adding a link between the national parliamentary outcome and government formation.[28] In parliamentary systems, members of parliament select the cabinet and prime minister (collectively, the government). The specific details of this process vary from system to system, but in general a potential government is proposed and then voted on by parliament.[29] If the government gains majority support, it forms. If it fails to gain majority support, it does not form and another proposed government may be put forward in its place until a government with majority support is determined. The government formation process inherently involves human discretion and therefore represents a behavioral link.

Because of this behavioral link, contextual factors may well influence whether a government is a majority, minority, or coalition government. The formation and maintenance of single-party majority governments, for example, depend on party cohesion. Party cohesion is often very high in parliamentary systems but may be lower in newer, less-consolidated democracies, and where ballot structure forces party members to compete against each other. In the absence of a majority party in parliament, formal investiture rules play a large role. Without a formal investiture requirement, minority governments, which draw support in parliament from shifting outside parties, become more likely.[30]

Figure 2.4: **Governance in Parliamentary Systems**

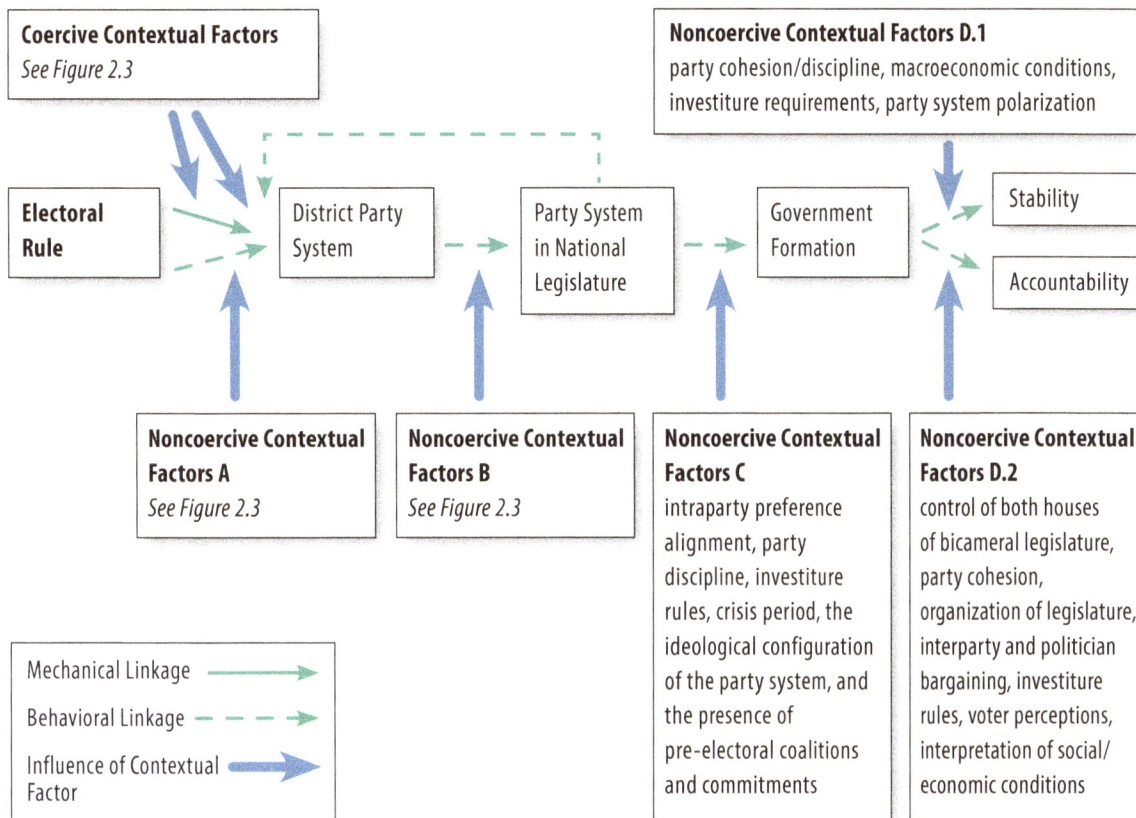

Source: Ferree, Powell and Scheiner, Task Force on Electoral Rules and Democratic Governance

Contextual factors—most notably, the ideological positions of parties—also determine which parties are included in governments. Extremist parties are unlikely to be included in coalitions. Collective governments (coalitions or minority governments) typically include the median party, the plurality party, or both[31] and are more likely to be between ideologically proximate parties.[32] Finally, pre-electoral coalitions also shape the composition of governments.

In sum, the causal chain linking electoral rules to government formation in parliamentary systems involves numerous behavioral linkages, providing significant opportunities for contextual factors to shape outcomes and attenuate the effects of electoral rules.

Government Formation in Presidential Systems

Many of the same causal processes we discussed previously in regard to legislative elections also apply to presidential elections. As highlighted in Figure 2.5, one important distinction is that in most presidential elections there is no district-level outcome that is distinct from the national outcome, so the projection stage in the legislative causal chain has no corollary in the presidential one.[33]

Figure 2.5: **Governance in Presidential Systems**

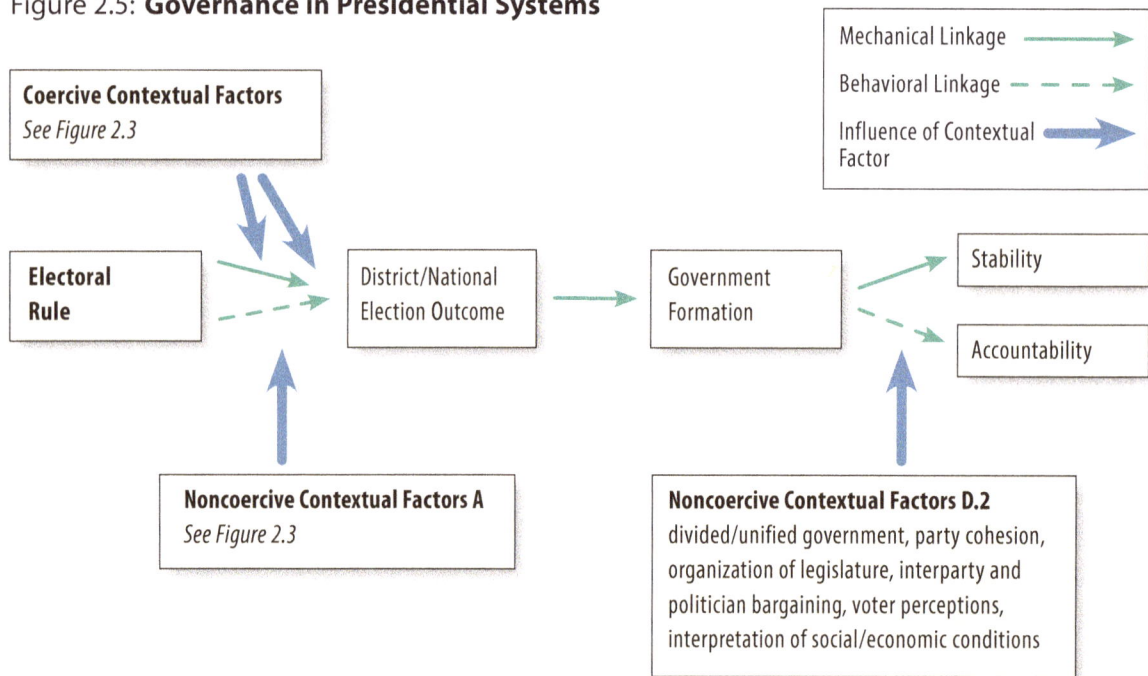

Source: Ferree, Powell and Scheiner, Task Force on Electoral Rules and Democratic Governance

The causal chain linking electoral rules to government formation is shorter in presidential systems than in parliamentary systems and involves a greater percentage of mechanical linkages. Regardless of context, government formation in presidential systems is almost entirely the result of the mechanical translation—based on the rules—of the popular vote into electoral victory for a single candidate.[34] In contrast, the influence of contextual factors does not end with the election of parliament in parliamentary systems.

Government Stability and Accountability

For both presidential and parliamentary systems, stability and accountability occur many steps downstream from the electoral institutions themselves (see Figures 2.4 and 2.5). Compared to presidential systems, parliamentary regimes contain a larger number of behavioral linkages between rules and stability/accountability, thus providing more opportunities for contextual factors to influence the outcomes, but, in fact, in both types of systems context heavily shapes governance outcomes.

Government Stability

Parliamentary systems. Parliamentary executives can be terminated by a vote of no confidence by parliament or premature resignation—that is, different types of discretionary human action—thus providing significant opportunities for context to shape stability.

More specifically, several types of contextual factors influence government stability in parliamentary systems (see Box D.1 in Figure 2.4). Government stability hinges critically on party cohesion. Party discipline, the power of the party leaders to sanction wayward members, helps sustain that cohesion. Absent party discipline, the risk of instability increases for all types of parliamentary government. Negative economic conditions, such as inflationary or unemployment shocks, are also likely to make all kinds of governments less durable. Governments that have had to pass formal investiture requirements are more durable than those that have not. Finally, a major contextual condition is the polarization of the party system, which is associated especially with less-durable minority and coalition governments. In polarized settings, minority governments struggle to gain stable support from nongoverning parties and coalition governments must contend with internal diversity.[35] Single-party governments may be more immune to some of these factors and therefore relatively more stable than minority or coalition governments.

Presidential systems. A defining feature of presidential regimes is the fixed term of office. Short of special, quasi-judicial action, presidents cannot be removed.[36] We therefore characterize the link between government formation and government stability in presidential systems as (near) mechanical and expect noncoercive contextual factors to play a minimal role in shaping the stability of presidential governments.

Government Accountability

Accountability implies that voters have the ability to remove the government from office if it fails to perform, and this, purportedly, motivates governments to perform as expected by voters. To establish and maintain accountability, voters must be able to assign responsibility for the outcome in question to the government and, within the government, to an identifiable actor or party.[37] In addition, voters must be assured that sanctioning of the government actually delivers the desired result: electorally unpopular leaders or parties must fail to retain office—or, at the very least, see their influence in government significantly wane.

Parliamentary systems. Accountability in parliamentary systems is contingent upon contextual factors because the ability to assign responsibility to the government, and within government to an identifiable actor or party, depends on behavioral factors such as party cohesion and voter perceptions. Accountability is likely to be reduced under minority and coalition governments, and when there is a lack of party cohesion.[38] Parties in coalitions may attempt to push the blame for poor performance onto their partners in government.[39] Even when a single party controls both cabinet and parliament, attribution within government may still be complicated if the party lacks cohesion. If the backbenchers claim party leadership is to blame for poor outcomes, and leadership blames backbenchers, voters may struggle to assign responsibility for actions. Parliamentary institutions like strong committee systems that give the opposition influence over policy[40] may also complicate attribution, even in single-party majority systems, by permitting the ruling party to claim, often credibly, that the opposition interfered with its policies or their implementation. Moreover, governments can credibly blame factors, such as the political, social, or economic context that they inherited from their predecessor or international interdependence and a global economic downturn, for a variety of failings, such as the state of the economy.[41]

There are important differences among types of parliamentary systems with respect to sanctioning. In single-party majority governments, voters have a clear ability to sanction majority governments by taking their majority away, and, thus, eliminating a party's ability to govern without restraint. In this way, the link between government formation and accountability is relatively mechanical for majority party governments in parliamentary systems. In contrast, the sanctioning component of accountability is behavioral for minority governments. Voters can strip a minority party of support if it performs poorly, but they cannot guarantee that the party will lose its ability to shape policy, since it can convince other parties to not oppose its place in the government. In this scenario, elite behavior within the legislature can mitigate the sanctioning power of voters.

The link between government formation and accountability is also behavioral for coalition governments. As with minority governments, voters can sanction the parties involved in the coalition, but the reduction of the influence of those parties depends on legislator/party behavior. Elites can opt to ignore the signal coming from voters and put back in government a party that has lost support at the polls. This behavior may respond to the same kinds of contextual conditions that gave rise to the coalition or minority government in the first place, such as the ideological configuration of the parties, the investiture and vote of confidence rules, and interpretation of economic shocks.

Presidential systems. If we look only at the executive branch, then presidential systems offer clear lines of accountability in a way unmediated by behavior. By taking away enough electoral support, voters remove presidents (or their party) from office. In this sense, presidential systems mechanically provide for accountability: voters can attribute and sanction in a way unmediated by behavioral factors.

However, if we take a more expansive view of government and allow that the president is but one actor in a complex system and that outcomes reflect the interaction of the presidential and legislative branches of government, then both attribution and punishment become more complicated. The division of responsibility between branches of government varies with presidential powers that differ per different constitutions, and is open to interpretation and persuasion. Are presidents responsible for poor economic outcomes, or are their opponents in the legislature to blame? Even when the same party controls the legislative and the executive branches, they may not present a unified front.[42] When there is strong party cohesion and the same party controls both branches, attribution may be relatively easy. But when elites within the same party refuse to stand together and accept responsibility, and when different parties control different parts of government, and the government itself may be only partially responsible for outcomes, attribution becomes highly complicated. And when attribution is complicated, sanctioning becomes difficult. Because the institutions do not clarify responsibility in a way that is immune to behavioral interventions, contextual factors may play a large role in determining accountability in presidential systems.

In sum, as we emphasize throughout this report, the numerous causal links between electoral rules and accountability and the behavioral nature of many of those links provide numerous points at which contextual factors can intervene.

Representation

Representation is a central concept in contemporary political science, with many different meanings and dimensions. Here we focus on two: the representation of ideological and geographic interests.

Representation of Ideological Interests

One dimension of representation is the extent to which the ideological position of the median voter is represented in government, or "congruence." Figure 2.6 shows the links between electoral rules and ideological representation for parliamentary systems. As the figure makes clear, the relationship between rules and ideological representation is long and involves many behavioral links. We therefore expect contextual factors to heavily mediate the relationship between rules and representation. The first several links in this chain replicate the initial steps in Figure 2.4, from electoral rules to government formation. In Figure 2.6, we add a new link—from government formation to the degree of ideological representation.

The causal mechanisms linking government formation to representation differ depending on whether 1) two large parties compete for power and a single-party majority

Figure 2.6: **Representation—Ideological Congruence of Voters and the Government**

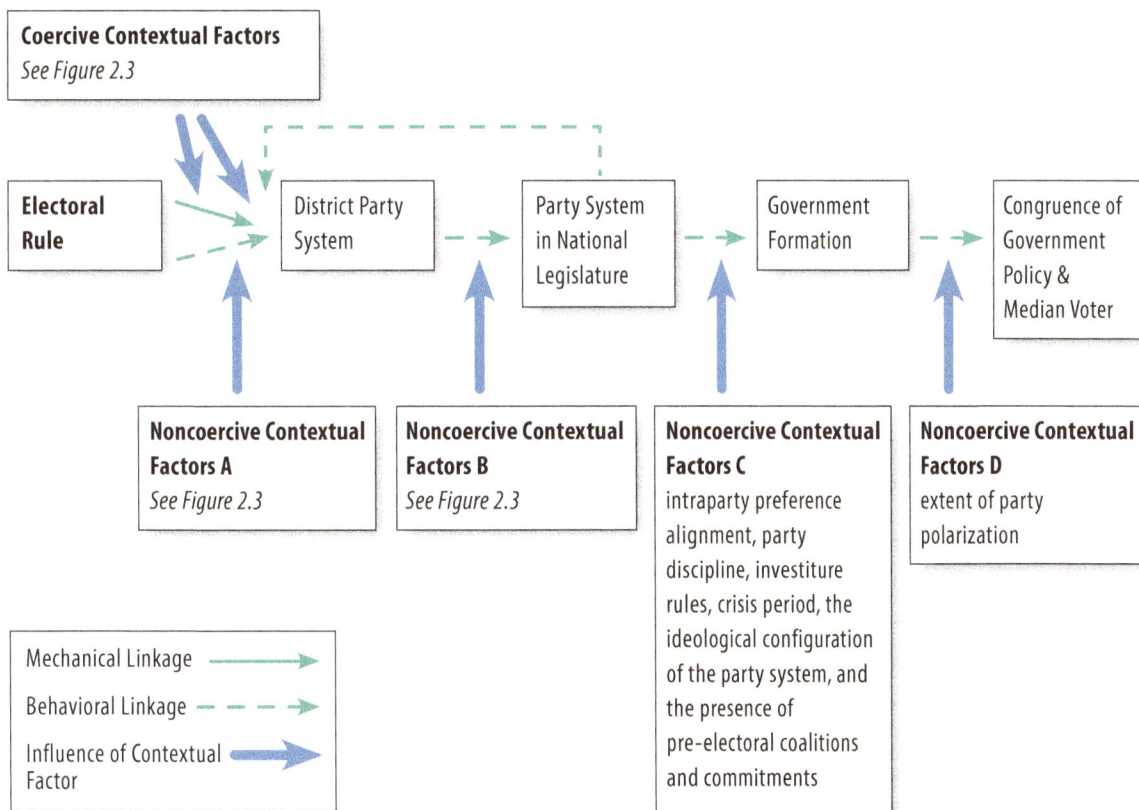

government forms or 2) many parties compete for power and a minority or coalition government forms.[43] When two large parties compete and win the most parliamentary seats, the link runs through Anthony Downs's[44] median voter theorem, which predicts that the legislative majority party should be close to the median voter. In contrast, when many parties divide up parliament, the link runs through the inclusion of the median or plurality party in the governing coalition, or both.[45] Regardless of the causal route, both mechanisms are behavioral. The median voter theorem assumes that parties and voters choose to act in specific ways. When behavior departs from assumptions, parties' full convergence to the policies of the median voter is not guaranteed. Indeed, substantial research suggests that full convergence often fails, underlining the contingency of the outcome. Moreover, while the median or plurality party (or both) is often included in governing coalitions, this inclusion is contingent on the decisions of elites—and elites could opt for coalitions that poorly represent the median voter.

For several decades following World War II, legislatures and governments in PR systems in developed democracies more consistently matched the issue positions of the median voter (i.e., created close ideological congruence) than those in SMD systems,[46] apparently because of breakdowns in Duverger-Downsian convergence in the SMD systems. However, studies of a more recent time period (roughly 1997–2004) indicate that the greater congruence under PR election rules has disappeared.[47] A contextual factor—specifically, the changing context of party system polarization—seems to be responsible for this change. Higher levels of party system polarization in the SMD systems, found in the immediate post-WWII decade and again in the 1970s and 1980s, limited Downsian convergence. Although such polarization also limited the formation of coalitions close to the median voter in the PR systems, the effects were larger and more direct in single-party majority SMD governments.[48] With declining polarization in the SMD systems during the 1997–2004 period, ideological congruence in SMD and PR systems still follows different causal paths but now has similar levels of congruence between the policy positions of the median voter and the legislature/government. This shift illustrates our central contention that ideological congruence is connected to election rules by a number of causal steps, and this lack of proximity (of the outcome to the electoral rule), as well as the role of multiple behavioral processes, render it vulnerable to contextual effects like polarization.

Representation of Geographic Interests

Electoral systems have a substantial impact on the representation of geographically concentrated interests, privileging some and disadvantaging others. There are at least two dimensions to such representational differences. On one hand, electoral systems differ in the breadth or narrowness of the interests represented in the legislature. Single-member districts and small-district magnitude PR (high-threshold PR) produce electoral responsiveness to interests that are geographically concentrated within district boundaries. High-magnitude PR districts, culminating in the extreme case of electoral systems in which the entire country is a single, large PR district, favor large, geographically dispersed interests. (The number of parties and the size of the legislature may determine mechanically how large in the aggregate these interests must be.)

However, Fiona McGillivray[49] argues that the degree of party system cohesion—a contextual factor that operates through a behavioral mechanism—creates different strategic incentives as to which geographically concentrated interests will be the focus of representation. Thus, behavioral linkages connect electoral rules to patterns of representational advantage. In strong party systems with few parties and party cohesion, parties will converge on closely competitive districts[50]; interests that are geographically concentrated in those districts will be targets of promises from both parties and be generally advantaged in representation as a result. In party systems with less cohesion, individual legislators will seek to represent dominant interests in their narrow geographic districts, and legislative advantage will emerge from coalitions constructed between these individual legislators. Consequently, the number of national parties (discussed earlier and in Figure 2.3) and the cohesion of the political parties are important contextual factors shaping representation of geographic interests. Party cohesion is itself shaped by parliamentary/presidential executives and the ballot structure of the election rules, as well as internal party organizational structures.[51] Once again, for outcomes distantly connected to rules through a number of behavioral mechanisms, contextual factors strongly mediate the effects of electoral rules.

Conclusion

Political analysts tend to agree that electoral rules play a significant part in shaping political outcomes, but rules do not work in a vacuum. A polity's context—whether social, economic, or political—shapes political outcomes as well. In this essay, we developed a framework for understanding when context mediates the effect of electoral rules on political outcomes and when the rules are more likely to work in an unadulterated fashion. In particular, contextual factors will have few mediating effects on outcomes directly and mechanically linked to electoral rules, such as disproportionality, but significant mediating effects on outcomes, such as the number of parties in the national party system, separated from electoral rules by many intervening stages, especially when those stages involve human discretion (what we have termed "behavioral" causal links). As the causal chain grows still longer, from electoral rules to, for example, issues of governance and ideological representation, the number of opportunities for contextual factors to shape outcomes grows dramatically. We do not expect uniform effects of rules on such outcomes. Rather, we can think of electoral engineering in such cases as similar to tossing a stone into the middle of a large lake. The stone will generate ripples on the shore, but the size, direction, and shape of those ripples will depend critically on objects encountered along the way, as well as prevailing winds, the depth of the lake, the distance to shore, and many other factors.

The framework we have laid out in this essay is not specific to the outcomes we have discussed, and ought to apply to numerous other important political outcomes—such as government stability and accountability, descriptive representation, the extent of party cohesion, the nature of the linkage between politicians and citizens, types of policies emphasized by the national government, and the degree to which politicians engage in corrupt practices. Our argument is not simply that context matters and that all analysis must be country-specific. There is no reason to think that every unique feature of a given country will mediate the effects of electoral rules. Rather, we suggest that context shapes the effects of electoral rules in *specific* ways. When rules have mechanical effects, involving no human discretion, contextual factors will have little influence, but when outcomes are a product of human behavior, contextual factors may be powerful forces.

Armed with this information, constitutional engineers will be better able to design institutions. Understanding the effects of electoral rules and specific contextual factors is important for any country, but especially so for new democracies that are only just beginning to implement new constitutions and electoral systems, and may have markedly different social, economic, and political foundations from established democracies.

3

Electoral Rules and Political Inclusion

Mona Lena Krook and Robert G. Moser

The inclusion of members of politically salient social categories within elected parliaments is an essential part of the democratic process. Legislatures that do not reflect society are typically deemed less legitimate and less likely to protect the interests of marginalized groups, and they can even spur excluded marginalized groups to destabilize the polity.[1] Although there is a thriving debate on whether political inclusion leads to advocacy to promote the interests of marginalized groups,[2] it can be reasonably assumed that groups lacking a visible legislative presence face strong impediments to making their concerns heard.[3] Scholars have tended to focus on how electoral rules affect the size and types of party systems, but a growing body of research indicates that these structures also have a crucial impact on who gets elected. Both *electoral systems*, which translate votes into seats, and, more specifically, *electoral regulations*, which directly attempt to influence the election of targeted groups, affect how much access members of politically salient social categories have to political decision-making bodies through elections.

Our aim in this article is to generate a framework for understanding how electoral rules influence patterns of political inclusion, concentrating on women and ethnic minorities. In short, we argue that electoral rules affect political inclusion by increasing or decreasing incentives for elites to nominate female and minority candidates and for voters to support them. These dynamics, however, are mediated in significant ways by contextual factors, including the level of social acceptance of women or minorities as political leaders, the commitment to the political incorporation of certain social categories, and the mode of electoral mobilization of these particular groups. Following the logic of the arguments made by Ferree, Powell, and Scheiner in this report, we propose that these two elements interact in a structured way: 1) electoral systems affect political inclusion in more indirect ways through psychological effects on elites and voters and thus are shaped much more by contextual factors, whereas 2) electoral quotas have more direct consequences on the election of historically marginalized groups by requiring the nomination and election of targeted groups and thus are shaped less by political context.

Electoral Systems and Political Inclusion

Electoral systems govern the translation of votes into seats. We distinguish here between the two most common electoral systems, proportional representation (PR) and plurality/ single-member district (SMD-plurality) elections. These two categories are internally differentiated by such features as district magnitude, legal thresholds, allocation formulas, and open-list versus closed-list competition. Electoral systems are identified as a primary factor influencing the election of women and ethnic minorities. PR is often cited as being more conducive to the election of both groups but for different reasons, as shown in Figure 3.1. The basic logic is that closed-list PR elections promote party-centric, multiparty contests that increase the incentives of parties and voters to support "diversity" candidates.

Figure 3.1: **Electoral Systems and Descriptive Representation**

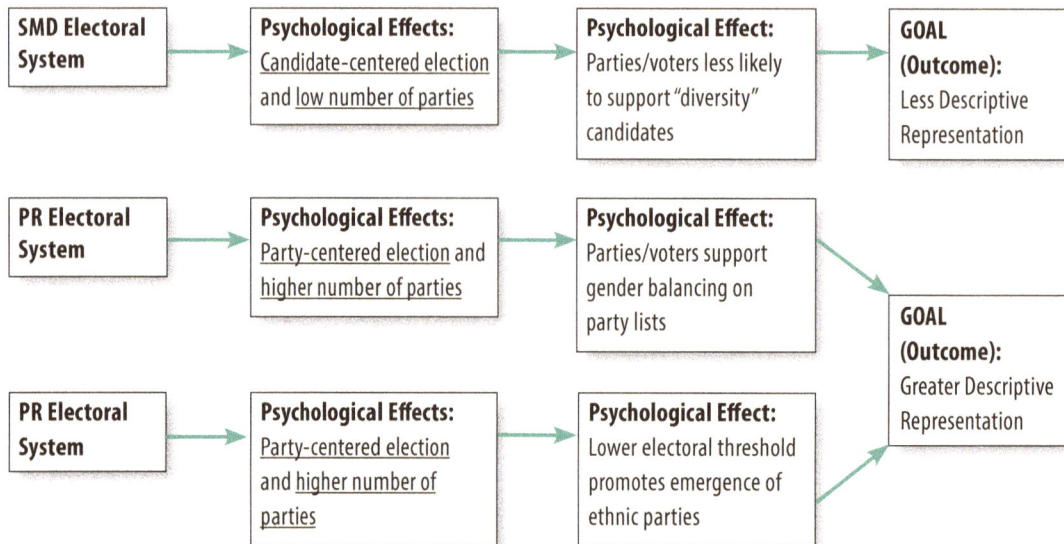

SMD Electoral System	→	Psychological Effects: Candidate-centered election and low number of parties	→	Psychological Effect: Parties/voters less likely to support "diversity" candidates	→	GOAL (Outcome): Less Descriptive Representation
PR Electoral System	→	Psychological Effects: Party-centered election and higher number of parties	→	Psychological Effect: Parties/voters support gender balancing on party lists	→	GOAL (Outcome): Greater Descriptive Representation
PR Electoral System	→	Psychological Effects: Party-centered election and higher number of parties	→	Psychological Effect: Lower electoral threshold promotes emergence of ethnic parties	→	

Source: Krook and Moser, Task Force on Electoral Rules and Democratic Governance

Party-centric contests make the personal characteristics of individual candidates less influential as voting cues. At the same time, the increased number of parties reduces the electoral threshold of representation, providing more potential avenues for the election of a diverse set of candidates. Conversely, when confronted with candidate-centered elections, all else being equal, voters and parties have fewer incentives to support women and ethnic minorities. Faced with a higher electoral threshold and the increased importance of candidate traits in SMDs, parties and voters are more apt to support candidates viewed as "safe and mainstream," which they see as more likely to win election.[4] Moreover, as Torben Iversen and Frances Rosenbluth[5] have noted in relation to gender, the career trajectories of men tend to create the backgrounds and financial/political connections most conducive to election in candidate-centered contests.[6] These socioeconomic disadvantages in SMDs are likely to extend to economically marginalized ethnic minorities as well.

While the disadvantages of SMD elections are similar for female and minority candidates, the advantages of PR for these groups display important differences. For women, multiparty competition based on party lists is expected to spur increased demand for and supply of female candidates across the party spectrum through a process of gender-balancing.[7] These dynamics culminate in many instances in the adoption of gender quotas,[8] which are also generally more straightforward to implement in PR systems due to the use of lists.[9] Consequently, parties anticipate electoral rewards for placing women on closed-party lists and penalties for failing to do so. For ethnic minorities, the primary vehicle of representation in PR elections is the ethnic party, in which parties appealing to particular ethnicities emerge due to the lower electoral threshold necessary to gain representation.[10]

Nonetheless, despite widespread agreement that PR tends to be more inclusive of women and ethnic minorities than SMD elections, empirical studies have produced a variety of different findings on this relationship. Richard Matland[11] finds that PR promotes the election of women in advanced democracies, but not developing countries. In contrast, Robert G. Moser and Ethan Scheiner[12] and Moser[13] conclude that PR does not promote the election of women more than SMD elections under certain circumstances. Lastly, Andrew Reynolds[14] observes that majoritarian elections tend to elect ethnic minorities in greater numbers than PR.

These varied findings suggest that context mitigates the impact these electoral rules have on the election of women and ethnic minorities. For example, the PR advantage for women presumes that parties will see the nomination of women as an electorally advantageous endeavor and electoral thresholds will be lower under PR than SMD. In party systems with dramatic party fragmentation even in plurality elections, women can gain election at higher rates in SMDs due to lower electoral thresholds. Yet they may gain less representation in PR elections due to lower party magnitude, which results in small parties that do not elect members from far enough down their party lists to reach female candidates.[15]

In societies with biases against women, female candidates are unlikely to gain election under any electoral system.[16] As Moser and Scheiner[17] show, in states with low support for women as political leaders and high party fragmentation—for example, post-Communist states—women are elected at the same rates under both PR and SMD rules. At the same time, women's higher socioeconomic status may lessen the disadvantages of candidate-centered elections for women by enlarging the pool of viable female candidates. In short, the impact that different electoral systems have on the election of women is contingent upon factors—cultural attitudes toward women, the socioeconomic status of women, and party system characteristics—that can lessen the disadvantages of SMDs and undermine the advantages of PR (see Figure 3.2).

As for the PR advantage in the election of ethnic minorities, different contextual factors can disrupt the logic that, in ethnically divided states, more parties under PR give rise to ethnic parties that can serve as a vehicle for minority representation. In particular, demographic characteristics of specific ethnic groups can alter the incentives for parties and voters to support minority candidates. Ethnic minorities that are geographically concentrated may reach a critical mass that prompts large, mainstream parties to nominate minority candidates in these regions. Under such conditions, SMD elections may result in similar or even greater levels of minority representation than PR elections.[18]

Yet the logic of ethnic parties serving as the main avenue of minority representation rests on a presumption of ethnic voting. However, the level of ethnic voting may vary across countries and groups and thus alter incentives for the formation of ethnic parties and the

Figure 3.2: **Context, Electoral Systems and the Election of Women**

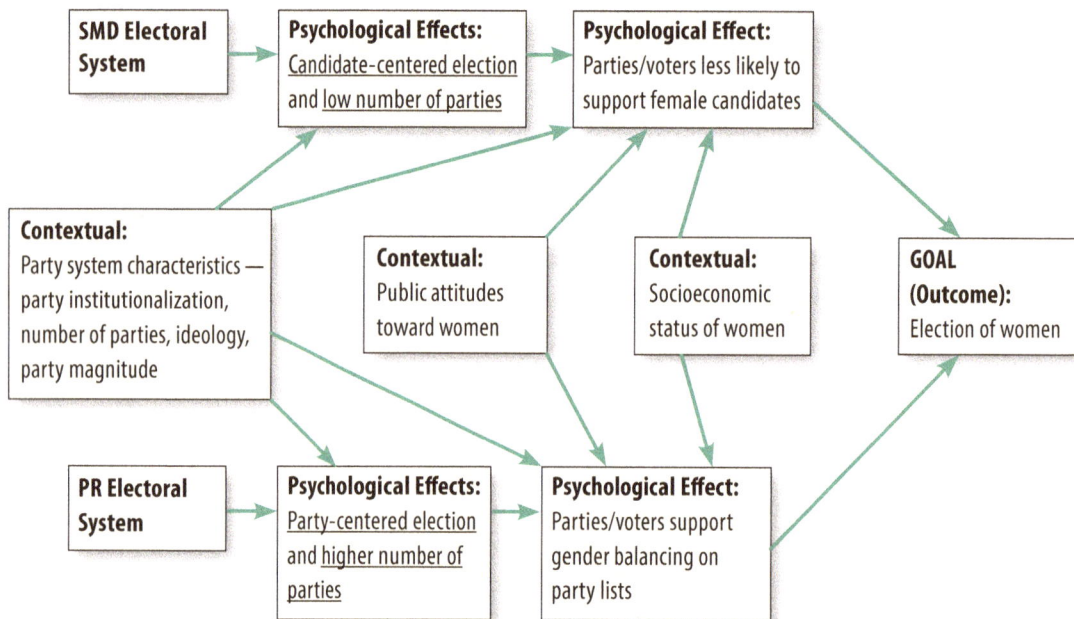

Source: Krook and Moser, Task Force on Electoral Rules and Democratic Governance

nomination of minority candidates by mainstream parties. Moser finds,[19] for example, that more assimilated ethnic minorities in Russia manage to gain election to the national legislature in roughly equal numbers under the PR and SMD tiers of the mixed-member electoral system. Popular attitudes toward minorities can have the same effect. As Reynolds notes, the ethos of inclusion in South Africa facilitated the nomination of minority candidates in parties across the political spectrum.[20] Thus, to an even greater extent than women's representation, the effects of electoral systems on the election of ethnic minorities are contingent upon the broader context (see Figure 3.3).

Electoral Regulations and Group Representation

Electoral regulations are provisions specifically designed to increase the election of a particular group. These policies have received a variety of labels, but are most often described as "quotas," "reservations," or "majority-minority districts." Like electoral rules, electoral regulations are subject to significant internal variation based on the location of the mandate at the state or party level, the proportion of seats affected, the existence of placement provisions, the specificity of requirements, and mechanisms of enforcement.

Preferential rules have gained prominence recently in discussions of political inclusion due to their introduction in a broad array of countries, most within the last 10 to 15 years. In all, more than 100 countries have witnessed the adoption of gender quotas, with slightly fewer than half being introduced through legal or constitutional reform. Diversity in their design means that quotas have not led to a uniform rise in women's representation; some

Figure 3.3: **Electoral Systems and the Election of Ethnic Minorities**

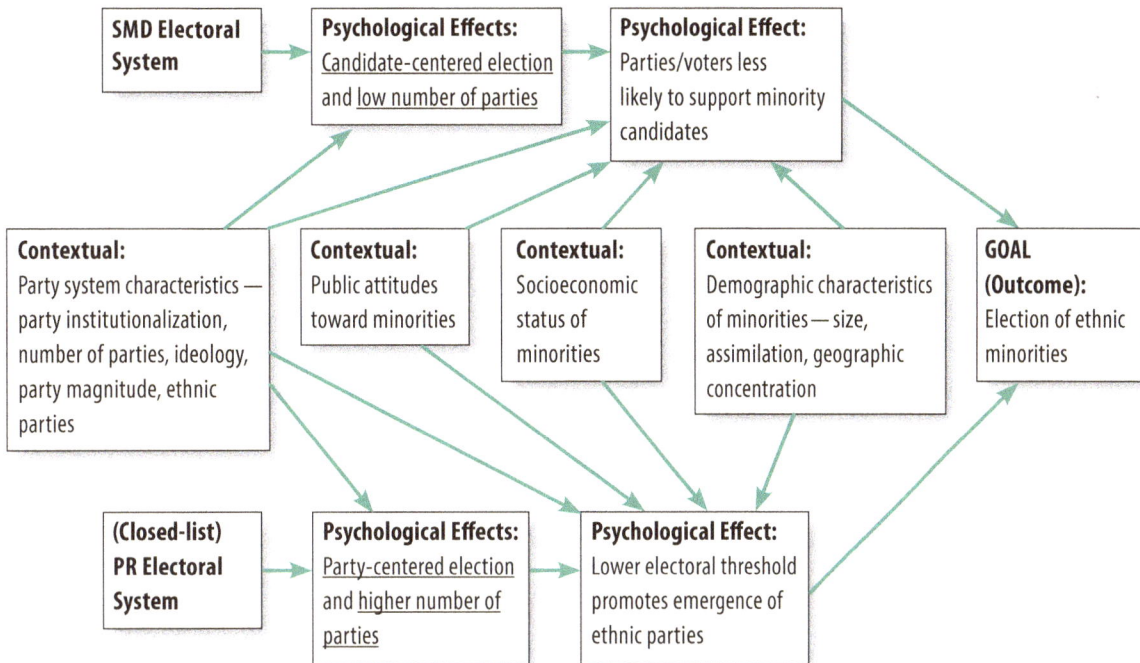

| SMD Electoral System | → | Psychological Effects: Candidate-centered election and low number of parties | → | Psychological Effect: Parties/voters less likely to support minority candidates |

Contextual: Party system characteristics — party institutionalization, number of parties, ideology, party magnitude, ethnic parties

Contextual: Public attitudes toward minorities

Contextual: Socioeconomic status of minorities

Contextual: Demographic characteristics of minorities — size, assimilation, geographic concentration

GOAL (Outcome): Election of ethnic minorities

(Closed-list) PR Electoral System → Psychological Effects: Party-centered election and higher number of parties → Psychological Effect: Lower electoral threshold promotes emergence of ethnic parties

Source: Krook and Moser, Task Force on Electoral Rules and Democratic Governance

countries have seen strong increases, whereas others have witnessed more modest changes or even setbacks in the proportion of women elected. Most explanations for these variations focus not on aspects of the broader social, economic, and political contexts, but rather on differences in their design and how they interact with other types of political institutions.[21]

Contextual elements, however, have featured prominently in accounts of gender quota introduction.[22] The mobilization of women's groups inside and outside parties, for example, has been seen as crucial in getting quotas on the political agenda, both in well-established democracies[23] and in societies experiencing dramatic changes in gender roles due to political transitions or reconstruction following years of violent conflict.[24] Indeed, demands for quotas may be particularly effective during periods of democratic transition, as the policy may be seen to help establish the legitimacy of the new political system.[25]

Case studies also signal the strategic incentives of elites in pursuing quota reform, which may emerge at moments of heightened competition among political parties[26] or when party leaders and incumbents seek to portray themselves—usually insincerely—as open to women and their concerns.[27] The support of international and transnational actors is an additional factor,[28] with many international organizations—most notably the United Nations—issuing declarations recommending that member-states aim for 30% women in all political bodies. The states most subject to international and transnational influence tend to be post-conflict societies and developing countries, where outside actors may play a larger role in shaping electoral structures via moral or material pressures.[29] Quotas featured prominently, for example, in discussions surrounding the creation of new political structures in the wake of the Arab Spring.[30]

Measures for minorities, in comparison, exist in nearly 40 countries and apply to a wide array of groups—many, but not all, of which may be subsumed under the "ethnic minority" label. Nearly all involve reserved seats, although the proportion and identities in question vary enormously across cases. These policies tend to have one of two goals: "protection" or power-sharing,[31] which highlights the importance of national context in defining salient groups and their share of reserved seats.

Protection entails allocating seats to groups that constitute a relatively small contingent of the population, including indigenous peoples, members of minority religions and nationalities, and class- or caste-based groups. The provisions are generally minimal, involving as little as 1 or 2% of all seats.[32] In instances of protection, the aim is often to compensate for past oppression. Reserved seats typically numerically overrepresent the minority in question.[33] Historical grounds often trump other considerations and include dealing with colonial legacies,[34] although transnational influences have grown more important both in cases of conflict and as a means for promoting indigenous rights.[35]

In contrast, power-sharing arrangements involve dividing up most or all seats in the legislature between two or more factions, defined by ethnicity, religion, or language. These policies entail a higher proportion of seats, often as much as 25 to 70%, and exist in most regions, including Africa, Europe, the Middle East, and the Pacific. In cases of power-sharing, the goal is to ensure democratic stability in a divided society.[36] Reserved seats grant group members a guaranteed voice in the political system as a means of preventing their defection which, it is feared, might provoke collapse of the state.[37] In the wake of conflict, several countries have devised power-sharing provisions based on historical practices of group representation or as part of international efforts to promote consociational political arrangements.[38]

Tensions in Promoting Political Inclusion

As shown in Figure 3.1, women and ethnic minorities are expected to gain election through different avenues. As Htun has observed, these different routes to electoral representation tend to be translated into distinct institutional mechanisms—quotas for women and reserved seats for minorities.[39] One consequence of these differences may be that electoral rules, in particular PR, may result in outcomes that favor one social category at the expense of another. Ethnic minorities, particularly smaller groups, arguably benefit from a more fragmented party system, with smaller parties that give rise to ethnic parties. However, women tend to gain election through larger, mainstream parties that require a higher party magnitude—the likelihood of winning more seats in a given district—to reach female candidates farther down the party list.

In general, through the manipulation of district magnitude or legal thresholds, PR systems can promote either more fragmented party systems with many parties and low electoral thresholds or less fragmented party systems with fewer parties and higher electoral thresholds. Moreover, ethnic parties themselves may undermine the election of women through their emphasis on ethnic cleavages.[40] Preferential electoral rules, in particular gender quotas with placement mandates,[41] can potentially remedy this situation by removing party magnitude as a factor in women's representation and requiring all parties to nominate women in winnable positions.

On the other hand, preferential electoral regulations may also lead to tradeoffs in political inclusion. By targeting one social category, preferential rules such as quotas, reserved seats, and majority-minority seats may undermine the election of the other historically marginalized groups that have not been targeted. Crucially, in most countries where such regulations exist, only one group is likely to receive representational guarantees.[42] Such dynamics can be addressed explicitly during quota debates, such that the granting of quota policies for one group opens up—rather than forecloses—options for additional groups.[43]

Moreover, as scholars of "intersectionality" have argued, focusing exclusively on one dimension of exclusion—for example, sex or race but not both—can strengthen dominant subgroups over marginalized ones.[44] For instance, as Melanie Hughes shows, countries with minority quotas tend to elect fewer women than countries without measures to increase minority representation. However, in cases in which electoral regulations are in place for both women and ethnic minorities ("tandem quotas"), elections have sometimes markedly increased the election of minority women.[45] A closer look suggests, nonetheless, that this can come at the cost of electing majority women and minority men—and can, in fact, bolster the electoral share of majority men in the process.[46]

Conclusion

Debates over the political inclusion of marginalized groups have emerged in recent decades leading to flourishing—although often disparate—literatures on electoral structures and group representation. This article reviews and reflects upon this research as it concerns women and ethnic minorities, highlighting some parallels but also some crucial differences when it comes to designing electoral institutions that might facilitate the greater inclusion of these two groups. A notable finding is that distinct electoral rules may shape the electoral prospects of women and ethnic minorities in opposing ways, although there is by no means a firm consensus within the literature—highlighting, in turn, the importance of the broader social, economic, and cultural contexts in mediating the effects of electoral structures.

The tendency to focus on women *or* ethnic minorities has led to a compartmentalization of research, limiting opportunities for cross-fertilization of insights. Moreover, this tendency has contributed to a general neglect of individuals—minority women—who lie at the intersection of these identities and thus are doubly marginalized, not only in politics but also in the literatures. This combined state of affairs points to a rich frontier for potential future research, deepening existing insights on women and minorities, exploring tensions and complementarities between these two groups, and taking a serious look at how intersectionally marginalized groups fare, all in relation to the rules, regulations, and contextual factors that shape the contours and outcomes of the political process.

4

Why Ballot Structure Matters

Matthew S. Shugart

When political scientists speak of ballot structure, attention is drawn to one critical variable: Does the ballot permit voters to cast a vote below the party level, or only at that level? That is, do voters have a choice of candidates within a party or not? There are numerous other variations, but this is the big way in which ballot structure makes a difference.

Ballot structure matters because of its impact on the collective action of political parties. A party can be thought of broadly as being like any other collective actor: it functions as a unitary organization only to the extent that the incentives of its individual members are aligned with the collective goals of the organization. In the case of political parties, it can be assumed that the dominant collective goal is to win seats in the legislature, because most other party goals are subordinated to this task, including forming or affecting the support of governments, passing policy, etc. The key impact of ballot structure lies in its potential to reinforce or undercut this goal. If ballot structure permits votes below the party level, it may undermine to varying degrees the alignment of these collective goals and the individual goals of its candidates and legislators.

The impact of ballot structure can be encapsulated by reference to the two dimensions of Table 4.1. The most basic meaning of ballot structure is simply whether voters are able to cast a vote for one (or sometimes more than one) of the candidates nominated by their preferred party. The top row of the figure, indicated as "open" ballots, shows election rules in which the ballot permits a candidate-level vote. The alternative to this is a "closed" ballot structure, in which case the vote is strictly at the party level.

Table 4.1: **Two Dimensions of Ballot Structure**

		Vote Pooling?	
		No	Yes
Ballot Structure	Open (vote for candidate)	Single- (Non-) Transferable Vote	Open-list PR
	Closed (vote for party)	N/A	Closed-list PR

Source: Shugart, Task Force on Electoral Rules and Democratic Governance

The second dimension considers what happens after the vote is cast. Does it stay only with the candidate for whom it was cast, or does it "pool" at the party level? The former case is pure candidate-based allocation: candidates win seats based solely on votes cast for them as individuals, as with the single-nontransferable vote (SNTV), as indicated in the upper-left cell of Table 4.1. So-called ordinal ballots that allow voters to rank their choices among multiple candidates, as in the single-transferable vote (STV), likewise belong to this category of open ballots without vote pooling.

By contrast, if there is vote pooling, the vote first is counted toward a list of candidates nominated by a party (or alliance of parties). At this first stage of counting, the two systems indicated in the right column as having vote pooling are identical. In either open-list or closed-list proportional representation (PR), the first criterion is to determine the proportional distribution of seats among competing lists. If the list is closed, voters have voted only for a list, and candidates win seats within the list in the order in which they are ranked by the party before the election. By contrast, the combination of open ballots with vote pooling—open-list PR (the upper-right cell of Table 4.1)—is a proportional system based on pooled votes at the party level (to determine proportionality), followed by candidate-based votes that determine the order of election within each list.

There are also intermediate types of list systems, which are known as either "flexible" or "semi-open" lists. Like open or closed lists, these entail vote pooling. They also offer voters an open ballot, in that candidate-level choice is offered. However, unlike the purely open lists, there is a party-determined order and only those candidates who obtain some stipulated quota of votes cast specifically for them have a chance to move up the list ranking. Otherwise, seats are filled by list order. Such semi-open list systems are quite common, and given that often most seats in such systems do not depend on candidates' own "preference" votes, it is important not to conflate them with purely open lists.

So far, the focus of this essay has been on multiseat districts—PR systems, SNTV, and STV. What about single-seat districts? Fully candidate-based ballots are the norm when single-seat districts are used—such as the plurality systems of Canada, the United Kingdom, and the United States, or the two-round system of France. However, in terms of the impact of ballot structure on intraparty choice, plurality and majority systems are not normally any different from a closed list: there are only M candidates per party, where M refers to the district magnitude (the number of seats in the district) and $M=1$, because there is no intraparty competition at the general election stage.[1] Similarly, even with ranked-choice ballots, if there is only one seat at stake only one candidate per party is the norm, and hence there is no voter choice below the party level.

Political Parties and Ballot Structure

Open ballot structure—even with, but especially without, vote pooling—potentially threatens the collective action of political parties. It pits a party's candidates against one another for seats whenever the party has more candidates than seats it could possibly win. Thus, in multiseat districts, such as those used for either type of PR or for SNTV or STV, parties need to reconcile the incentives of their competing candidates with the collective pursuits of the party as a whole.

This is not to say that the collective action of political parties is determined only by ballot structure. The electoral system—of which ballot structure is a critical variable—is not destiny. There are other aspects of party organization and the broader political context that may work to reinforce or undermine collective action. In parties organized around a specific ideology or programmatic agenda, organizational tools such as candidate selection rules and disciplinary tactics (e.g., offering or denying desirable intralegislative or executive posts) may be used to stymie careers, and in any case, potential candidates will tend to self-select based on their commitment to the party's broader political goals.[2] Other parties are more loosely identified with specific policy commitments, or are "clientelistic"—organized around the exchange of material benefits—and such parties may display less cohesiveness and adopt more permeable selection procedures.

Prominent institutional factors that shape how well parties behave as collective actors include the executive-legislative structure—presidential, parliamentary, or semipresidential or other hybrid. In situations in which parties are directly involved in seeking to place one of their own in a top executive position that is dependent on the legislature—as in a parliamentary democracy—intraparty incentives are more strongly aligned than when there is a separate election to constitute executive power.[3] For all these reasons and more, it should not be surprising when a direct link between ballot structure (or other electoral-system features) and various outcome variables of interest is not immediately apparent. Nor should it be surprising when different studies find different effects, such as in the literature on corruption, as noted later. One must be cognizant of what it is that ballot structure does, as well as how it fits into the broader context.

The Impact of District Magnitude

District magnitude, M, is the number of seats in a district. When there are single-seat districts, $M=1$, and only one candidate per party, any limitations on the collective action of a party are not the result of ballot structure. In terms of the simple process of determining the winners of the election, candidate and party incentives are perfectly aligned: whenever one of its candidates has won his or her district contest, the party has picked up an additional seat. Any deviation of candidates from the party line in their campaign strategy or of elected legislators in their floor votes must stem from cross-district differences or individual characteristics, not from ballot structure.

In multiseat districts, on the other hand, the relationship of collective and individual incentives is quite different and conditional upon ballot structure. Without getting too technical, some systematic basic notation will be helpful. As already noted, M is used to refer to district magnitude, the number of seats in a district. In addition, the number of seats any given party wins in a district can be denoted by s, and the number of candidates it endorses in the district as c. Thus when $M=1$, it is almost always the case that $c=M$, and for the winning party, $s=c=M$ (whereas for all other parties, $s=0$, $c=M$). In other words, due to the ballot structure, as well as the party nomination strategy (partly) derived from that structure, there is no vote below the party level and hence no intraparty competition or misalignment of incentives, at least within any one district. However, things change as M increases, such that when $M > 1$, often $c \geq M$, but even for the most successful parties, usually $s < c$. This is a way of stating that there is internal competition for a scarce resource, since the party has more candidates than it can realistically elect.

The main systems using multiseat districts can be arrayed along a continuum[4] from most party-centric to increasingly candidate-centric as follows:

Closed list > Semi-open lists > Open lists > STV > SNTV.

It should be noted that the relative position of the last two systems is not straightforward, given that neither has vote pooling. Nonetheless, STV facilitates the exchange of preferences among candidates of the same party; SNTV does not. Of course, unlike any list system, STV also permits voters to rank candidates without regard to party affiliation, and both STV and SNTV can be employed in nonpartisan elections.

At the opposite end of the continuum, when lists are closed, the only competition within a party occurs in advance of the election, over who gets the best (or "safest") list ranks. Once the election comes around, incentives are perfectly aligned between individual candidates and their party: if the party—as a collective actor with a brand identity among voters—prospers, a candidate's chances of election increase. Candidates thus have an overriding incentive to cultivate a party vote.[5]

However, with any other ballot structure, there is at least some chance that candidates' entrepreneurial activities can increase their election chances independent of the party reputation. The greater the weight the rules put on candidate votes rather than a pre-fixed list order (if there is one), the more the candidates have an incentive to cultivate a personal vote. Carey and Shugart[6] showed how different electoral formulas affect the incentive to cultivate a personal vote, considering the interaction of preference voting and district magnitude. A simplified form of the Carey-Shugart hypothesis[7] is depicted in Figure 4.1, in which the incentive to cultivate a personal vote is shown to decrease with district magnitude when there is no intraparty competition, and to increase with district magnitude when there is such competition.

In closed-list systems, the value of the personal vote decreases as magnitude

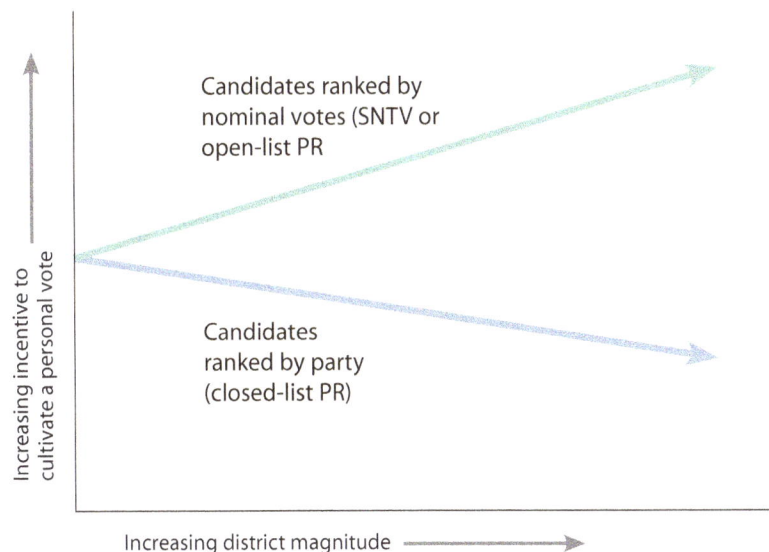

Figure 4.1: **The Differential Effect of District Magnitude on the Intraparty Dimension**

Candidates ranked by nominal votes (SNTV or open-list PR

Candidates ranked by party (closed-list PR)

Increasing incentive to cultivate a personal vote

Increasing district magnitude

Source: Shugart, Task Force on Electoral Rules and Democratic Governance

increases, because any entrepreneurial behavior by candidates has an imperceptible effect on their probability of election. Only pre-election party rankings matter. However, given small magnitude, with a correspondingly smaller number of candidates, the activities of the leading (and perhaps also marginal) candidates to highlight their personal record or characteristics may affect their election chances by drawing voters who would not otherwise have voted for the party. Thus, personal campaigning may affect some candidates' election prospects under closed ballots when M is low, but any such affect diminishes the more M rises.

On the other hand, when ballots are open, an increase in magnitude increases the incentive to cultivate a personal vote. When preference votes for candidates determine candidates' order of election, as under open lists, SNTV, or STV, only those candidates who are successful at drawing votes to themselves are likely to prosper. As M increases, each candidate in a party typically must compete against a greater number of copartisans. As a result, a higher M generates greater incentives to distinguish oneself in order to stand out in the larger crowd. The effect should be similar under semi-open lists, albeit attenuated, to the extent that the rules may permit many candidates to win based on having safe list ranks provided by their party.

There is now a rich literature on SNTV, the system that most induces personal vote-seeking incentives in individual candidates. Examples include the various contributions to Grofman et al.,[8] as well as burgeoning single-country literatures on Japan and Taiwan.[9] This impressive body of literature has generated certain propositions about the effects of SNTV, many of them tied to the practices parties must employ to manage the system. For instance, parties under SNTV are not rewarded for their aggregate level of support in an electoral district, but instead for having fielded an optimal number of candidates and having divided the votes optimally among them. Managing the system often implies heavy use of pork-barrel politics to ensure the loyalty of voters to one candidate over another. The remainder of this essay does not consider the increasingly rare—if still theoretically interesting—case of SNTV. Instead, the focus is on closed- and open-list systems. This narrowed focus is not intended to deny important differences among SNTV, STV, and open-list PR[10]; however, most of the key contrasts are between this set of open-ballot systems and other systems with a closed ballot structure. This latter term refers primarily to closed party lists, but would also encompass most ballots used in single-seat districts, due to the lack of voter choice *within parties* in these systems.

Impact on Legislative Behavior

The literature with regard to the effect of electoral institutions on behavior in the legislative arena is an established and fast-growing subfield.[11] More often than not, however, studies easily leap from the formal properties of electoral institutions to legislative behavior, failing to identify the causal mechanism responsible for generating incentives for voters, parties, and individual legislators. Not much is known about the manner in which the formal properties of the electoral institutions translate into conflicting incentives. Nor is much known about how individual legislators choose between the multiple behavioral repertoires commonly called "personal vote-seeking."

Previous sections have already detailed the impact of ballot structure on electoral competition. When ballots are closed, the dominant dimension of competition is interparty, due to the basic alignment of the incentives of individual candidates with the collective goals of their party. However, with open ballots, electoral competition occurs on both the interparty and intraparty levels, with individual vote-seeking potentially undermining party collective action. Here, I now turn to the impact ballot structure has on democratic accountability, specifically on whether legislative structure and behavior are geared toward legislators' desire to be personally recognized, and rewarded, by groups of voters (individual accountability) or toward enhancing the collective reputations of parties (collective accountability).

With open ballots, the threat to an individual legislator's pursuit of reelection—or to any new candidate's prospects of first election—comes primarily from other candidates of the same party (or political camp). This threat supplies the motivational drive to use the scarce perquisites of office to nurture a personal reputation.[12] Some will look after constituents' individual and collective interests; others champion a particular social group; and still others seek to translate the party's platform pledges into legislation.

Ballot structure both enables and constrains voters' abilities to monitor and sanction legislators' performance, thus shaping the balance between individual and collective accountability. For instance, if parties control nominations but voters determine ranks on a list, legislators answer to multiple principals, which creates potential problems for the cohesiveness of a party in the legislature.[13]

The legislator who is the sole representative of a district bears the responsibility of promoting its interests.[14] In these circumstances, constituents have only the actions of one legislator to monitor, increasing his or her name recognition.[15] When constituents are represented by many legislators, on the other hand, the cost of monitoring quickly exceeds the time and effort that voters will typically devote to politics.[16] To some degree, shirking and free-riding will ensue in any context of multiseat districts because constituents must monitor multiple representatives,[17] and voters are less likely to recall candidate names as there are more legislators elected from their district.[18] However, the monitoring problem is potentially exacerbated by open ballots and high district magnitude.

When ballots are closed, voters have no means to sanction individuals, even if they are aware of undesirable traits or actions by one or more of them. All voters can do is sanction the party as a whole by voting for a different one next time. Moreover, with closed ballots, party organizations need to cope with potential free-riding problems, given that the individual legislative candidates' actions have so little impact on their election prospects. (On the other hand, if party leaders are aware of a legislator who shirks on the party, they have the individual sanction of denying renomination or moving a candidate down to a marginal or even hopeless list position.) When ballots are open, in principle, voters have the option to sanction an incumbent for poor performance and vote for a copartisan instead, whether a different incumbent or one of several challengers. However, there is often a tension between competitiveness and accountability: On the one hand, higher intraparty competition implies a strong incentive for individual legislators to cultivate ties to voters (as argued in the previous section). On the other hand, the more candidates in competition for a limited number of seats, the less effective individual "credit-claiming" for services rendered can be. When responsibility is divided among several legislators, each seeking personal votes, the ability to hold any one of them accountable for his or her actions is lessened.

Empirical research linking incentives to cultivate a personal vote with legislative behavior faces a fundamental problem: while the incentives of different ballot structures can be clearly articulated, incentives, per se, are unobservable. They can be inferred only from the behavioral patterns they instigate.[19] Some legislators initiate bills or amendments that primarily benefit their local community; others hold frequent surgeries and redress constituents' grievances; and still others take positions that defy the party whip. As Audrey André and Sam Depauw[20] note, the implicit assumption that grew out of the personal vote literature is that incentives will translate into all of the behavioral repertoires and outcomes commonly considered to be personal vote-seeking. Scott Morgenstern and Javier Vázquez-D'Elía[21] emphasize, however, that electoral institutions are but the rules of the game; they do not impose a particular course of action. More important, one personal vote-seeking course of action may be substituted for another.[22] Since research has focused on one single indicator of personal vote-seeking at a time,[23] little is known about the manner in which legislators choose between different courses of action that are equally personal vote-seeking, leading to a risk of underestimating personal vote-seeking.[24]

The tensions between collective and individual incentives in political parties shape the balance between personal- and constituency-oriented behavior of legislators on the one hand and their cultivation of a party reputation and adherence to a party line on the other. Nonetheless, it is important to remember that party leaders frequently have the ability to directly affect the behavioral repertoires on which a legislator's personal reputation is built. On the one hand, party leaders will seek to constrain a legislator's personal vote-seeking when such behavior would be detrimental to the party's collective reputation. On the other hand, party leaders may require legislators to engage in behavior from which they do not personally benefit.[25] The ability to thwart electoral incentives critically depends on the means at the disposal of the party leadership to monitor and sanction an individual legislator's behavior. These means include control over career advancement, staff allocation, and numerous procedural advantages in the legislative arena (e.g., through committee assignment and agenda control).[26] More important, parties more often than not control access to the party label in elections: via candidate nomination, they have the ability to coordinate intraparty competition and thereby manage the vote in systems under which unequal dispersion of candidates votes might cost the party, such as SNTV and STV.[27]

Impact on Ties to Interest Groups and the Prospects for Corruption

Some of the literature on the impact of ballot structure has attempted to link variation on the intraparty level to behavioral patterns and macrolevel outcomes that go well beyond the immediate impact on party and personal vote cultivation. There is an evolving tension in this area of the literature between those who see electoral systems that emphasize party-vote incentives as favoring the representation of unorganized voters and those who see the opposite effect. For those who emphasize the "particularistic" nature of the personal vote, electoral rules that strengthen the party at the expense of the individual legislator are understood to reduce particularism (i.e., the targeting of policy to favor narrow interests). The logic is that intraparty competition for personal votes encourages legislators to forge close relations with organized special interests that can either mobilize reliable voters to help legislators withstand competition with their copartisans or finance their campaigns. The result is recourse to the pork barrel[28]—that is, sponsoring legislation that targets spending on the interest groups or voter constituencies that members need for their personal vote—or outright corruption.[29] On the other hand, this perspective at least implicitly sees parties as encompassing organizations capable of overcoming the influence of special interests that competition for personal votes breeds.

However, an alternative perspective sees party leaders, not individual candidates, as the villains who distort popular sovereignty in favor of narrow interests. When party leaders control the prospects for the election of rank-and-file legislators, they can shield members and themselves from electoral accountability and provide favors to interest groups that lack a popular constituency.[30] Disentangling the conditions under which one electoral system or another advances in general over narrow interests should be a high priority item on the agenda of electoral systems researchers. However, before this research agenda can advance, progress must be made in basic data availability.

Conclusion

Ballot structure can reinforce or undermine the collective action of political parties. When ballots permit voters to make only a single choice, the structure reinforces the collective action of a party by aligning the incentives of the candidate (get more votes, be more electorally secure) with those of the party (win another seat). When the ballot structure is open, voters are able to make one or more choices of candidates below the party level. This structure tends to undermine the collective action of a party because it pits candidates of the same party against one another. Variations within open ballots—for example, open- and semi-open (flexible) lists, ranked-choice ballots, nontransferable votes that are not also party votes—can further shape the degree to which ballot structure affects parties. Since numerous other factors shape parties' collective action, ballot structure is not destiny. It does, however, critically shape the relationships among voters, candidates, and political parties.

5

Policy Consequences of Electoral Rules

John Carey and Simon Hix

Electoral Rules, Policy, and Narrow versus Broad Interests

One of the fastest growing areas of research on electoral systems in political science and political economy has been on the effects of electoral systems on policy outcomes. This agenda has sparked some lively controversies among prominent scholars. It has also generated new theoretical ideas and new data sets with which these ideas have been tested. Research has focused on the effect of electoral systems on a wide range of policy issues, including:

- redistribution of wealth through taxation and progressive social welfare policies
- redistribution of wealth through regulatory policies that affect consumer prices
- fiscal restraint versus profligacy of governments as measured by size of the public sector and government deficits
- government intervention in markets to protect workers and local industries
- levels of protectionism through tariffs, subsidies, exchange rate policies, and regulations on FDI
- the relative priority policy makers place on providing broad public goods versus goods targeted at narrow constituencies

Most arguments about how and why electoral systems shape policy outcomes rest on a distinction between "narrow" versus "broad" socioeconomic interests, advancing claims that the type of competition engendered by a particular electoral system favors one sort of interest or the other. How scholars conceive of narrowness and breadth, and the nature of the tradeoff between them, varies markedly. We see five distinct types of stories about what constitutes narrowness and breadth—that is, whose economic interests are properly conceived as narrow and whose as broad. Each type of story, moreover, is associated with a particular set of claims about how specific electoral systems shape the narrow/broad tradeoff.

The five main stories differ on whether narrow versus broad ought to be conceived according to:

- level of wealth
- economic sector
- access to economic rents
- geography
- nongeographic characteristics that nevertheless allow for targeted policies

We discuss each of these in turn, but we match the first three and the last two because the theoretical foundations of these sets are most directly comparable.

Redistribution: Governing Coalitions, Voter Leverage, and Rents

The first approach takes as a starting point the fact that the distribution of wealth in every democracy is skewed such that the median voter's wealth is below the mean level, so that a progressive redistribution of wealth could appeal to electoral majorities. From that premise, narrow interests are those of the minority rich, whereas broad interests are those of the numerically larger middle-class and poor groups. In a competing approach, by contrast, the narrow versus broad distinction is not about level of wealth, but rather about economic sector. Those whose livelihoods derive directly from domestic industries whose production costs and market positions are shaped by government regulatory policies are characterized as narrow, whereas broad interests are those of all others in low consumer prices.

The key division in this literature is over how electoral rules act as a source of the relative political leverage for the narrow versus the broad. The landmark arguments here are advanced by Torben Iversen and David Soskice (and Thomas Cusack) on one side, and by Ronald Rogowski (with various coauthors) on the other, and by Torsten Persson and Guido Tabellini (and Gerard Roland), who offer combinations and alternative permutations of arguments from both sides.[1] For the Iversen and Soskice camp, redistribution primarily takes the form of taxation by the government and transfers from richer to poorer groups, so the crucial form of government intervention in the economy is progressive. For the Rogowski et al. camp, the vehicles of redistribution are regulatory and trade policies that favor the narrow interests of producer groups, but raise prices for everyone. Consequently, these researchers characterize government intervention in the economy as primarily regressive.[2] For Persson and Tabellini, redistribution takes the form of rents extracted from state coffers by politicians and political parties, both in the form of fiscal transfers and regulatory protection for favored groups. In either case, the effect of government intervention in the economy is to transfer resources from the broader population to politically privileged constituencies, and so is regarded as regressive. The logics of the various arguments are as follows.

Pivotal Median Parties

Iverson and Soskice (2006, 2009) start with a three-class model of society, with low-income (L), middle-income (M), and high-income (H) citizens. Governments have three policy options: (A) no redistribution, (B) moderate redistribution (from H to M and L), or (C) radical redistribution (from H and M to L). The social groups have preferences toward these policies such that: L prefers C to B to A; M prefers B to A to C; and H prefers A to B to C.

The electoral system shapes policy outcomes by influencing which parties exist and which governments form as a result. Proportional representation (PR) systems lead to one party representing each of the social groups (L, M, and H, respectively), and coalition governments either between LM or MH. M is the pivotal player and can decide which government forms and which policy results. M's first choice is to coalesce with L to pursue a policy that redistributes from H to M and L. As a result, PR electoral systems lead to moderate levels of economic redistribution (e.g., welfare states and high levels of public spending).

Single-member district (SMD) systems, meanwhile, lead to two broad-based parties: LM and MH. M is split between the two parties, and hence is weaker than the other social group within the respective parties. As a result, M cannot guarantee that its partner will not seize control of policy and pursue its own first preference: policy C (radical redistribution) in the case of LM, or policy A (no redistribution) in the case of MH. Unable to guarantee itself policy B, and preferring A to C, M's voters prefer to ally with group H under SMD competition. The consequence is lower levels of economic redistribution in SMD systems compared to PR systems. Note that this argument hinges on SMD competition yielding a policy outcome that deviates from the median group's preference, whereas PR competition allows the median group to determine policy.

Vote-seat Elasticity and Competition

In contrast, Rogowski and Mark Andreas Kayser[3] focus on how electoral rules shape the relationship between the proportion of votes parties receive and the proportion of seats they win.[4] Because vote swings between parties lead to disproportionately larger seat swings under SMD than under PR, the value of the marginal vote is higher under SMD than under PR. As a result, parties pay closer attention to the median voter in SMD systems than in PR systems, and conversely, politicians in PR systems are more likely to be "captured" by producer interests that deviate from median-voter preferences than are politicians in SMD systems.[5]

By this account, the level of consumer prices is the main policy manifestation of the differing electoral incentives in SMD versus PR systems. Consumers make up the larger share of the electorate, and thus include the median voter, who prefers policies that yield lower consumer prices. Such policies include lower import tariffs, a lighter regulatory footprint, and more competition among producers. Producers are a smaller group than consumers, and prefer policies that yield higher consumer prices (and so, producer rents), such as import duties, regulatory standards that protect favored sectors, industrial subsidies, and industrial concentration and "national champions." If politicians in SMD systems are more keenly attuned to consumers than are politicians in PR systems, then consumer prices should be lower in the former and higher in the later. The evidence supports this proposition.[6]

Combining the Competitiveness and Coalition Formation Perspectives

Persson and Tabellini[7] initially developed a similar logic to Rogowski et al., embracing the vote-seat elasticity premise to argue that political competition between politicians and parties is stiffer in SMD systems than in PR systems, and therefore that politicians will be more responsive— and more accountable—to voters' preferences in SMD than in PR systems. This not only relates to the policies politicians deliver to secure their re-election (the primary focus of Rogowski et al.), but also the policies politicians pursue to promote their own personal interests, such as seeking political rents and engaging in corruption. The policy consequences, they suggest, are that SMD systems lead not only to less public goods provision but also to lower rents for politicians than PR systems.[8]

Building on this argument, Persson, Roland, and Tabellini[9] contend that electoral rules also have indirect policy consequences, via their impact on party and government formation. The focus on coalition bargaining would appear to put Persson, Roland, and Tabellini on the same page as Iversen and Soskice,[10] but whereas Iversen and Soskice's model is spatial, and contends that two-party systems yield governments that embrace non-median policies, Persson et al.[11] focus on accountability and efficiency. Specifically, SMD systems lead to fewer parties, which makes single-party government more likely, clarifying government accountability and yielding more efficient policies. In contrast, PR systems lead to more parties and incentives for each party in a government coalition to "overgraze the fiscal commons," spending money on its own supporters while free-riding on the accountability deficit implied by lower clarity of responsibility within coalition governments.

The Diversity of Perspectives on Narrowness, Breadth, and Redistribution

These various sets of authors derive opposing inferences about policy outcomes from the same sets of electoral rules at least in part because their categories of narrow and broad are defined differently. All might agree that PR electoral rules are more likely than SMD rules to yield labor market regulations that boost industrial wages and compensation, but Iversen and Soskice would interpret the result as redistribution from citizens in the "narrow" (richer) category to those in the "broad" (poorer) category; Rogowski et al. would see the same policies as redistributing from "broad" (consumer) to "narrow" (producer) interests, and Persson et al. would just see political and economic rents. This particular brand of inefficiency—identified by Persson et al.[12]—suggests a way to reconcile the account of Iversen and Soskice with that of Rogowski et al. Median voters may favor both moderate redistribution via taxation and transfer (per Iversen and Soskice) and low consumer prices (per Rogowski et al.), and PR systems may tend to produce cabinets with pivotal parties closer to the median voter than do SMD systems.[13] In the operation of coalition government, however, the pivotal centrist party may be better able to deliver on its fiscal promises of moderate redistribution than on its commitment to refrain from regulatory policy that drives up consumer prices, owing precisely to the spending dynamics and the common-pool resource problems that Persson and Tabellini et al. emphasize. Indeed, Iversen and Soskice,[14] hold that PR encourages political coalitions that support broad wage protection policies, although they may attach to this brand of regulatory intervention a different normative implication from Rogowski et al. or Persson and Tabellini.

Apart from the empirical evidence summoned by each set of authors reviewed so far, what does the broader literature say about whether and how electoral systems affect redistribution? A variety of authors support the claim that PR encourages more progressive redistribution of wealth by governments than does SMD.[15] Alberto Alesina, Edward Glaeser, and Bruce Sacerdote[16] qualify the argument, maintaining that whereas PR may encourage redistribution in advanced (i.e., OECD) democracies, there is little evidence of this effect in developing countries. One explanation may be that the Iversen and Soskice result of progressive redistribution hangs on the logic of government formation in a parliamentary system, with party competition along a single, left-right dimension. Under presidentialism or less-well-ordered ideological competition among parties, both of which are prevalent in less-developed regions, the PR-progressivity logic may not apply. A related line of argument, by Francesc Amat and Erik Wibbels,[17] also suggests low redistribution under PR in environments in which parties have not developed ideological foundations. The rationale is that the low thresholds for representation characteristic of PR systems encourage parties based on group identity, and that strong in-group identification discourages voter support for globally redistributive policies.

Finally, as with all research based largely on cross-national comparisons, there is the persistent question of identifying causal effects, and, specifically, the extent to which electoral systems drive policy interventions that affect redistribution, as opposed to the distribution of economic resources driving electoral system choice. Cusack, Iversen, and Soskice[18] acknowledge that the choice of the electoral system might be endogenous, since high local economic coordination (such as common interests between employers and unions in common assets) appears to have facilitated the adoption of inclusive PR electoral rules in many European contexts in the early 20th century. Countries with traditionally low economic policy coordination and adversarial relations between employers and craft-based unions—in other words, where there were conflicts between higher-/middle- and lower-income groups—tended to choose SMD systems. In contrast, countries with high economic coordination and common interest between employers and industrial unions—where there was a more consensual relationship between higher-/middle- and lower-income groups—tended to choose PR.

Geography and Targeted versus Universal Appeals

Geography First

The electoral systems literature also contains an entirely different set of competing claims about narrow versus broad interests. As with the schools of thought reviewed earlier, the distinction between SMD and PR enters these debates, but some of these stories push further into the details of electoral rules to develop hypotheses about narrowness and breadth. The key distinction among these accounts is whether the main driver of narrowness is the geographical scope of the districts in which legislators are elected, or, conversely, whether other factors can drive the narrowness of candidates' electoral appeals and their policy preferences once in office.

For the geography-first approach, the key distinction is between SMD systems and the rest—perhaps with a further distinction among PR systems according to district magnitude. The central premise is that SMD elections privilege more narrow interests than do PR elections because (assuming a fixed assembly size) SMDs mean the geographical scope of each district must necessarily be smaller. Therefore, the priorities of representatives seeking to advance their constituents' interests are going to be geographically targeted.[19] Patricia Funk and Christina Gathmann,[20] for example, find that PR leads to spending on broader public goods, like education, rather than targeted goods, like roads and agricultural subsidies. Along the same lines, but with analysis at the level of individual legislators, Stefano Gagliarducci, Tommaso Nannicini, and Paolo Naticchioni[21] found that, during Italy's use of a mixed electoral system, SMD-elected members proposed geographically targeted spending projects more than PR-elected members did.

Research in international political economy has mirrored that on public spending, with protectionist trade policies in the role of budget largess. For example, several scholars claim that SMDs encourage high tariffs because small districts encourage protection of narrow interests.[22] Dong-Hun Kim[23] finds that politicians in SMD systems tend to restrict mergers and acquisitions more than those in PR systems, arguing that the reason is that SMD representatives are more inclined to protect firms in their home districts that might be adversely affected by mergers and acquisitions. Moving in a slightly different direction, Kare Vernby[24] argues that strikes are more common in SMD systems than in PR systems, and diminish under PR as district magnitude grows. His explanation is that unions recognize that strikes are more electorally costly to incumbents under SMD, where vote-seat elasticity is greater, and so they deploy that strategy more readily.

The scholarship reviewed up to now either posits that electoral competition is more intense in SMD systems than in PR, or relies on aggregate measures of vote-seat elasticity. But competitiveness varies across districts. A more subtle extension of the general argument that SMD elections encourage narrowly targeted policy benefits posits that the effect of electoral system is conditional on district-level characteristics—for example, the geographical concentration of voters with shared interests. The logic for this argument rests on the marginal bang for the buck politicians get from distributing resources in pursuit of votes. Thus, in SMD systems, narrow interests—for example, in subsidies for a particular industry—are more likely to be privileged in policy when voters who share that interest are geographically concentrated, whereas the distribution of such benefits is unrelated to geographical concentration in PR systems.[25] Stephanie J. Rickard[26] also finds that violations of GATT/WTO (General Agreement on Tariffs and Trade/World Trade Organization) agreements—which favor narrow, sectoral interests—tend to be more frequent in SMD countries than in PR countries.

There is, however, an additional condition implicit in this account—district-level competitiveness. Politicians only want to lavish additional goods, like subsidies, on a geographically concentrated voting bloc when that bloc is pivotal. If a group of voters with a shared interest is geographically concentrated, but those districts are either already safely in the government's column or are unwinnable, then policy benefits should be targeted elsewhere. This logic implies a compound conditionality (electoral system * geographical concentration * district-level competitiveness) to the effect of electoral system on the geographical concentration of benefits. There is some suggestive evidence in favor of such a relationship. McGillivray[27] advances the case that, under SMD systems, protectionism is targeted at geographically concentrated industries located in electorally marginal districts. Michael Neugart[28] also argues that under SMD systems, worker protection tends to be narrowly targeted at voters in pivotal districts, whereas PR systems encourage policies with broader protection against unemployment because parties need to take the employment risks of all voters into account. Vaughan Dickson[29] also provides some support for this proposition with evidence that Canadian governments target spending toward provinces with greater vote-seat elasticity.

Even the compound conditionality described here may understate the complexity of the relationship between SMDs and targeted benefits, however. Consider how this argument jibes with the Rogowski et al. logic of vote-seat elasticity in SMDs. Rogowski's pro-consumer effect depends on large numbers of competitive SMDs, such that modest vote swings across parties are amplified into larger seat swings. The contention is that district-level competitiveness under SMDs should motivate universal, public goods–oriented policies targeted at the broadest possible swath of voters (i.e., consumers). Arguments that competitive SMDs encourage targeted economic largesse, by contrast, posit an electoral strategy that identifies district-level groups whose affections can be won with district-specific favors. The conditions under which district-specific favors should generate a larger electoral bang for the buck in SMDs than do universalistic policies—and under which this difference induces more targeting under SMD competition than under PR elections—remain to be specified.

Nongeographical Targets

There are also arguments in regard to narrowness versus breadth of interests that do not privilege geography as a point of departure. By this account, the geographical scope of districts is one possible driver of narrowness versus breadth, but not necessarily the most decisive. Ideological differences among parties are an alternative potential source of narrow appeals. One manifestation of this is entirely consistent with the Rogowski et al. account of appeals to narrow, sectoral economic interests in electoral systems with low thresholds for representation. Jong Hee Park and Nathan Jensen, for example, argue that the low thresholds for representation that characterize inclusive PR systems encourage parties organized around appeals to narrow constituencies, which in turn produce high levels of agricultural subsidies and protectionism.[30] McGillivray argues that the dispersion of stock prices among firms in different industries is an indicator of the degree to which governments favor some economic sectors over others, and shows that dispersion is generally higher under PR than SMD systems, which suggests more policy favoritism under PR than SMD.[31] Along the same lines, Rickard finds that responsiveness to surges in demand for narrow transfers is greater in PR systems than in SMD systems.[32]

An extension of this logic posits a conditional effect of ballot structure on district magnitude, whereby intraparty competition in high-magnitude districts encourages candidates to appeal to highly specific (i.e., narrow) groups of voters for personal support.[33] In high-magnitude districts, which tend to be large and highly populated, these targeted benefits might be geographically specific, but they need not be, and policies targeted by sector or industry, demographic criteria, or partisanship are equally feasible. Brian F. Crisp et al. and Charles R. Hankla both present evidence that, under PR, stronger incentives to cultivate a personal vote (as, for example, in open-list or transferable vote systems) encourage protectionism through particularistic subsidies and regulations for targeted industries.[34] Tanya Bagashka argues that electoral rules that allow for personal votes discouraged market-oriented reforms in post-Communist countries.[35] Megumi Naoi and Ellis Krauss demonstrate that pre-reform Japan's SNTV system, which privileged personal vote-seeking in multimember districts, encouraged lobbying by locally oriented interest groups and organizations with strong ties to individual legislators, whereas the shift to a mixed-member electoral system diminished the policy concessions, in the form of subsidies and regulatory protection, awarded to these specialized interest groups.[36] Sean D. Ehrlich also argues that the more government access points are available to lobbyists, the more protectionism that should be observed, and further, that the more electoral districts there are (e.g., under SMD), or the lower the party discipline (e.g., under open-list PR), the more access points are available to lobbyists.[37] Thus, protectionism should be greater either under SMD elections or under PR systems that allow personal votes, but lower under closed-list PR.

Scholarship on Italian politics has also produced evidence that electoral incentives to cultivate personal votes in open-list PR systems encourage targeted infrastructure spending.[38] Miriam A. Golden and Lucio Picci maintain that where electoral incentives to cultivate personal votes encourage narrowly targeted spending projects, senior legislators in the governing coalition tend to be advantaged in obtaining such projects.[39] Meanwhile, Chang and Golden show that, in Italy under open-list elections, waste and corruption in public works spending was greatest in the high-magnitude districts where competition for personal votes was the most intense.[40]

Electoral Systems, the Fiscal Commons, and Economic Growth

Finally, scholarship in political economy has reached beyond examination of targeted benefits to advance even broader claims about the relationship between electoral systems and macroeconomic performance. Since the work of Persson and Tabellini in the late 1990s, there has been growing support, mainly by economists, for the claim that SMD electoral systems tend to produce lower government spending, lower public deficits, and less government rent-seeking than PR systems.[41]

The broad claims about SMD versus PR elections, however, have not gone unchallenged in the empirical literature. Gian Maria Milesi-Ferretti, Roberto Perotti, and Massimo Rostagno concur that more proportional systems lead to higher spending in OECD countries, but they find no evidence of a difference in Latin America.[42] Bernardin Akitoby and Thomas Stratmann, meanwhile, present evidence that, contrary to Persson and Tabellini, SMD elections produce *higher* government spending than PR elections, and more penalization of governments by financial markets via higher bond yield spreads.[43]

In work echoing that on targeted benefits, some scholars have distinguished the fiscal incentives generated by strong incentives for personal vote-seeking within PR systems. In a classic study of Brazil's open-list elections, for example, Barry Ames found that high-magnitude PR with intraparty competition fosters particularistic spending.[44] More recently, and with a broader comparative perspective, Mark Hallerberg and Patrik Marier found that budget procedures that strengthen the executive's formal authority produce lower deficits when the electoral system for legislators generates strong incentives for personal votes, but yield no impact when legislators' incentives for personal votes are low (e.g., in closed-list PR systems).[45] In addition, Edwards and Thames found that higher–district magnitude systems tend to produce greater overall spending and more public goods provision when elections are party-centered (e.g., under closed lists), but lower overall spending, and they focus on particularistic goods when elections are candidate-centered (e.g., under open lists).[46] Other research tested similar propositions by exploiting variations within mixed-member systems. Edwards and Thames found that mixed-member parallel systems produce lower overall spending than mixed-member compensatory systems (which more closely approximate PR), and that spending is higher in parallel systems the greater the share of seats allocated by PR.[47]

To widen the lens even further, a number of scholars advance arguments about the effects of electoral system on the motivations and the capacities of politicians to manage the economy. Here again, the hypotheses as well as the evidence are mixed. Carl Henrik Knutsen argues that PR encourages policies that pursue broader public goods than does SMD, and so produces more economic growth in the long run.[48] Sergio Béjar and Bumba Mukherjee argue that SMD elections produce more volatility in government spending policies and growth rates than PR systems, because single-party governments are more inclined and better positioned to engage in pro-cyclical spending.[49] Pursuing a related theme, Bortolotti and Pinotti argue that majoritarian electoral systems expedite privatization reforms because single-party governments are more decisive and face fewer veto points.[50] William Bernhard and David Leblang and Barry Eichengreen and Leblang argue that SMD elections encourage floating exchange rates, because single-party governments value the associated policy flexibility, whereas the coalition governments more prevalent under PR encourage fixed exchange rates as a commitment measure to resolve policy disputes among parties, and as a means for coalition partners to monitor the Finance Ministry.[51]

Finally, in a familiar move that distinguishes among PR systems according to the incentives to cultivate personal votes, Joseph Wright argues that foreign aid stimulates economic growth in countries with closed lists—that is, no preference votes—but depresses growth in countries with systems with preference voting and strong incentives to cultivate personal votes, because aid is channeled toward spending on broad-based public goods in the former but to narrowly targeted spending projects in the latter.[52]

As will be familiar by now, the common theme running through the scholarship on the downstream policy effects of electoral rules is that of narrowness versus breadth. Claims that some electoral rules favor narrow interests whereas others favor broad ones are everywhere. The distinctions scholars draw, however, between narrow and broad do not always align, nor do their claims regarding which types of rules privilege which types of interests.

Conclusion and Avenues for Future Research

Research on the effect of electoral systems on policy outcomes is at a relatively early stage compared to the decades of work on the impact of electoral systems on the party system, the relationship between votes and seats in parliaments, and the number of parties in government. Nevertheless, a lot of progress has been made in a very short time.

There are now some reasonably clear empirical regularities in terms of the effect of the two main types of electoral systems—majoritarian and proportional—on some major economic policies. In particular, whereas proportional systems tend to produce higher public spending, majoritarian systems tend to produce lower public deficits and lower consumer prices. Furthermore, at a lower level of aggregation, SMD systems tend to produce policies targeted at pivotal voters in marginal districts, whereas PR systems tend to produce more general public goods—although there are inconsistencies in how the field defines "narrow" and "broad" interests and policies, as we discussed.

Also, the causal mechanisms behind the connection between electoral systems and these (and other) policy outcomes are not yet fully understood. There are two main reasons for this. First, it remains unclear whether the electoral system effects are *direct*, a result of different sociogeographic campaigning incentives for parties and politicians under the different electoral systems, or *indirect*, a result of the processes of government formation and operation, such as the difference between single-party government and coalition government. For example, on this latter point, higher public spending and higher public deficits tend to be associated with coalition governments, which are correlated with PR systems. Yet single-party governments exist in PR systems, and coalition governments exist in majoritarian systems. The challenge, though, is that identifying these separate effects is difficult with the available data.

This leads to the second reason: only a small number of countries have switched between a majoritarian and a proportional electoral system since the 1950s. This means that most of the key empirical results are drawn from cross-sectional (cross-country) data rather than cross-time data. The problem with cross-country data, though, is that it is difficult to identify the effect of electoral systems independent of other factors that vary systematically across countries, such as parties, governments, other political institutions, and voters' preferences. In addition, electoral systems are endogenous to political factors that also vary across countries, such as the number of parties and the conflictual or consensual nature of relations between groups in society. Hence, without sufficient within-country cross-time variation in electoral systems, it is almost impossible to isolate a clear causal connection between a particular electoral system and a particular set of policy outcomes.

Recognizing these challenges, researchers have begun to look at within-country variations. For example, several scholars have looked at mixed-member electoral systems, in which politicians in the same country at the same time are elected by either SMD or PR rules. This has allowed researchers to identify the types of policies the two sets of politicians seek. Extrapolating from this microlevel behavior to macropolicy outcomes, such as public spending or trade tariffs, is not straightforward. Nevertheless, we believe that a lot more can be learned, at both an empirical and a theoretical level, by focusing on the short- and long-term policy effects of changes in electoral rules within countries over time, such as changes in district magnitude or switches from closed-list to open-list PR.

6

Designing Electoral Systems: Normative Tradeoffs and Institutional Innovations

Andrew Rehfeld and Melissa Schwartzberg

As many of the essays in this report suggest, electoral rules have a dramatic effect on political outcomes. These rules also enable the achievement of different normative ends. These normative aims range broadly, but include maximizing the likelihood that every citizen votes for a candidate who wins, maximizing the correspondence of policy outcomes to citizen preferences, and ensuring an ethnically diverse legislature, among many other desiderata. Since electoral rules do not equally achieve each of these goals, and since some of these aims are incompatible with some others, the choice of an electoral system will have normative consequences. For instance, in choosing an electoral rule, the goal that every citizen votes for a candidate who wins may have to be sacrificed so as to maximize the likelihood that policy outcomes correspond to majority preferences.

In this brief essay, we seek to highlight the normative implications of electoral reforms, while recognizing the tradeoffs that instantiating commitments in political institutions necessarily entail. To preserve even a core value such as political equality in an electoral system may entail unacceptable sacrifices of a competing value—or even a sacrifice of equality on a different dimension. As such, engaging in political experimentation and innovation may be the best hope of expanding the range of institutions available to realize these commitments and of clarifying where normative priorities rest.

※ ※ ※ ※

Democracy is committed, in the first instance, to political equality. In ancient Athens, this entailed the equal right to put oneself forward to hold political office and the equal probability, via the lot, of being selected (for most magistracies). Yet it is far from clear what equality among citizens ought to mean in modern representative democracies. Under universal suffrage—one person, one vote—all citizens in principle ought to have equal opportunity to choose the candidate they believe will best protect their interests. Robert Dahl has famously defined democracy by reference to the "responsiveness of the government to the preferences of its citizens, considered as political equals."[1] Note, however, that already there are potential tensions between the equal capacity to choose a candidate and the ability to have one's preferences count equally: my preferred candidate may have no chance of winning; my candidate, even if elected, may be in the position of a permanent minority and have no means of realizing my policy preferences; and even if elected and in the majority, my representative's votes may not always track my policy preferences.

Even if the specific aim is to improve political equality in one form, the result may end up increasing inequality measured in a different fashion. As Charles Beitz has suggested, the decision might be made that political equality should be obtained primarily in reference to the legislation created rather than to voting or to the likelihood of electing a candidate.[2] In that case, a commitment to proportionality may or may not lead to a greater chance of achieving legislative outcomes. Greater homogeneity within a district may increase the capacity of constituents to choose a representative who shares their values and interests, but at the cost of having a representative who may be marginalized once he or she enters the legislature. This is what David Lublin nicely titled the "paradox of representation."[3] The alternative he suggests is to have minorities remain within single-member districts at a high enough level to affect some moderating influence on the resulting election, even if their numbers are not large enough to elect their own candidate. Although Lublin was discussing only minorities, the point can be generalized to party affiliation as well, were small parties to be represented proportionately in legislatures. So, maximizing political equality in the sense of having representatives who reflect the distinct interests of particular populations may lead to a loss of equality measured in terms of political outcomes.

Any institutional instantiation of a normative principle, such as political equality, will necessarily involve intervening choices and costs. Quota laws that guarantee candidacies or seats to women and minorities, like all qualifications for office, violate two presumptions of democratic government: that voters have the freedom to choose whomever they want as their representatives, and that all citizens have a right to run for the offices by which they are ruled. If quota laws are justified, they are only to correct a problem of systemic political inequality that has systematically denied the achievement of those two presumptions to minorities and women throughout many societies. Thus, as Philip Pettit has expressed, sometimes a restriction on values in one area is justified to maximize the total amount of the value throughout the system.[4]

Although achieving a perfect harmony of values is unrealizable, there are dimensions on which existing electoral institutions fall short and might be subject to improvement. As such, it is worth exploring whether serious institutional innovations might help realize normative aims. History provides evidence that imaginative ideals have led to lasting political changes. When Thomas Hare proposed a proportional system as an alternative to majority rule to elect representatives for the English House of Commons, it was derided for being absurdly complicated because it required every voter to rank order hundreds of candidates on a list. Who would have predicted that his ideas would lead to the single-transferable voting system ("preference voting") and other forms of proportional representation in practice today, thanks in part to Mill's own account of Hare's system in *Considerations on Representative Government*? Today, organizations around the world—from local nonprofit groups to national governments—use a variety of these schemes to translate underlying voter preferences into the institutions of government.

Political theorists have recently focused attention on the incentives of representatives to act in ways that may fail to realize the interests of their constituents, or may promote the interests of their constituents at the expense of the national interest or "common good" more generally. Insofar as these issues entail the question of how best to ensure the equal consideration of citizens' interests, they are importantly connected to the issues of political equality addressed earlier. But they also transcend these issues to raise normative questions of the ethics of political representatives, and the responsibility of citizens to monitor their agents. Two institutional innovations designed to address these issues help both to clarify both some of the deficiencies in current electoral systems and to reimagine the possibilities of electoral democracy.

Alternative Constituency Design

Nearly every democracy groups voters into territorial subgroups before counting their votes. This is a historical artifact, however, and may be less important to large states now than it was three centuries ago and continues to be in smaller communities. The original justification for territorial districts may have been the close ties voters within a district had with one another, a justification that was plausible when the average size of a colonial district was roughly 3,000 people. Today, however, districts are much more densely populated. In the United States, for example, electoral constituencies for the House of Representatives number about 600,000 people, much larger than the original number of 30,000 set in the Constitution in 1789—and that original number was on average 10 times the size of districts for colonial legislatures.

The fact that electoral constituencies are based on geographical lines creates incentives for representatives to spend locally as part of serving their constituencies. Sometimes this spending is also in the national interest; other times, local spending is simply a way to deliver resources to secure votes. The reason that "pork" is a political problem is not because politics is naturally local. Rather, politics is local to the extent that representation is institutionalized along geographical lines. The most common alternative to territorial districting is national proportional representation, in which electoral constituencies are essentially formed by voters who cast a vote for national parties. Other alternatives include functional representation and representing individuals by profession or other organized interests. These systems do not eliminate special interest spending in the name of the national good so much as they move local spending to spending on other interests on which the constituency is defined (e.g., interest group, political party, and profession).

Thomas Pogge[5] has gone so far as to recommend "self-constituting constituencies" that would allow individuals to have their votes counted in whatever way they choose. Such an alternative has the benefit of leaving to the group the manner by which it is represented, and to define for the group what it means, for example, to be represented as a woman, even as it raises the likelihood that one of its own members is elected. Pogge's recommendation maximizes the value of autonomy by placing the choice of a constituency in the hands of voters. Autonomy at the level of constituency definition, however, is likely to leave districts more homogenous, since they will attract like-minded voters—all of whom want to be represented by their party identification, or by their interest in whatever feature it is by which they would choose to be defined. This may generate the paradox of representation described earlier. So, it might be that autonomy should be sacrificed instead to achieve better policy outcomes.

In contrast to territorial representation or more concentrated interest representation, we can imagine electoral constituencies defined by the national interest, rather than the interest of a part. This could involve randomizing the assignment of citizens to permanent, involuntary, heterogeneous electoral constituencies, producing nonterritorial districts of which each would look like the nation as a whole.[6] In a legislature of, say, 4535 seats (the number in the US Congress) each voter would randomly draw a number between 1 and 4535 (inclusive), and he or she would be a member of that constituency for the rest of his or her life. The random district would reduce partisanship by having each representative pursue his or her own constituents' interests, even as that would mean pursuing the nation's interest as a whole. In addition, the permanence of such districts would enable the same group of voters to authorize a representative to act for them and then reward or punish this person at election time.

The use of randomization is in part designed to promote the inclusion of diverse social groups. The membership of each constituency would be national and demographically identical to one other, as well as to the nation as a whole. The median voter would not only prevail within a constituency, the median national voter would by extension prevail. The hope, often implicitly, is that through capturing the diversity of the citizen body as a whole, the institutions will better reflect the common good, or at least not be subject to the systematic distortions and partiality associated with electoral systems (again, perhaps most important, wealth). The resulting policy implication is that issues for which there are clear national majorities would have constant support within Congress. Issues on which the nation is divided, however, would be the primary ones on the basis of which representatives might distinguish themselves from each other.

Since the constituents of each district would be nationally distributed, campaigns would not find it effective to advertise using broadcast media, but rather only the use of direct e-communications, dramatically lowering the costs of campaigns and thus reducing the influence of media in politics. In Congress, spending and other decisions would still be based on serving the good of a representative's constituents, but now the constituency's interests and the nation's interests would be identical.

Accountability and the Euthynai

That elections are insufficient for accountability is a familiar lament, but a justifiable one. Monitoring one's representatives is very costly for voters, even when aided by the critical reviews of opposing parties; representatives have an incentive to conceal bargains that constituents would reject. Further, the bluntness of the vote makes it imperfect as a mechanism of retrospective accountability for several reasons, among them the fact that it entails both a retrospective assessment of the representative's performance in office, which is itself comprised of a multitude of votes, and a prospective judgment as to whether an opponent is likely to perform better.[7]

In recent years, theorists have begun to defend the value of extra-electoral mechanisms of political accountability. Jeffrey Green has recently argued that the primary role of the people in contemporary democracy is to be "spectators" of their leaders, and, as such, the critical ideal ought to be *candor*: "the institutional requirement that leaders not be in control of the conditions of their publicity."[8] He defends the increased use of public inquiries, in which leaders are subject to explicitly political investigation and trial, holding that such inquiries would encourage direct scrutiny while removing the power from the leaders under examination to shape the spectacle. John McCormick[9] praises Machiavelli's defense of political trials and urges contemporary republicans to endorse them as a means of improving the accountability of representatives and fostering citizens' control over the wealthy elites who today dominate political office.

Though Green in particular offers suggestions for how some of the obvious risks associated with political trials might be mitigated, nonetheless, it still may not be desirable to develop a political institution that could so readily be subject to partisan abuse. Nor would it necessarily be desirable to have an accusatory framework for such an accountability mechanism. Yet the public nature of rendering accounts, especially given the incentives on the part of incumbents to obfuscate features of their record, might well have benefits. Ancient Athens offers a model of one such mechanism. Magistrates and other public officials there were subject to scrutiny after their term in office, a mechanism of "rendering accounts" called *euthynai*. A first stage was focused on financial improprieties, but the second phase entailed a mechanism by which any citizen or metic could present a written accusation of malfeasance; if the "corrector" for the magistrate's tribe deemed the charge justified, it would be handled by public or private prosecution.[10]

One might suggest that such an institution is unnecessary, because opposing candidates will have an incentive to monitor and disclose evidence of wrongdoing or simply votes that are at odds with the public interest, as construed by the competing candidate. However, because opposing candidates themselves have a strong incentive to characterize the record in a negative light or to misrepresent the incumbent's position, there is reason to think that the voters would not, and should not, necessarily trust a challenger's presentation of the incumbent's performance. As such, and given the limited incentives on the part of the incumbent to provide a full rendering of performance, an additional mechanism might be necessary.

Imagine, then, a public hearing at which the incumbent would present his or her voting record and, perhaps, other evidence of performance in office, and would be subject to challenge on this record by a panel of judges. Though it is surely the case that this would expose the incumbent to substantial criticism that might well benefit the challenger, it is not obvious that this is unattractive; the incumbency advantage is so strong that mitigating it on the basis of a careful evaluation should not raise serious concerns. Further, to the extent that the prospect of this scrutiny encourages closer relationships with constituents, and public reason-giving for unpopular decisions, the performance of representatives might be enhanced.

One might ask how different the euthynai is from what the free press already does in contemporary society. Journalists regularly compel politicians to render accounts in public forums such as press conferences and televised interviews. Citizens also participate in this process by submitting questions, a process that the growth of the Internet has facilitated. Yet the profit interests of the media and its penchant for spectacle frequently reduce the process of rendering accounts to the exchange of sound bites. The public emerges more entertained than informed. Nonetheless, as Green would argue, stripping away the leaders' own power to orchestrate the euthynai makes it a spectacle worthy of public observation.

Like any institutional choice, however, again a tradeoff among competing values must be confronted. Here, a tradeoff between the desire to (re-)elect whichever candidate one might wish, and the value of transparency can be imagined. A voter may wish to re-elect a representative simply on the grounds of ideological congruence, regardless of any shirking or malfeasance; witness, for instance, the career of Charles Rangel, among others. Yet heightened public scrutiny may lead voters to choose a different candidate, or parties to find competing candidates to run aggressive primary campaigns.

Conclusion

As we have hoped to suggest, electoral rules necessarily entail compromises and tradeoffs among different values—and even the particular manifestation of these values, as the discussion of political equality explored. Within democracies, there is likely to be disagreement about the relative weight that should be ascribed to these values. Because of the technical nature of electoral systems, citizen engagement in electoral reform tends to be relatively limited—except, perhaps, where redistricting is concerned. As we hopefully have shown, however, the normative consequences of electoral design are significant.

Though there are serious costs associated with instability in an electoral system, there are also substantial liabilities to sclerosis: electoral reform in many ways constitutes an ongoing process. Remarkably, perhaps because of the desire to enable electoral rules to remain flexible enough to cope with important demographic or political changes, electoral rules are rarely given constitutional status. Although the flexibility of electoral rules may generate an incentive for temporarily dominant parties to lock in advantages, it also provides citizens and their representatives an opportunity to ensure that electoral rules reflect their normative commitments—indeed, an opportunity to reflect on the nature of these commitments and their limits. The realization of ambitions for democracy more generally, however, may require creative thought about institutional innovations beyond elections.

7

Report from the Field: Two Surveys of Political Scientists

John Carey, Simon Hix, Shaheen Mozaffar, Andrew Reynolds

This task force sought to address the following questions: What goals do political scientists value in electoral systems? In light of these goals, how do they rate various systems? And how have they have applied their knowledge of system design in the service of electoral reform?

We conducted two surveys. The first recruited participants from a random sample drawn from APSA's member base, asking about normative goals and for respondents' evaluations of an array of commonly used electoral systems. The second survey was aimed at a much smaller respondent group—political scientists who have served as electoral reform consultants in various countries over the span of the last several decades. It asked about the context in which they did their work, the political actors with whom they interacted, the type of counsel they offered, and how that counsel was received.[1]

Representational Goals and Electoral Systems

The APSA-wide survey presented two main batteries of questions to respondents. One asked respondents to rate, on a five-point scale from "Not Important" to "Top Priority," the priority afforded to various normative goals associated with the rules used to elect legislators. These goals included decisiveness, partisan proportionality, individual accountability, government stability, party cohesiveness, representation of women and minority groups, single-party government, and correspondence to preferences of a median voter. The other questions asked respondents to rate various electoral systems on a five-point scale from "Very Bad" to "Very Good." These included: single-member district systems, both plurality (SMD-P) and two-round/run-off varieties (SMD-TR and SMD-AV); the single-transferable vote system (STV); proportional representation systems, both closed-list (CL-PR) and open-list (OL-PR); and mixed-member systems, both parallel (MM-P) and compensatory (MM-C).[2]

As an assist to respondents who may have been unfamiliar with the lexicon of electoral systems, the survey provided examples of national parliaments elected under each type of rule. To prevent question order from driving the results, both the order of the two batteries and the ordering of the items within each battery were randomized. The survey also asked for respondents' nationality, their country of residence, age, sex, minority group status, and a self-assessment of their expertise on electoral systems. The full survey is available in Appendix E.

Of the APSA members contacted, 703 took at least part of the survey and 611 completed it.[3] Almost all respondents registered opinions about the various normative goals. Response rates for evaluations of electoral systems were lower, most likely due to unfamiliarity with some of the systems. Still, about 70–85% (depending on the system) of those who rated the representational goals also rated the systems.

Overall Ratings of Goals and Systems

Figure 7.1 shows the mean rating for each of the nine representational goals included in the survey on the 1–5 scale from highest to lowest. Interestingly, government stability rated high, right alongside individual accountability, whereas single-party government rated by far the lowest, while the other six goals were clumped nearer the middle of the scale.

Figure 7.1: **Mean Value Assigned to Electoral System Goals**

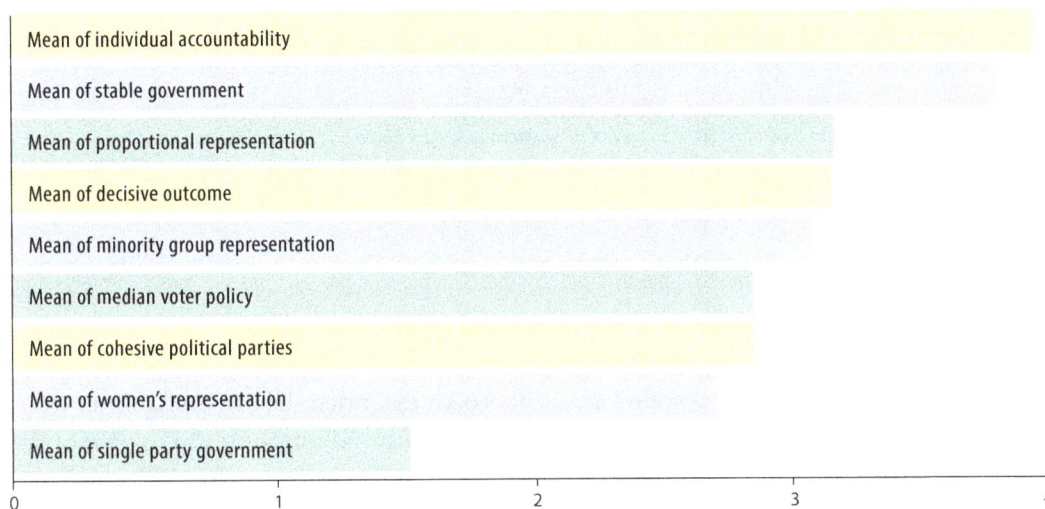

Source: Carey, Hix, Mozaffar, and Reynolds, 2012 Survey of APSA Members, Task Force on Electoral Rules and Democratic Governance

Our survey allowed us to identify female from male respondents, and those who self-identified as members of ethnic, racial, religious, or linguistic minorities. This led us to ask whether women valued the representation of women more than men do, and whether those who identified as a member of a minority valued the representation of minorities more than nonminorities do. The answers, for this set of respondents, appeared to be "yes" and "no," respectively. Women valued both women's representation and minority representation more than men. By contrast, self-identified minority respondents gave no higher priority to minority representation than did nonminority respondents, and valued partisan proportionality (often regarded as protective of minority interests) even less.

Figure 7.2 shows the mean ratings of electoral systems across all respondents. Although the overall rankings suggest a mild collective preference for multiple-winner systems over single-winner systems, the lack of variance in the mean ratings is as striking as anything about the rank order. By contrast with the representational goals (Figure 7.1), on which aggregate opinions varied starkly, the range of mean ratings for electoral systems is compressed.

Figure 7.2: **Mean Rating Assigned to Electoral Systems**

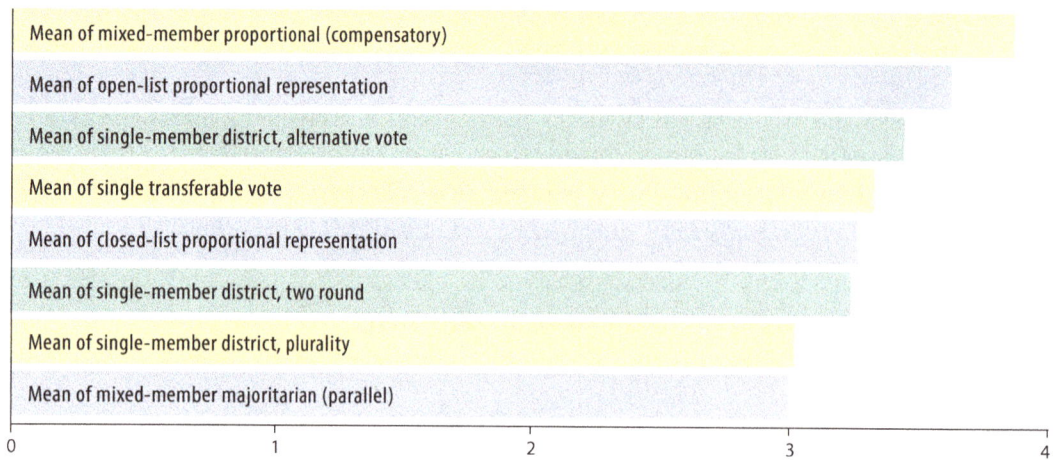

Mean of mixed-member proportional (compensatory)				
Mean of open-list proportional representation				
Mean of single-member district, alternative vote				
Mean of single transferable vote				
Mean of closed-list proportional representation				
Mean of single-member district, two round				
Mean of single-member district, plurality				
Mean of mixed-member majoritarian (parallel)				

Source: Carey, Hix, Mozaffar, and Reynolds, 2012 Survey of APSA Members, Task Force on Electoral Rules and Democratic Governance

How Do Political Scientists Link Systems to Goals?

Beyond these summary statistics, we were interested in whether and how respondents' stated representational goals connected to their preferences over electoral systems. Much of the scholarly literature on electoral systems amounts to an extended debate on whether the design of electoral rules systematically affects representational outcomes[4]: Do proportional systems protect minority interests? Do they produce unstable governments? Do systems in which voters can indicate preferences for specific candidates enhance individual accountability? Does closed-list PR produce disciplined and cohesive parties? Does the alternative vote (also known as instant run-off) find Condorcet winners who represent the elusive median voter? Does SMD-plurality yield decisive outcomes? The APSA-wide survey allowed us to explore whether political scientists' preferences over electoral systems were systematically linked to the values they prioritized.

Our primary approach was to regress respondents' ratings of a given electoral system on the series of nine representational ideals included in the goals battery of the survey. So, for example, to the extent that political scientists bought into the idea that closed-list PR generates strong parties, but makes coalition government almost inevitable,[5] then we might expect the coefficient on the cohesive parties explanatory variable to be strongly positive (the more respondents valued these, the more they favored closed-list PR), and the single-party government explanatory variable to be strongly negative (the more respondents valued this, the less inclined they were toward closed-list PR).

Rather than present a mass of coefficients and diagnostics, we distill the results from all those regressions in Table 7.1, which is organized such that the representational goals are listed down the rows in descending order of how highly they are valued overall among respondents (by mean survey response), and the electoral systems are listed across the columns in descending order of how much they are favored (also by mean survey value). The interior cells show whether the estimated effect of valuing some goal (e.g., accountability, proportionality, decisiveness) was statistically discernible from zero, and, if so, whether the estimated effect was positive (+) or negative (-). By convention, the number of markers (+, ++, +++) indicates whether the effect was distinguishable at better than 0.1, 0.05, or 0.01, respectively. The bottom row of the table also shows the "baseline" level of support for each type of electoral system; that is, the coefficient on the constant term in each regression, which can be interpreted as the expected level of support for a respondent who cared not a hoot about any of the goals we included in the survey.

Table 7.1: **Relationship between Representational Goals and Evaluation of Different Electoral Systems**

	MM-Compensatory	OL-PR	AV	STV	CL-PR	SMD-TR	SMD-P	MM-Parallel
Individual Legislator Accountability	--				-	+	+++	
Stable Governments						++	+++	
Partisan Proportionality	+++	+++	---	+++	+++	---	---	
Decisive Outcome						++	+++	++
Representation of Minority Groups	+	+++		++	+++		---	
Policies Preferred by Median Voter			++					
Cohesive Parties		--					+	
Representation of Women		++		--				+
Single-party Government						++		
Baseline (Coefficient on Constant)	2.9	2.6	3.1	2.8	2.5	2.3	3.0	2.4

Note: Cells indicate the direction (positive or negative) and statistical significance of the estimated effect of representational goals on respondents' assessments of electoral systems. Empty cells indicate that no relationship between a given goal and a given system was discernible.

Source: Carey, Hix, Mozaffar, and Reynolds, 2012 Survey of APSA Members, Task Force on Electoral Rules and Democratic Governance

The results are consistent with many of the expectations inherent in the electoral systems literature in political science. First, the goal that respondents appeared to connect most clearly and consistently with the choice of electoral system was partisan proportionality, which probably reflects how well-developed the scholarly literature on this representational ideal is.[6] Caring more about proportionality was strongly associated with favoring MM-compensatory, list PR, or single-transferable vote (STV) systems, and just as strongly negatively associated with support for all the single-winner systems—alternative vote, two-round, or plurality—whereas valuing proportionality provided no guidance to a respondent's evaluation of MM-parallel systems.

Some other goals also predictably mapped onto electoral system preferences. Respondents who valued decisive electoral outcomes favored SMD two-round and plurality elections, as well as MM-parallel systems that include SMD contests and do not attempt to compensate for their results in awarding list-PR seats.[7] Respondents who valued minority representation were more inclined to favor list-PR systems (including MM-compensatory) and STV elections, and much less likely to favor SMD-plurality.[8] The more a respondent valued median-voter outcomes, the stronger the inclination toward elections by alternative vote, which is touted precisely as a system designed to reward moderation.

Other results sit slightly less comfortably with the established wisdom. For example, those who valued women's representation leaned toward OL-PR and appeared indifferent to CL-PR. This is interesting in light of the long-standing hypothesis that closed lists are more favorable to women than open lists,[9] although it might reflect movement on current debates within the electoral systems literature over the effects of preference voting on women's representation.[10] It is also worth noting that the most highly valued representational goal overall was individual accountability, and the most favored electoral system was MM-compensatory, yet valuing individual accountability was negatively associated with favoring mixed-compensatory systems! Political scientists as a group could connect their goals to electoral systems that would likely advance those goals, and the connections between goals and systems as well to arguments developed in the electoral systems scholarship. There was, however, considerable heterogeneity in both values and system preferences within the profession.

Taking Electoral Systems Expertise to the Field

Participation by social scientists in the design of democratic institutions generally, and electoral systems more specifically, has a long—if not always happy—pedigree. The involvement of legal theorist Hugo Preuss and sociologist Max Weber in the construction of the Weimar Constitution is well documented.[11] In recent years, electoral systems scholars have increasingly been invited to provide guidance to electoral reformers, sometimes via governmental and diplomatic contacts, other times through nongovernmental organizations, and other times via academic institutions.[12] To evaluate how political scientists are engaging with those who design electoral institutions, we designed the Consultant Survey (included in this report) specifically for scholars who have participated in electoral consulting missions abroad. Note that the invitation letter (also included in this report) requested that survey participants provide a separate response for each such consulting mission. We sent the invitation to 39 political scientists known by members of the task force to have participated in electoral reform consulting missions abroad, and we received 67 distinct responses.

Figure 7.3 shows the distribution over time of the consulting missions for which survey respondents provided information. The data are inevitably biased toward currently active professionals and should not be viewed as providing a precise estimate of rates of engagement by political scientists in this activity, yet we suspect that the general upward trend reflected in the figure is accurate for two reasons. First, the events of the Arab Spring and other regime changes in the Middle East and Central Asia have produced a boomlet in

Figure 7.3: **Year of Consulting Mission** (or first year if multiyear)

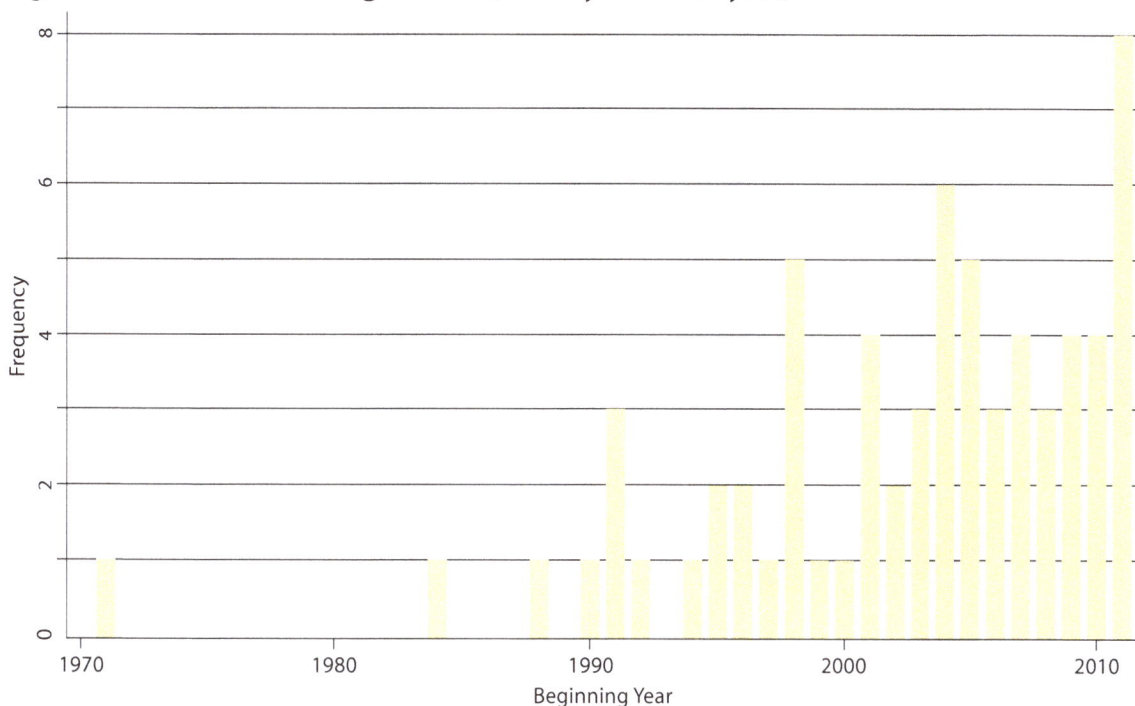

Source: Carey, Hix, Mozaffar and Reynolds, 2011–2012 Consultant Survey, Task Force on Electoral Rules and Democratic Governance

electoral systems design activity. Second, democracy promotion organizations have grown increasingly active and frequently draw on academics to support their efforts. Our survey asked respondents to identify what organization, if any, recruited them and organized their consulting activities.

The most commonly cited contracting organizations were democracy promotion NGOs, such as the International Foundation for Electoral Systems and the National Democratic Institute, often under contracts from governments or supragovernmental organizations, including the US Agency for International Development, the UN Development Program, and the European Union. In addition, survey responses pointed to the US Department of State, the US Information Agency, the government of South Africa, the government of Colombia, the British House of Commons, the Danish parliament, the senate of Mexico, the regional government of Iraqi Kurdistan, the Latvian Department of Local Government, the Organization for Security and Cooperation in Europe, the Goethe Institute in Beirut, the Inter-Disciplinary Center in Herziliya (Israel), and the Salvadoran Foundation for Economic Development (FUSADE).

Figure 7.4 illustrates the great diversity among consultants in prior knowledge of the countries where they advise on reform. Only about 10% were native, whereas about 30% each reported minimal, moderate, and extensive background knowledge of the politics and political actors involved. Most missions themselves, moreover, were of a short duration, as shown in Figure 7.5, with two-thirds of consultants spending two weeks or less in country,

Figure 7.4: **Consultant Prior Knowledge of Country**

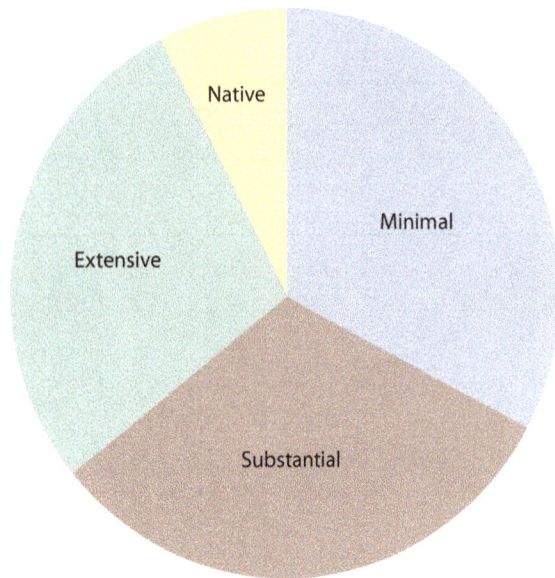

Source: Carey, Hix, Mozaffar, and Reynolds, 2011–2012 Consultant Survey, Task Force on Electoral Rules and Democratic Governance

Figure 7.5: **Time Spent in Country**

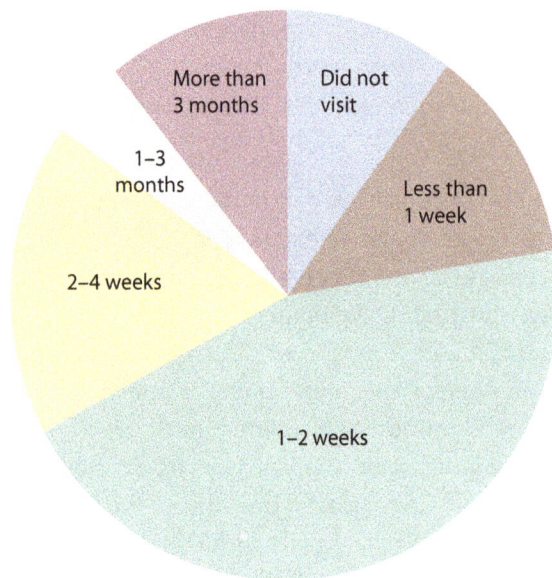

Source: Carey, Hix, Mozaffar, and Reynolds, 2011–2012 Consultant Survey, Task Force on Electoral Rules and Democratic Governance

and fewer than 20% spending more than a month. Moreover, those with less prior knowledge did not compensate by spending more time. Indeed, of the seven longest missions reported in our survey, those of more than three months, four were conducted by natives. Those cases aside, there was no correlation between prior knowledge and time spent in country.

One might question whether political scientists with less than extensive prior knowledge, spending between one and two weeks in country (30% of survey responses share these traits), were qualified to offer advice on electoral system design. As occasional consultants, the authors regard skepticism along these lines as entirely reasonable. The best response is, perhaps, that the imperative for extensive case knowledge depends on the nature of the consulting job. In many instances, consultants were not asked to offer specific proposals for how electoral rules ought to be designed, but rather to provide academic seminars on electoral systems for politicians whose baseline familiarity with the topic was limited.

One of the authors of this report, for example, conducted crash courses running from one day to about a week for members of parliament in Yemen and Jordan, countries with limited democratic experience in a region with sparse history of competitive elections. In both cases, the executive branch had made a public commitment to send an electoral reform proposal to parliament, but most members of parliament themselves had little idea what the range of reform alternatives actually consisted of. Consulting, in these cases, amounted to providing politicians who would be asked to evaluate and approve (or disapprove or amend) electoral reform proposals with a grasp of basic concepts (e.g., what a list proportional system is, what a mixed system is, how various formulas for converting votes to seats operate), and with accounts of how various electoral systems have operated in other countries (e.g., how open-lists have worked in Brazil, how mixed SMD-PR systems worked in Russia and Ukraine before they were jettisoned, how the combination of block vote with list-PR used for the 2006 Palestinian Authority elections differs from other mixed systems). In these instances, very little of the substance of consulting involved deep knowledge of the case immediately at hand. That knowledge was not lacking in country. The relative needs were for technical expertise and informed perspectives about experiences elsewhere.

How broadly does this reflect the experience of electoral consultants surveyed? Figure 7.6 shows the proportion of consulting missions that interacted with various categories of actors in country. Most consultants interacted with a range of actors, but most missions put consultants in contact with government officials at the level of cabinet ministers, national legislators, and electoral commissioners, as well as political party officials.

We also asked respondents whether, in their interactions with these actors, they offered specific recommendations for electoral system design or offered more technical information and analysis. Figure 7.7 indicates that, although slightly fewer than half of the missions produced specific endorsements, consultants rarely (10%) refrained completely from offering recommendations. In 40% of cases, the recom-

Figure 7.6: **Points of Contact**

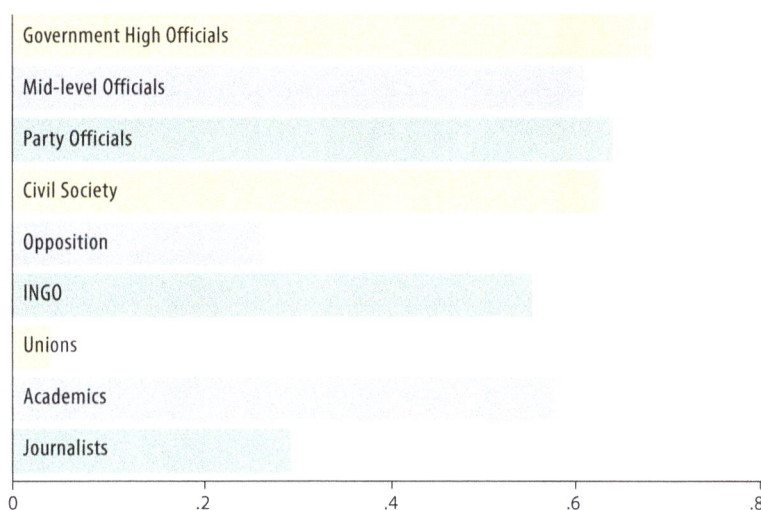

Source: Carey, Hix, Mozaffar, and Reynolds, 2011–2012 Consultant Survey, Task Force on Electoral Rules and Democratic Governance

mendations took the shape of negative assessments of specific reform proposals on the table, although without an explicit endorsement of any specific reform solution.

What are the issues on which consultants are asked to weigh in? Figure 7.8 illustrates that in more than three-quarters of instances, agendas included whether parliamentary elections should be single-winner or multiple-winner contests (or some combination of these), questions of the size and structure of electoral districts, the choice of electoral formula and thresholds for representation, and the design of ballot structure. More technical questions about the process of voter registration, election monitoring, vote counting, fraud, and arbitration lagged substantially in the consulting dossiers of our survey respondents, but we suspect that is because the same organizations that recruit political scientists to consult on matters of

Figure 7.7: **Content of Consultant's Advice**

Technical advice or endorsement of specific reforms

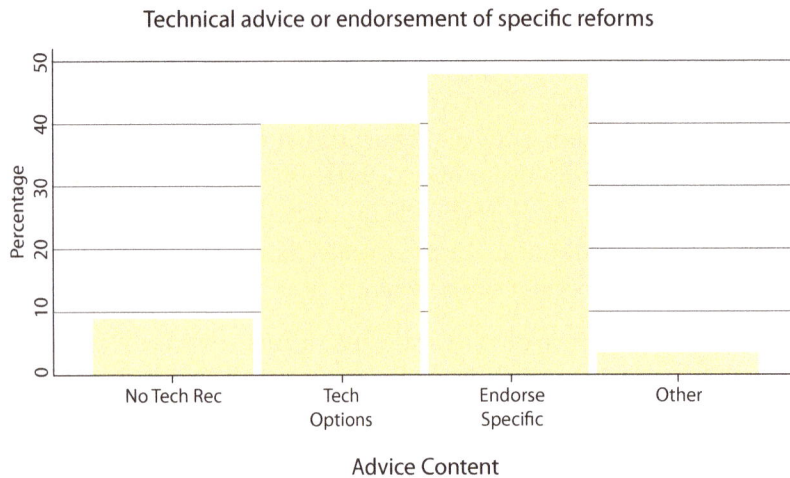

Source: Carey, Hix, Mozaffar, and Reynolds, 2011–2012 Consultant Survey, Task Force on Electoral Rules and Democratic Governance

system design generally lean on legal scholars and former government officials with specific electoral commission experience to consult on matters of electoral administration and dispute resolution.

We were also interested in the reform goals of the electoral reformers with whom consultants interact. We asked survey respondents to evaluate on a four-point scale running from "Not Concerned" to "Central Goal" the priority given to various electoral reform goals among the political actors they met. Figure 7.9 displays histograms of the distribution of responses on each potential goal listed in the survey. As above, the histograms are ordered—from top to bottom of each column in the figure, and from left to right across the page—according to the mean evaluation, so higher priorities are top and left whereas lower are bottom and right.

Many of the goals included in the consultants' survey replicated those included

Figure 7.8: **Consulting Agenda**

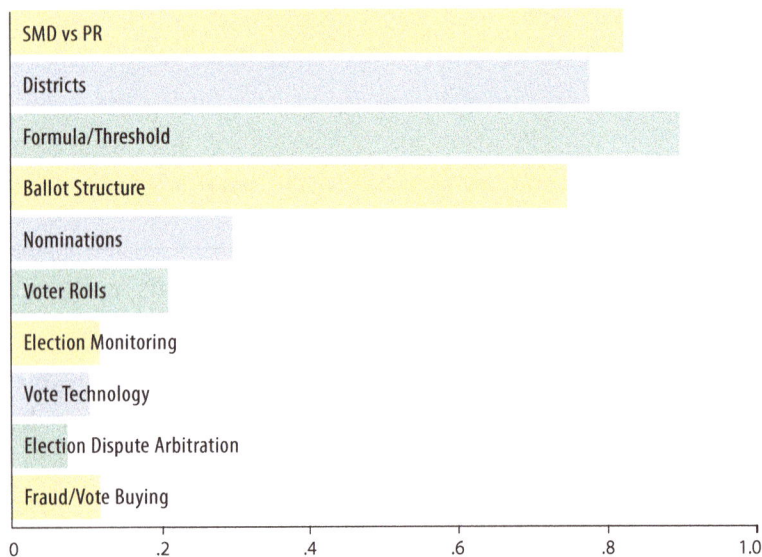

Source: Carey, Hix, Mozaffar, and Reynolds, 2011–2012 Consultant Survey, Task Force on Electoral Rules and Democratic Governance

in our APSA-wide survey, although the correspondence was not perfect. Where the surveys corresponded, making comparison straightforward, the correlation of priorities across our two surveys was noteworthy.[13] Stable government and the accountability of individual representatives came out at the top, party cohesiveness and women's representation landed at the bottom, and representation for marginalized groups fell in between.

Figure 7.9: **Relative Weight Given by Local Actors to Various Potential Reform Priorities**

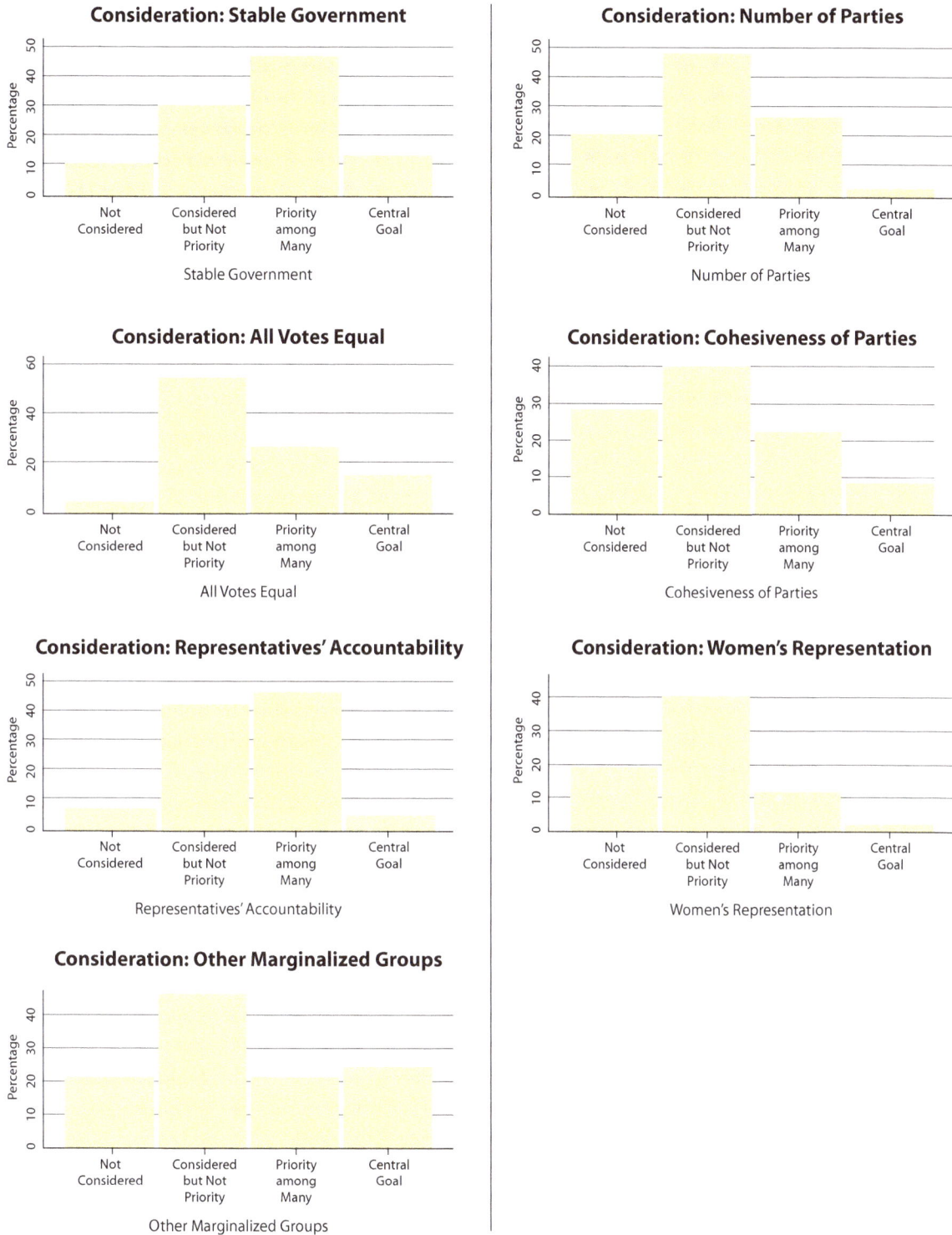

Consideration: Stable Government

Consideration: Number of Parties

Consideration: All Votes Equal

Consideration: Cohesiveness of Parties

Consideration: Representatives' Accountability

Consideration: Women's Representation

Consideration: Other Marginalized Groups

Source: Carey, Hix, Mozaffar, and Reynolds, 2011–2012 Consultant Survey, Task Force on Electoral Rules and Democratic Governance

Figure 7.10: **Reaction by Political Actors to Consultant's Advice**

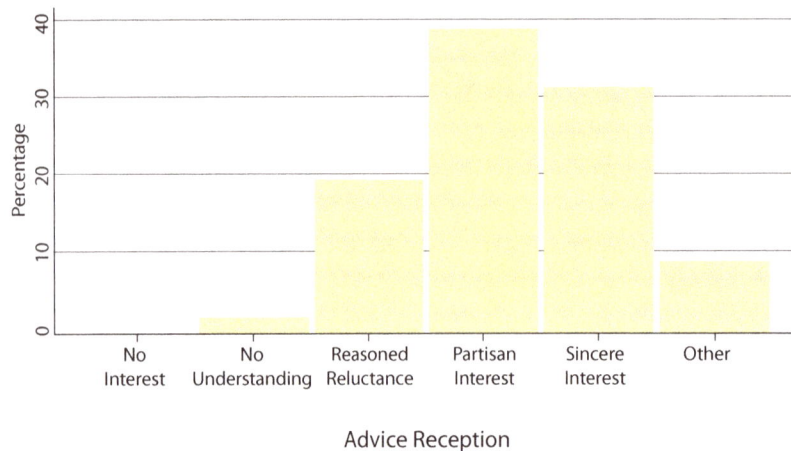

Source: Carey, Hix, Mozaffar, and Reynolds, 2011–2012 Consultant Survey, Task Force on Electoral Rules and Democratic Governance

The last two questions in the consultants' survey addressed how the political scientists' advice was received. Figure 7.10 shows consultants' subjective assessments of political actors' reactions, whereas Figure 7.11 illustrates the bottom line—at least as understood by those consultants who offered specific recommendations. None of our consultants found their audiences to be completely uninterested in their input, and almost none regarded them as baffled by the topic.[14] The most common subjective assessment, in almost 40% of cases, was that local political actors were motivated primarily by partisan (or personal, sectarian, movement) concerns, and inclined to draw on the content provided by academic consultants selectively, when that content could be used to bolster positions motivated by other factors.

Figure 7.11 displays the consultants' assessments of the outcomes of the reform episodes in which they participated. For consultants who offered specific advice, the modal response was that it had no impact on the outcome. Yet episodes in which some or all of the consultants' advice was heeded outnumbered those in which it was ignored entirely, and, of course, in a substantial set of cases, the reform debates are ongoing.

Conclusion

One of the core competences of modern political science is the design of electoral systems. So, what do political scientists think they know about this issue? And, how has this knowledge been

Figure 7.11: **How Much of Consultant's Advice Implemented?**

Source: Carey, Hix, Mozaffar, and Reynolds, 2011–2012 Consultant Survey, Task Force on Electoral Rules and Democratic Governance

translated to practitioners of electoral systems design in the real world? Our survey of APSA members revealed that political scientists' preferences about electoral systems were broadly consistent with their normative goals for what electoral systems should aim to achieve, as well as with existing knowledge in the discipline. Respondents did not separate cleanly into distinct camps, however—whether majoritarian versus proportional, or governability versus inclusivity, or what have you. Respondents showed an inclination to value multiple goals and to try to balance among these. This is perhaps what is reflected in the substantial support for mixed-member compensatory systems, famously characterized as the "best of both worlds" by Shugart and Wattenberg.[15] We also found strong support for the open-list form of PR, perhaps reflecting a growing concern in the discipline that closed-list PR delivers too much power to party leaders as opposed to individual voters.

In answering the second question, our survey of practical experience suggested that political scientists are increasingly engaged in designing electoral systems for governments, and that many of the central areas of research in contemporary electoral studies map closely onto the issues on which electoral reformers seek guidance. That said, reformers seek advice for various reasons, among which pursuit of the best science may not predominate. Political scientists can transmit their knowledge—and the discipline has produced many results relevant to reformers in recent decades—but reformers will deploy that knowledge to their own ends.

References

Akitoby, Bernardin, and Thomas Stratmann. "Fiscal Policy and Financial Markets." *Economic Journal* 118 no. 533 (2008): 1971–85.

Alesina, Alberto, Edward Glaeser, and Bruce Sacerdote. "Why Doesn't the US Have a European-Style Welfare System?" NBER Working Paper 8524, National Bureau of Economic Research, Cambridge, MA, 2001.

Alionescu, Ciprian-Calin. "Parliamentary Representation of Minorities in Romania." *Southeast European Politics* 5 no. 1 (2004): 60–75.

Amat, Francesc, and Erik Wibbels. "Electoral Incentives, Group Identity and Preferences for Redistribution." Estudio/Working Paper 2009/246, Juan March Institute, Madrid, 2009.

Ames, Barry. "Electoral Rules, Constituency Pressures, and Pork Barrel: Bases of Voting in the Brazilian Congress." *Journal of Politics*. 57 no. 2 (1995a): 324–43

———. "Electoral Strategy under Open-List Proportional Depresentation." *American Journal of Political Science* 39 no. 2 (1995b): 406–33.

Andersen, Jørgen Juel, and Silje Aslaksen. "Constitutions and the Resource Curse." *Journal of Development Economics* 87 no. 2 (2008): 227–46.

André, Audrey, and Sam Depauw. "District Magnitude and Home Styles of Representation in European Democracies." Paper presented at the ECPR Joint Sessions of Workshops, Antwerp, April 11–15, 2012.

André, Audrey, Sam Depauw, and Matthew S. Shugart, "The Effect of Electoral Institutions on Legislative Behavior." in *The Oxford Handbook of Legislative Studies*, edited by Shane Martin, Thomas Saalfeld, and Kaare Strøm. Oxford: Oxford University Press, 2013.

Atkeson, Lonna, Lisa Bryant, Thad Hall, Kyle Saunders, and Michael Alvarez. "A New Barrier to Participation: Heterogeneous Application of Voter Identification Policies." *Electoral Studies* 29 no. 1 (2010): 66–73.

Austen-Smith, David. "Redistributing Income under Proportional Representation." *Journal of Political Economy* 108 no. 6 (2000): 1235–69.

Bagashka, Tanya. "The Personal Vote and Economic Reform." *Electoral Studies* 31 (2012): 562–75.

Baldez, Lisa. "Elected Bodies: Gender Quotas for Female Legislative Candidates in Mexico." *Legislative Studies Quarterly* 29 no. 2 (2004): 231–58.

Banducci, Susan A., and Jeffrey A. Karp. "Perceptions of Fairness and Support for Proportional Representation." *Political Behavior* 21 no. 3 (1999): 217–38.

Barkan, Joel. "Elections in Agrarian Societies." *Journal of Democracy* 6 no. 4 (1995): 106–16.

Bauer, Gretchen, and Hannah Britton. "Women in African Parliaments: A Continental Shift?" In *Women in African Parliaments*, edited by Gretchen Bauer and Hannah Britton. Boulder: Lynne Rienner, 2006.

Bawn, Kathleen, and Frances Rosenbluth. "Short versus Long Coalitions: Electoral Accountability and the Size of the Public Sector." *American Journal of Political Science* 50 no. 2 (2006): 251–65.

Bawn, Kathleen, and Michael F. Thies. "A Comparative Theory of Electoral Incentives: Representing the Unorganized under PR, Plurality and Mixed-Member Electoral Systems." *Journal of Theoretical Politics*. 15 no. 1 (2003): 5–32.

Beckwith, Karen, and Kimberly Cowell-Meyers. "Sheer Numbers: Critical Representation Thresholds and Women's Political Representation." *Perspectives on Politics* 5 no. 3 (2007): 553–65.

Béjar, Sergio, and Bumba Mukherjee. "Electoral Institutions and Growth Volatility: Theory and Evidence." *International Political Science Review* 32 no. 4 (2011): 458–79.

Beitz, Charles. *Political Equality*. Princeton: Princeton University Press, 1989.

Benedetto, Giacomo, and Simon Hix. "The Rejected, the Ejected, and the Dejected: Explaining Government Rebels in the 2001–2005 British House of Commons," *Comparative Political Studies* 40 no. 7 (July 2007): 755–81.

Benoit, Ken. "Electoral Laws as Political Consequences: Explaining the Origins and Change of Electoral Institutions." *Annual Review of Political Science* 10 (2007): 363–90.

Bergman, Matthew E., Matthew S. Shugart, and Kevin A. Watt. "Patterns of Intra-Party Competition in Open-List and SNTV Systems." *Electoral Studies* 32 no. 2 (2013): 321

Birch, Sarah. *Electoral Malpractice*. New York: Oxford University Press, 2012.

———. "Perceptions of Electoral Fairness and Voter Turnout." *Comparative Political Studies* 43 no. 12 (2010): 1601–22.

———. "Electoral Systems and Electoral Misconduct." *Comparative Political Studies* 40 no. 12 (2007): 1533–56.

Bernhard, William, and David Leblang. "Democratic Institutions and Exchange Rate Commitments." *International Organization* 53 no. 1 (1999): 71–97.

Birchfield, Vicki, and Markus M. L. Crepaz. "The Impact of Constitutional Structures and Collective and Competitive Veto Points on Income Inequality in Industrialized Democracies." *European Journal of Political Research* 34 no. 2 (1998): 175–200.

Bird, Karen. "The Political Representation of Women and Ethnic Minorities in Established Democracies." Paper presented at the Academy of Migration Studies at Aalborg University, Denmark, 2003.

Bjarnegård, Elin. *Gender, Informal Institutions and Political Recruitment Explaining Male Dominance in Parliamentary Representation*. New York: Palgrave, 2013.

Blais, Andre, and Marc A. Bodet. "Does Proportional Representation Foster Closer Congruence between Citizens and Policymakers?" *Comparative Political Studies* 39 (2006): 1243–63.

Blume, Lorenz, Jens Müller, Stefan Voigt, and Carsten Wolf. "The Economic Effects of Constitutions: Replicating—and Extending—Persson and Tabellini." *Public Choice* 139 nos. 1–2 (2009): 197–225.

Boix, Carles. "Electoral Markets, Party Strategies, and Proportional Representation." *American Political Science Review* 104 no. 2 (2010): 404–13.

Bortolotti, Bernardo, and Paolo Pinotti. "Delayed Privatization." *Public Choice* 136 nos. 3–4 (2008): 331–51.

Bowler, Shaun. "Parties in Legislature: Two Competing Explanations." In *Parties without Partisans: Political Change in Advanced Industrial Democracies*, edited by R.J. Dalton and M.P. Wattenberg, 157–79. Oxford: Oxford University Press, 2002.

Bowler, Shaun, and David M. Farrell. "Legislator Shirking and Voter Monitoring: Impacts of European Parliament Electoral Systems upon Legislative-Voter Relationships." *Journal of Common Market Studies* 31 no. 1 (1993): 45–69.

Bronner, Ethan. "Legal Battles Erupt Over Tough Voter ID Laws." *New York Times*, July 19, 2012. Available at http://www.nytimes.com/2012/07/20/us/politics/tougher-voter-id-laws-set-off-court-battles.html?ref=voterregistrationandrequirements.

Brownlee, Jason, Tarek Masoud, and Andrew Reynolds. *The Arab Spring: The Politics of Transformation in North Africa and the Middle East*. New York: Oxford University Press, forthcoming.

Buck, J. Vincent, and Bruce E. Cain. "British MPs in Their Constituencies." *Legislative Studies Quarterly* 15 no. 1 (1990): 127–43.

Burnheim, John. *Is Democracy Possible?* 2nd edition. Sydney: Sydney University Press, 2006.

Bush, Sarah Sunn. "International Politics and the Spread of Quotas for Women in Legislatures." *International Organization* 65 no. 1 (2011): 103–37.

Cain, Bruce E., John A. Ferejohn, and Morris P. Fiorina. *The Personal Vote: Constituency Service and Electoral Independence*. Cambridge, MA: Harvard University Press, 1987.

Cameron, Charles, David Epstein, and Sharyn O'Halloran. "Do Majority-Minority Districts Maximize Substantive Black Representation in Congress?" *American Political Science Review* 90 no. 4 (1996): 794–812.

Carey, John M. "Competing Principals, Political Institutions, and Party Unity in Legislative Voting." *American Journal of Political Science* 51 no. 1 (2007): 92–107.

———. *Legislative Voting and Accountability*. Cambridge: Cambridge University Press, 2009.

Carey, John M., and Simon Hix. "The Electoral Sweet Spot: Low-Magnitude Proportional Electoral Systems." *American Journal of Political Science* 55 (2011): 383–97.

Carey, John M., and Matthew S. Shugart. "Incentives to Cultivate a Personal Vote: A Rank Ordering of Electoral Formulas." *Electoral Studies* 14 no. 4 (1995): 417–39.

Carreras, Miguel, and Yasemin Irepoglu. "Perceptions of Electoral Integrity, Efficacy, and Support for Democratic Institutions in Latin America." Paper prepared for the Workshop on Electoral Integrity, Madrid, July 7, 2012.

Celis, Karen, Sarah Childs, Johanna Kantola, and Mona Lena Krook. "Rethinking Women's Substantive Representation." *Representation* 44 no. 2 (2008): 99–110.

Celis, Karen, Mona Lena Krook, and Petra Meier. "The Rise of Gender Quota Laws: Expanding the Spectrum of Determinants for Electoral Reform." *West European Politics* 34 no. 3 (2011): 514–30.

Chang, Eric C.C. "Electoral Incentives and Budgetary Spending: Rethinking the Role of Political Institutions." *Journal of Politics* 70 no. 4 (2008): 1086–97.

Chang, Eric C.C., and Miriam A. Golden, "Electoral Systems, District Magnitude and Corruption." *British Journal of Political Science* 37 no. 1 (2006): 115–37.

Chang, Eric C.C, Mark A. Kayser, Drew A. Linzer, and Ronald Rogowski. *Electoral Systems and the Balance of Consumer-Producer Power*. Cambridge: Cambridge University Press, 2011.

Chang, Eric C.C., Mark A. Kayser, and Ronald Rogowski. "Electoral Systems and Real Prices: Panel Evidence for the OECD Countries, 1970–2000." *British Journal of Political Science* 38 no. 4 (2008): 739–51.

Chhibber, Pradeep, and Ken Kollman. *The Formation of National Party Systems: Federalism and Party Competition in Canada, Great Britain, India, and the United States*. Princeton: Princeton University Press, 2004.

Collier, Paul, and Pedro C. Vicente. "Violence, Bribery, and Fraud: The Political Economy of Elections in Sub-Saharan Africa." *Public Choice* 53 nos. 1, 2 (2012): 117–47.

Colomer, Josep M. *Political Institutions: Democracy and Social Choice*. New York: Oxford University Press, 2001.

Cowhey, Peter F. "Domestic Institutions and the Credibility of International Commitments: Japan and the United States." *International Organization* 47 no. 2 (1993): 299–326.

Cox, Gary W. *Making Votes Count: Strategic Coordination in the World's Electoral Systems*. New York: Cambridge University Press, 1997.

Crepaz, Markus M.L. "Inclusion versus Exclusion: Political Institutions and Welfare Expenditures." *Comparative Politics* 31 no. 1 (1998): 61–80.

Crisp, Brian F. "Incentives in Mixed-Member Electoral Systems: General Election Laws, Candidate Selection Procedures, and Cameral Rules." *Comparative Political Studies* 40 no. 12 (2007): 1460–85.

Crisp, Brian F., Maria C. Escobar-Lemmon, Bradfod S. Jones, Mark P. Jones, and Michelle M. Taylor-Robinson. "Vote-Seeking Incentives and Legislative Representation in Six Presidential Democracies." *Journal of Politics* 66 no. 3 (2004): 823–45.

Crisp, Brian F., Nathan M. Jensen, Guillermo Rosas, and Thomas Zeitzoff. "Vote-Seeking Incentives and Investment Environments: The Need for Credit Claiming and the Provision of Protectionism." *Electoral Studies* 29 no. 2 (2010): 221–26.

Curtice, John, and Phillips Shively. "Who Represents Us Best? One Member or Many?" In *The Comparative Study of Electoral Systems*, edited by H.D. Klingemann, 171–92. Oxford: Oxford University Press, 2009.

Cusack, Thomas R., Torben Iversen, and Philipp Rehm. "Risks at Work: The Demand and Supply Sides of Government Redistribution." *Oxford Review of Economic Policy* 22 no. 3 (2006): 365–89.

Cusack, Thomas R., Torben Iversen, and David Soskice. "Coevolution of Capitalism and Political Representation: The Choice of Electoral Systems." *American Political Science Review* 104 no. 2 (2010): 393–403.

———. "Economic Interests and the Origins of Electoral Systems." *American Political Science Review* 101 no. 3 (2007): 373–91.

Dahl, Robert. *Polyarchy*. New Haven: Yale University Press, 1971.

Dahlerup, Drude, ed. *Women, Quotas, and Politics*. New York: Routledge, 2006.

Dehon, Catherine, Gassner Marjorie, and Verardi Vincenzo. "Beware of 'Good' Outliers and Overoptimistic Conclusions." *Oxford Bulletin of Economics and Statistics* 71 no. 3 (2009): 437–52.

Diamond, Larry. "Three Paradoxes of Democracy." *Journal of Democracy* 1 no. 3 (Summer 1990): 48–60.

Dickson, Vaughan. "Seat-Vote Curves, Loyalty Effects and the Provincial Distribution of Canadian Government Spending." *Public Choice* 139 nos. 3–4 (2009): 317–33.

Downs, Anthony. *An Economic Theory of Democracy*. N.Y.: Harper and Row, 1957.

Drometer, Marcus, and Rincke Johannes. "The Impact of Ballot Access Restrictions on Electoral Competition: Evidence from a Natural Experiment." *Public Choice* 138 nos. 3–4 (2009): 461–74.

Duch, Raymond M., and Randolph T. Stevenson. *The Economic Vote: How Political and Economic Institutions Condition Election Results*. New York: Cambridge University Press, 2008.

Duffield, John S., and Charles R. Hankla. "The Efficiency of Institutions Political Determinants of Oil Consumption in Democracies." *Comparative Politics* 43 no. 2 (2011): 187–205.

Duverger, Maurice. *Political Parties: Their Organization and Activity in the Modern State*. New York: John Wiley, 1954.

Edwards, Martin S., and Frank C. Thames. "District Magnitude, Personal Votes, and Government Expenditures." *Electoral Studies* 26 no. 2 (2007): 338–45.

Ehrlich, Sean D. "Access to Protection: Domestic Institutions and Trade Policy in Democracies." *International Organization* 61 no. 3 (2007): 571–605.

Eichengreen, Barry, and David Leblang. "Exchange Rates and Cohesion: Historical Perspectives and Political-Economy Considerations." *Journal of Common Market Studies* 41 no. 5 (2003): 797–822.

Ellis Valdini, Melody. "Electoral Institutions and the Manifestation of Bias: The Effect of the Personal Vote on the Representation of Women." Paper prepared for presentation at the annual meeting of the Western Political Science Association, Portland, OR, March 2012.

Esping-Andersen, Gosta. *The Three Worlds of Welfare Capitalism*. Princeton: Princeton University Press, 1990.

Estevez-Abe, Margarita. *Welfare Capitalism in Postwar Japan*. New York: Cambridge University Press, 2008.

Evans, Carolyn L. "A Protectionist Bias in Majoritarian Politics: An Empirical Investigation." *Economics and Politics* 21 no 2 (2009): 278–307.

Fabrizio, Stefania, and Ashoka Mody. "Can Budget Institutions Counteract Political Indiscipline?" *Economic Policy* 21 no. 48 (2006): 689–739.

Farrell, David M., and Roger Scully. *Representing Europe's Citizens? Electoral Institutions and the Failure of Parliamentary Representation*. Oxford: Oxford University Press, 2007.

Ferree, Karen. *Framing the Race in South Africa: the Political Origins of Racial-Census Elections*. New York: Cambridge University Press, 2011.

Ferree, Karen, Clark Gibson, and Barak Hoffman. "Social Diversity, Electoral Rules, and South Africa's Local Party Systems." Unpublished manuscript, University of California, San Diego, 2011.

Ferree, Karen, and James Long. "Violating the Secret Ballot: The Political Logic of Vote Monitoring in Ghana's 2008 Elections." Unpublished manuscript, University of California, San Diego, 2012.

Ferree, Karen, G. Bingham Powell, Jr., and Ethan Scheiner. "APSA Presidential Task Force on Electoral Rules and Democratic Governance—How Context Shapes Electoral Rule Effects" Prepared for delivery at the American Political Science Association Meeting, New Orleans, LA, August 30–September 2, 2012.

Filippov, Mikhail, Peter Ordeshook, and Olga Shvetsova. "Party Fragmentation and Presidential Elections in Post-Communist Democracies." *Constitutional Political Economy* 10 no. 1 (1999): 1–24.

Franchino, Fabio, and Marco Mainenti. "Electoral Institutions and Distributive Policies in Parliamentary Systems: An Application to State Aid Measures in EU Countries." Working Paper, University of Milan, 2011.

Fréchette, Guillaume R., Francois Maniquet, and Massimo Morelli. "Incumbents' Interests, Voters' Bias and Gender Quotas," *American Journal of Political Science* 52 no. 4 (2008): 891–909.

Freidenvall, Lenita, Drude Dahlerup, and Hege Skjeie. "The Nordic Countries: An Incremental Model." In *Women, Quotas, and Politics,* edited by Drude Dahlerup. New York: Routledge, 2006.

Funk, Patricia, and Christina Gathmann. "How Do Electoral Systems Affect Fiscal Policy? Evidence from State and Local Governments, 1890 to 2005." CESifo Working Paper 2958, Center for Economic Studies, Munich, 2010.

Gagliarducci, Stefano, Tommaso Nannicini, and Paolo Naticchioni. "Electoral Rules and Politicians' Behavior: A Micro Test." *American Economic Journal-Economic Policy* 3 no. 3 (2011): 144–74.

Gallagher, Michael. "Proportionality, Disproportionality and Electoral Systems." *Electoral Studies* 10 (1991): 33–51.

Gallagher, Michael, Michael Laver, and Peter Mair. *Representative Government in Modern Europe*. 4th ed. New York: McGraw Hill, 2006.

Garland, Marshall W., and Glen Biglaiser. "Do Electoral Rules Matter? Political Institutions and Foreign Direct Investment in Latin America." *Comparative Political Studies* 42 no. 2 (2009): 224–51.

Geddis, Andrew. "A Dual Track Democracy? The Symbolic Role of the Maori Seats in New Zealand's Electoral System." *Election Law Journal* 5 no. 4 (2006): 347–71.

Golden, Miriam A., and Eric C. Chang. "Competitive Corruption: Factional Conflict and Political Malfeasance in Postwar Italian Christian Democracy." *World Politics* 53 no. 4 (2001): 588–622.

Golden, Miriam A., and Lucio Picci. "Pork-Barrel Politics in Postwar Italy, 1953–94." *American Journal of Political Science* 52 no. 2 (2008): 268–89.

Gourevitch, Peter, and Michael Hawes. "The Politics of Choice among National Production Systems." *L'Année de la régulation* 6 (2002): 241–71.

Green, Jeffrey. *The Eyes of the People: Democracy in an Age of Spectatorship*. Oxford: Oxford University Press, 2011.

Grilli, Vittorio, Donato Masciandaro, Guido Tabellini, Edmond Malinvaud, and Marco Pagano. "Political and Monetary Institutions and Public Financial Policies in the Industrial Countries." *Economic Policy* 6 no. 13 (1991): 341–92.

Grofman, Bernard, Shaun Bowler, and Andre Blais. "Introduction: Evidence for Duverger's Law in Four Countries." In *Duverger's Law of Plurality Elections: The Logic of Party Competition in Canada, India, the United Kingdom, and the United States,* edited by B. Grofman, A. Blais, S. Bowler. New York: Springer, 2009.

Grofman, Bernard, and Arend Lijphart, ed. *Electoral Laws and their Political Consequences*. New York: Agathon Press, 1986.

Grofman, Bernard, Sung C. Lee, Edwin A. Winckler, and Brian Woodall *Elections in Japan, Korea and Taiwan under the Single Non-Transferable Vote. The Comparative Study of an Embedded Institution*. Ann Arbor, University of Michigan Press, 1999.

Hallerberg, Mark, and Patrik Marier. "Executive Authority, the Personal Vote, and Budget Discipline in Latin American and Caribbean Countries." *American Journal of Political Science* 48 no. 3 (2004): 571–87.

Hallerberg, Mark, Rolf Strauch, and Jürgen von Hagen. "The Design of Fiscal Rules and Forms of Governance in European Union Countries." *European Journal of Political Economy* 23 no. 2 (2007): 338–59.

Hankla, Charles R. "Party Strength and International Trade: A Cross-National Analysis." *Comparative Political Studies* 39 no. 9 (2006): 1133–56.

Hansen, Mogens Herman. *The Athenian Democracy in the Age of Demosthenes*. Oxford: Blackwell, 1991.

Hartzell, Caroline, and Matthew Hoddie. "Institutionalizing Peace: Power Sharing and Post–Civil War Conflict Management." *American Journal of Political Science* 47 no. 2 (2003): 318–32.

Hatfield, John William, and William R. Hauk Jr. "Electoral Regime and Trade Policy." Working Paper, Stanford University, Stanford, CA, and University of South Carolina, Columbia, 2010.

Hazan, Reuven Y., and Gideon Rahat. *Democracy within Parties: Candidate Selection Methods and Their Political Consequences*. Oxford: Oxford University Press, 2010.

Helmke, Gretchen. *Institutions on the Edge: Inter-Branch Crises in Latin America*. Rochester, New York, unpublished manuscript, 2012.

Hicken, Allen. *Building Party Systems in Developing Nations*. New York: Cambridge University Press, 2009.

Hicken, Allen, and Heather Stoll. "Presidents and Parties: How Presidential Elections Shape Coordination in Legislative Elections." *Comparative Political Studies* 44 no. 7 (2011): 854–83.

Ho, Daniel E. "Majoritarian Electoral Systems and Consumer Power: A Matching Rejoinder." Working Paper, Harvard University, Cambridge, MA, 2003.

Holmsten, Stephanie, Robert G. Moser, and Mary Slosar. "Do Ethnic Parties Exclude Women?" *Comparative Political Studies* 43 no. 10 (2010): 1179–1201.

Horowitz, Donald. "Electoral Systems: A Primer for Decision Makers." *Journal of Democracy* 14 no. 4 (2003).

———. *Ethnic Groups in Conflict*. Berkeley: University of California Press, 1985.

Horowitz, Jeremy, and James Long. "Does Ethnicity Reduce Strategic Voting? Unpublished manuscript, University of California, San Diego, 2012.

Htun, Mala. "Intersectional Disadvantage and Political Inclusion: Getting More Afrodescendant Women into Elected Office in Latin America." Inter-American Development Bank, Gender and Diversity Division, Program for Women's Leadership and Representation. Washington, D.C. October 2011. Available at: http://idbdocs.iadb.org/wsdocs/getdocument .aspx?docnum=36945627.

———. "Women, Political Parties and Electoral Systems in Latin America." In *Women in Parliament. Beyond Numbers. A New Edition*, edited by Julie Ballington and Azza Karam. Stockholm: International IDEA, 2005.

———. "Is Gender like Ethnicity? The Political Representation of Identity Groups." *Perspectives on Politics* 2 no. 3 (2004): 439–58.

Htun, Mala, and Mark Jones. "Engendering the Right to Participate in Decision Making: Electoral Quotas and Women's Leadership in Latin America." In *Gender and the Politics of Rights and Democracy in Latin America,* edited by Nikki Craske and Maxine Molyneux, 32–56. London: Palgrave, 2002.

Htun, Mala, and Juan Pablo Ossa. "Political Inclusion of Marginalized Groups: Indigenous Reservations and Gender Parity in Bolivia." *Politics, Groups, and Identities* 1 no. 1 (2013).

Huber, John D., and G. Bingham Powell, Jr. "Congruence between Citizens and Policymakers in Two Visions of Liberal Democracy." *World Politics* 46 (1994): 291–326.

Hughes, Melanie M. "Intersectionality, Quotas, and Minority Women's Political Representation Worldwide." *American Political Science Review* 105 no. 3 (2011): 604–20.

Hughes, Melanie, Mona Lena Krook, and Pamela Paxton. "Transnational Women's Activism and the Global Diffusion of Gender Quotas." Working Paper. 2012

Hyde, Susan D. *The Pseudo-Democrat's Dilemma*. Ithaca: Cornell University Press, 2011.

———. "The Observer Effect in International Politics: Evidence from a Natural Experiment." *World Politics* 60 no. 1 (2007): 37-63.

Ichino, Nahomi, and Matthias Schuendeln. "Deterring or Displacing Electoral Irregularities? Spillover Effects of Observers in a Randomized Field Experiment in Ghana." *Journal of Politics* 74 no. 1 (2012): 292–307.

Ingall, Rachael E., and Brian F. Crisp. "Determinants of Home Style: The Many Incentives for Going Home in Colombia." *Legislative Studies Quarterly* 26 no. 3 (2001): 487–512.

International Foundation for Election Systems, Middle East and North Africa. *Elections in Egypt: Analysis of the 2011 Parliamentary Electoral System*. IFES Briefing Paper. Washington, DC, 2011. Available at http://www.ifes.org/~/media/Files/ Publications/White%20PaperReport/2011/Analysis_of_Egypts_2011_Parliamentary_Electoral_System.pdf

International IDEA. *International Electoral Standards: Guidelines for Reviewing the Legal Framework of Elections*. Stockholm: International IDEA, 2002.

Iversen, Torben, and Frances Rosenbluth. *Women, Work, and Politics: The Political Economy of Gender Equality*. New Haven: Yale University Press, 2010.

———. "Work and Power: The Connection Between Female Labor Force Participation and Female Political Representation." *Annual Review of Political Science* 11 (2008): 479–95.

Iversen, Torben, and David Soskice. "Real Exchange Rates and Competitiveness: The Political Economy of Skill Formation, Wage Compression, and Electoral Systems." *American Political Science Review* 104 no. 3 (2010): 601–23.

———. "Distribution and Redistribution: The Shadow of the Nineteenth Century." *World Politics* 61 no. 3 (2009): 438–86.

———. "Electoral Institutions and the Politics of Coalitions: Why Some Democracies Redistribute More Than Others." *American Political Science Review* 100 no. 2 (2006): 165–81.

Jensen, Nathan M. "Rational Citizens against Reform: Poverty and Economic Reform in Transition Economies." *Comparative Political Studies* 36 no. 9 (2003): 1092–1111.

Johnson, Gregg B., and Brian F. Crisp. "Mandates, Powers, and Policies." *American Journal of Political Science* 47 no. 1 (2003): 128–42.

Johnson, Joel W., and Veronica Hoyo. "Beyond Personal Vote Incentives: Dividing the Vote in Preferential Electoral Systems." *Electoral Studies* 31 no. 1 (2012): 131–42.

Jones, Mark P. "Gender Quotas, Electoral Laws, and the Election of Women: Evidence from the Latin American Vanguard." *Comparative Political Studies* 42 no. 1 (2009), 56–81.

Kang, Shin-Goo, and G. Bingham Powell, Jr. "Representation and Policy Responsiveness: The Median Voter, Election Rules, and Redistributive Welfare Spending." *Journal of Politics* 72 no. 4 (2010): 1014–28.

Karol, David. "Does Constituency Size Affect Elected Officials' Trade Policy Preferences?" *Journal of Politics* 69 no. 2 (2007): 483–94.

Karpowitz, Christopher F., and Tali Mendelberg. "Do Women Deliberate with a Distinctive Voice? How Decision Rules and Group Gender Composition Affect the Content of Deliberation." Paper prepared for presentation at the annual meeting of the American Political Science Association, Seattle, WA, September 1–4, 2011.

Kayser, Mark Andreas. "The Price-Level Effect of Electoral Competitiveness." Working Paper, University of Oxford, Oxford, UK, 2004.

Key, V.O. *Southern Politics in State and Nation.* New York: A. A. Knopf, 1949.

Keyssar, Alexander. *The Right to Vote: The Contested History of Democracy in the United States.* New York: Basic Books, 2000.

Kim, Dong-Hun. "Making or Breaking a Deal: The Impact of Electoral Systems on Mergers & Acquisitions." *Kyklos* 63 no. 3 (2010): 432–49.

King, Gary, James Alt, Nancy Burns, and Michael Laver. "A Unified Model of Cabinet Dissolution in Parliamentary Democracies." *American Journal of Political Science* 34 (1990): 846–71.

Knutsen, Carl Henrik. "Which Democracies Prosper? Electoral Rules, Form of Government and Economic Growth." *Electoral Studies* 30 no. 1 (2011): 83–90.

Kolinsky, Eva. "Political Participation and Parliamentary Careers: Women's Quotas in West Germany." *West European Politics* 14 no. 1 (1991): 56–72.

Kono, Daniel Yuichi. "Market Structure, Electoral Institutions, and Trade Policy." *International Studies Quarterly* 53 no. 4 (2009): 885–906.

Krook, Mona Lena. "Minorities in Electoral Politics: Gender, Race, and Political Inclusion in Sweden, France, and Britain." In *European States and Their Muslim Citizens: The Impact of Institutions on Perceptions and Boundaries*, eds. John Bowen, Christophe Bertossi, Jan Willem Duyvendak, and Mona Lena Krook. New York: Cambridge University Press, forthcoming.

———. *Quotas for Women in Politics: Gender and Candidate Selection Reform Worldwide.* New York: Oxford University Press, 2009.

———. "Gender and Political Institutions: Implementing Quotas for Women in Politics." Paper presented at the annual meeting of the American Political Science Association, Chicago, IL, August 30-September 2, 2007.

Krook, Mona Lena, and Diana Z. O'Brien. "The Politics of Group Representation: Quotas for Women and Minorities Worldwide." *Comparative Politics* 42 no. 3 (2010): 253–72.

Krook, Mona Lena, Diana Z. O'Brien, and Krista M. Swip. "Military Invasion and Women's Political Representation." *International Feminist Journal of Politics* 12 no. 1 (2010): 66–79.

Kucuksenel, Serkan, and Osman Gulseven. "Electoral Systems and International Trade Policy." *Actual Problems of Economics* 121 (2011): 367–71.

Kunicova, Jana, and Susan Rose-Ackerman. "Electoral Rules and Constitutional Structures as Constraints on Corruption." *British Journal of Political Science* 35 no. 4 (2005): 573–606.

Laver, Michael. "Government Termination." *Annual Reviews of Political Science* 6 (2003): 23–40.

Laver, Michael, and Norman Schofield. *Multiparty Government: The Politics of Coalition in Europe.* New York: Oxford University Press, 1990.

Lehoucq, Fabrice Edouard. "Electoral Fraud: Causes, Types, and Consequences." *Annual Review of Political Science* 6 (2003): 233–56.

Lijphart, Arend. "Constitutional Choices for New Democracies." *Journal of Democracy* 15 no. 2 (2004): 96–109.

———. *Patterns of Democracy*. New Haven: Yale University Press, 1999.

———. *Electoral Systems and Party Systems*. New York: Oxford University Press, 1994.

Lijphart, Arend, and Bernard Grofman. *Choosing an Electoral System*. New York: Praeger, 1984.

Linzer, Drew A., and Ronald L. Rogowski. "Lower Prices: The Impact of Majoritarian Systems in Democracies around the World." *Journal of Politics* 70 no. 1 (2008): 17–27.

Longman, Timothy. "Rwanda: Achieving Equality or Serving an Authoritarian State?" In *Women in African Parliaments*, edited by Hannah Britton and Gretchen Bauer. Boulder: Lynne Rienner, 2006.

Lovenduski, Joni, and Pippa Norris, ed. *Gender and Party Politics*. London: SAGE, 1993.

Lublin, David. *The Paradox of Representation*. Princeton: Princeton University Press, 1999.

Manin, Bernard, Adam Przeworski, and Susan Stokes. "Elections and Representation." In *Democracy, Accountability, and Representation*, edited by Adam Przeworski, Susan C. Stokes, and Bernard Manin, 29–54. New York: Cambridge University Press, 1999.

Manow, Philip. "Electoral Rules, Class Coalitions and Welfare State Regimes, or How to Explain Esping-Andersen wit Stein Rokkan." *Socio-Economic Review* 7 no. 1 (2009): 101–21.

Mansbridge, Jane. "A 'Selection Model' of Political Representation." *Journal of Political Philosophy* 17 no. 4 (2009): 369–98.

———. "Should Blacks Represent Blacks and Women Represent Women? A Contingent Yes." *Journal of Politics* 61, no. 3 (1999): 628–657.

Mansfield, Edward D., and Marc L. Busch. "The Political Economy of Nontariff Barriers: A Cross-National Analysis." *International Organization* 49 no. 4 (1995): 723–49.

Martin, Lanny, and Randolph Stevenson. "Government Formation in Parliamentary Democracies." *American Journal of Political Science* 45 (2001): 33–50.

Matland, Richard. "Electoral Quotas: Frequency and effectiveness." In *Women, Quotas, and Politics*, edited by Drude Dahlerup. New York: Routledge, 2006.

———. "Women's Legislative Representation in National Legislatures: A Comparison of Democracies in Developed and Developing Countries." *Legislative Studies Quarterly* 28 no. 1 (1998): 109–25.

———. "Institutional Variables Affecting Female Representation in National Legislatures: The Case of Norway." *Journal of Politics* 55 no. 3 (1993): 737–55.

Matland, Richard, and Donley T. Studlar. "The Contagion of Women Candidates in Single Member and Multi-Member Districts," *Journal of Politics* 58 no. 3 (1996): 707–33.

McCormick, John. *Machiavellian Democracy*. Cambridge: Cambridge University Press, 2011.

———. "Contain the Wealthy and Patrol the Magistrates: Restoring Elite Accountability to Popular Government." *American Political Science Review* 100 no. 2 (2006): 147–63.

McDonald, Michael D., S. Mendes, and Ian Budge. "What Are Elections For? Conferring the Median Mandate." *British Journal of Political Science* 34 (2004): 1–26.

McGillivray, Fiona. *Privileging Industry: The Comparative Politics of Trade and Industrial Policy*. Princeton: Princeton University Press, 2004.

———. "Redistributive Politics and Stock Price Dispersion." *British Journal of Political Science* 33 no. 3 (2003): 367–95.

———. "Party Discipline as a Determinant of the Endogenous Formation of Tariffs." *American Journal of Political Science* 41 no. 2 (1997): 584–607.

Meier, Petra. "The Mutual Contagion Effect of Legal and Party Quotas: A Belgian Perspective." *Party Politics* 10 no. 5 (2004): 583–600.

Milesi-Ferretti, Gian Maria, Roberto Perotti, and Massimo Rostagno. "Electoral Systems and Public Spending." *Quarterly Journal of Economics* 117 no. 2 (2002): 609–57.

Mill, John Stuart. *Considerations on Representative Government*. Edited by C.V. Shields. Indianapolis: Bobbs-Merrill, [1861] 1958.

Milner, Helen V., and Benjamin Judkins. "Partisanship, Trade Policy, and Globalization: Is There a Left-Right Divide on Trade Policy?" *International Studies Quarterly* 48 no. 1 (2004): 95–119.

Mitchell, Paul. "Voters and their Representatives: Electoral Institutions and Delegation in Parliamentary Democracies." *European Journal of Political Research* 37 no. 3 (2000): 335–51.

Mitchell, Paul, and Benjamin Nyblade. "Government Formation and Cabinet Type." In *Cabinets and Coalition Bargaining*, edited by Kaare Strøm, Wolfgang Mueller, and Torgjoern Bergman, 201–36. New York: Oxford University Press, 2008.

Mommsen, Wolfgang J. *Max Weber and German Politics, 1890–1920*. Chicago: University of Chicago Press, 1959. English translation by Michael Steinberg, 1990.

Morgenstern, S. and J. Vázquez-D'Elía. "Electoral Laws, Parties, and Party Systems in Latin America." *Annual Review of Political Science* 10 (2007): 143–68.

Moser, Robert G. "Electoral Systems and the Representation of Ethnic Minorities: Evidence from Russia." *Comparative Politics* 40 no. 3 (2008): 273–92.

———. "The Effects of Electoral Systems on Women's Representation in Post-Communist States." *Electoral Studies* 20 no. 3 (2001): 353–69.

———. "Electoral Systems and the Number of Parties in Post-Communist States." *World Politics* 51 no. 3 (1999): 359–84.

Moser, Robert G., and Ethan Scheiner. *Electoral Systems and Political Context: How the Effects of Rules Vary Across New and Established Democracies*. New York: Cambridge University Press, 2012.

Moser, Robert G., Ethan Scheiner, and Caitlin Milazzo. "Social Diversity Affects the Number of Parties Even under First-Past-the-Post Rules." Unpublished manuscript, 2011.

Myerson, Roger B. "Incentives to Cultivate Favored Minorities under Alternative Electoral Systems." *American Political Science Review* 87 no. 4 (1993): 856–69.

Naoi, Megumi. "Shopping for Protection: The Politics of Choosing Trade Instruments in a Partially Legalized World." *International Studies Quarterly* 53 no. 2 (2009): 421–44.

Naoi, Megumi, and Ellis Krauss. "Who Lobbies Whom? Special Interest Politics under Alternative Electoral System." *American Journal of Political Science* 53 no. 4 (2009): 874–92.

Neugart, Michael. "Unemployment Insurance: The Role of Electoral Systems and Regional Labour Markets." *European Journal of Political Economy* 21 no. 4 (2005): 815–29.

Nielson, Daniel L. "Supplying Trade Reform: Political Institutions and Liberalization in Middle-Income Presidential Democracies." *American Journal of Political Science* 47 no. 3 (2003): 470–91.

Norris, Pippa. "Implementing Women's Representation in Afghanistan's Electoral Law: Options for Reserved Seats." Paper prepared for the Afghanistan Reconstruction Project, Center for International Cooperation, New York University, n.d. http://www.hks.harvard.edu/fs/pnorris/Acrobat/Afghanistan%20electoral%20law%20Norris.pdf.

———. "The Concept of Electoral Integrity." Symposium. Revised May 13, 2013. Available at: https://sites.google.com/site/electoralintegrityproject4/publications-1/links-to-other-publications/working-papers-list.

———. *Electoral Engineering: Voting Rules and Political Behavior*. New York: Cambridge University Press, 2004.

———. "Ballot Structures and Legislative Behavior: Changing Role Orientations via Electoral Reform." In *Exporting Congress? The Influence of the US Congress on World Legislatures*, edited by Timothy J. Power, and T.J. and Nicol C. Rae, 157–84. Pittsburgh, PA: University of Pittsburgh Press, 2006.

Park, Jong Hee, and Nathan Jensen. "Electoral Competition and Agricultural Support in OECD Countries." *American Journal of Political Science* 51 no. 2 (2007): 314–29.

Paxton, Pamela, and Melanie M. Hughes. *Women, Politics and Power: A Global Perspective*. Thousand Oaks, CA: SAGE, 2007.

Perez-Linan, Anabal. *Presidential Impeachment and the New Political Instability in Latin America*. New York, NY: Cambridge University Press, 2007.

Persson, Torsten. "Do Political Institutions Shape Economic Policy?" *Econometrica* 70 no. 3 (2002): 883–905.

Persson, Torsten, and Guido Tabellini. "Constitutional Rules and Fiscal Policy Outcomes." *American Economic Review* 94 no. 1 (2004): 25–45.

———. *The Economic Effects of Constitutions*. Cambridge, MA: MIT Press, 2003.

Persson, Torsten, Gerard Roland, and Guido Tabellini. "Electoral Rules and Government Spending in Parliamentary Democracies." *Quarterly Journal of Political Science* 2 no. 2 (2007): 155–88.

———. "The Size and Scope of Government: Comparative Politics with Rational Politicians." *European Economic Review* 43 nos. 4–6 (1999): 699–735.

Pettit, Philip. *Republicanism*. Oxford: Oxford University Press, 1997.

Phillips, Anne. *The Politics of Presence*. New York: Oxford University Press, 1995.

Pogge, Thomas. "Self-constituting Constituencies to Enhance Freedom, Equality and Participation in Democratic Procedures." *Theoria: A Journal of Social and Political Theory* 99 (2002): 26–54.

Powell, G. Bingham. "Party Polarization and the Ideological Congruence of Governments." In *Citizens, Context and Choice*, edited by Russell J. Dalton and Christopher J. Anderson, 197–213. New York: Oxford University Press, 2011.

———. "The Ideological Congruence Controversy." *Comparative Political Studies* 42 (2009): 1475–97.

———. Political Representation in Comparative Politics. *Annual Review of Political Science* 7 (2004): 273–96.

———. *Elections as Instruments of Democracy*. New Haven: Yale University Press, 2000.

———. *Contemporary Democracies: Participation, Stability and Violence*. Cambridge: Harvard University Press, 1982.

Powell, G. Bingham, and Georg Vanberg. "Election Laws, Disproportionality and Median Correspondence: Implications for Two Visions of Democracy." *British Journal of Political Science* 30 no. 3 (2000): 383–411.

Przeworski, Adam. "Institutions Matter?" *Government and Opposition* 39, 2 (2004): 527–40.

Primo, David M., and James M. Snyder Jr. "Party Strength, the Personal Vote, and Government Spending." *American Journal of Political Science* 54 no. 2 (2010): 354–70.

Przeworski, Adam, Susan Stokes, and Bernard Manin. *Democracy, Accountability, and Representation*. New York: Cambridge University Press, 1999.

Rae, Douglas. *The Political Consequences of Election Laws*. New Haven: Yale University Press, 1967.

Ramseyer, J. Mark, and Frances M. Rosenbluth. *Japan's Political Marketplace*. Cambridge, MA: Harvard University Press, 1994.

Reed Steven R. "Democracy and The Personal Vote" A Cautionary Tale from Japan." *Electoral Studies*. 13 no. 1 (1994): 17–28.

———. "Structure and Behavior: Extending Duverger's Law to the Japanese Case." *British Journal of Political Science* 20 no. 3 (1990): 335–56.

Rehfeld, Andrew. *The Concept of Constituency*. New York: Cambridge University Press, 2005.

Reynolds, Andrew. *Designing Democracy in a Dangerous World*. New York: Oxford University Press, 2011.

———. "Electoral Democratization in Nepal," *Journal of Contemporary Asia* 40 no. 3 (2010): 509–19.

———. "Reserved Seats in National Legislatures: A Research Note." *Legislative Studies Quarterly* 30 no. 2 (2005): 301–10.

Reynolds, Andrew, Ben Reilly, and Andrew Ellis. *Electoral System Design: The New International IDEA Handbook*. Stockholm: IDEA, 2005.

Rickard, Stephanie J. "A Non-Tariff Protectionist Bias in Majoritarian Politics: Government Subsidies and Electoral Institutions." *International Studies Quarterly* 56 no. 4 (2012a): 777–85.

———. "Electoral Systems, Voters' Interests and Geographic Dispersion." *British Journal of Political Science* (2012b).

———. "Democratic Differences: Electoral Institutions and Compliance with GATT/WTO Agreements." *European Journal of International Relations* 16 no. 4 (2010): 711–29.

———. "Strategic Targeting: The Effect of Institutions and Interests on Distributive Transfers." *Comparative Political Studies* 42 no. 5 (2009): 670–95.

Rigby, Andrew. "Lebanon: Patterns of Confessional Politics." *Parliamentary Affairs* 53 no. 1 (2000): 169–90.

Riker, William. *Liberalism Against Populism*. Long Grove, IL: Waveland Press, 1982a.

———. "The Two-party System and Duverger's Law." *American Political Science Review* 76 (1982b): 753–66.

Roelfsema, Hein. "Political Institutions and Trade Protection." Discussion Paper 04-06, Tjalling C. Koopmans Research Institute, Utrecht, 2004.

Rogowski, Ronald. "Trade and the Variety of Democratic Institutions." *International Organization* 41 no. 2 (1987): 203–23.

Rogowski, Ronald, and Mark Andreas Kayser. "Majoritarian Electoral Systems and Consumer Power: Price-Level Evidence from the OECD Countries." *American Journal of Political Science* 46 no. 3 (2002): 526–39.

Rule Wilma, and Matthew S. Shugart. "The Preference Vote and Election of Women: Women Win More Votes in Open List PR." In *Voting and Democracy Report 1995,* 177–178. Washington, DC: Center for Voting and Democracy, 1995.

Samuels, David J. "Incentives to Cultivate a Party Vote in Candidate-Centric Electoral Systems: Evidence from Brazil." *Comparative Political Studies* 32 no. 4 (2002): 487–518.

Samuels, David J., and Matthew S. Shugart. *Presidents, Parties, and Prime Ministers: How the Separation of Powers Affects Party Organization and Behavior*. New York: Cambridge University Press, 2010.

Sanders, David, Harold D. Clarke, Marianne C. Stewart, and Paul Whiteley. "Simulating the Effects of the Alternative Vote in the 2010 UK General Election." *Parliamentary Affairs* 64 no. 1 (2011): 5–23.

Scartascini, Carlos G. and W. Mark Crain. "The Size and Composition of Government Spending in Multi-party Systems." 2002. Available at SSRN: http://dx.doi.org/10.2139/ssrn.1353462.

Schedler, Andreas. The Menu of Manipulation." *Journal of Democracy* 13 (2002): 36–50.

Scheiner, Ethan. "Does Electoral System Reform Work? Electoral System Lessons from Reforms of the 1990s." *Annual Review of Political Science* 11 (2008): 161–81.

Schmidt, Gregory. "The Implementation of Gender Quotas in Peru: Legal Reform, Discourses, and Impacts." In *The Implementation of Quotas: Latin American Experiences*. Workshop Report for International IDEA Conference, Lima, February 23–24, 2003.

Schwindt-Bayer, Leslie. "Making Quotas Work: The Effect of Gender Quota Laws on the Election of Women." *Legislative Studies Quarterly* 34 no. 1 (2009): 5–28.

Schwindt-Bayer, Leslie A., Michael Malecki, and Brian Crisp. "Candidate Gender and Electoral Success in Single Transferable Vote Systems." *British Journal of Political Science* 40 no. 3 (2010): 693–709.

Schwindt-Bayer, Leslie A., and William Mishler. "An Integrated Model of Women's Representation." *Journal of Politics* 67 no. 2 (2005): 407–28.

Scott, Joan Wallach. "French Universalism in the Nineties." *Differences: A Journal of Feminist Cultural Studies* 15 no. 2 (Summer 2004).

Shugart, Matthew S. "Comparative Electoral Systems Research: The Maturation of a Field and New Challenges Ahead." In *The Politics of Electoral Systems,* edited by Michael Gallagher and Paul Mitchell, 25–56. Oxford: Oxford University Press, 2005.

———. "Presidentialism, Parliamentarism, and the Provision of Collective Goods in Less-Developed Countries." *Constitutional Political Economy* 10 (1999): 53–88.

Shugart, Matthew S., M.E. Valdini, and E. Suominen. "Looking for Locals: Voter Information Demands and Personal Vote-Earning Attributes of Legislators under Proportional Representation." *American Journal of Political Science* 49 no. 2 (2005): 437–49.

Shugart, Matthew S., and Martin P. Wattenberg, ed. *Mixed-Member Systems: The Best of Both Worlds?* Oxford: Oxford University Press, 2001.

Silver, Nate. "Measuring the Effects of Voter Identification Laws." *New York Times*, July 7, 2012. Available at http://fivethirtyeight.blogs.nytimes.com/2012/07/15/measuring-the-effects-of-voter-identification-laws.

Stein, Ernesto, Ernesto Talvi, and Alejandro Grisanti. "Institutional Arrangements and Fiscal Performance: The Latin American Experience." NBER Working Paper 6358 (January 1998).

Strolovitch, Dara Z. "Do Interest Groups Represent the Disadvantaged? Advocacy at the Intersection of Race, Class, and Gender." *Journal of Politics* 68 no. 4 (2006): 893–908.

Strøm, Kaare. "Rules, Reasons and Routines: Legislative Roles in Parliamentary Democracies." In *Members of Parliament in Western Europe: Roles and Behaviour*, edited by W.C. Müller and T. Saalfeld, 155–74. London: Frank Cass, 1997.

———.*Minority Government and Majority Rule*. New York, NY: Cambridge University Press, 1990.

Swain, Carole. *Black Faces, Black Interests: The Representation of African-Americans in Congress*. Cambridge: Harvard University Press, 1993.

Swindle, S.M. "The Supply and Demand of the Personal Vote: Theoretical Considerations and Empirical Implications of Collective Electoral Incentives." *Party Politics* 8 no. 3 (2002): 279–300.

Taagepera, Rein. *Predicting Party Sizes: The Logic of Simple Electoral Systems*. Oxford: Oxford University Press, 2007.

Taagepera, Rein, and Matthew S. Shugart. *Seats and Votes: The Effects and Determinants of Electoral Systems*. New Haven: Yale University Press, 1989.

Thames, Frank C., and Martin S. Edwards. "Differentiating Mixed-Member Electoral Systems: Mixed-Member Majoritarian and Mixed-Member Proportional Systems and Government Expenditures." *Comparative Political Studies* 39 no. 7 (2006): 905–27.

Ticchi, Davide, and Andrea Vindigni. "Endogenous Constitutions." *Economic Journal* 120 no. 543 (2010): 1–39.

Tollson, Michelle. ""Mongolian Women's Hard-Won Victory" Women's Media Center, October 22, 2012. Available at http://www.womensmediacenter.com/feature/entry/mongolian-womens-hard-won-victory.

Towns, Ann E. *Women and States: Norms and Hierarchies in International Studies*. Cambridge: Cambridge University Press, 2010.

Valenzuela, Arturo. "Latin American Presidencies Interrupted." *Journal of Democracy* 15 no. 4 (2004): 5–19.

Van Cott, Donna. "Building Inclusive Democracies: Indigenous Peoples and Ethnic Minorities in Latin America." *Democratization* 12 no. 5 (2005): 820–37.

Verardi, Vincenzo. "Electoral Systems and Income Inequality." *Economic Letters* 86 (2005): 7–12.

Vernby, Kare. "Strikes are More Common in Countries with Majoritarian Electoral Systems." *Public Choice* 132 nos. 1–2 (2007): 65–84.

Warwick, Paul V. *Government Survival in Parliamentary Democracies*. New York: Cambridge University Press, 1994.

Waylen, Georgina. *Engendering Transitions*. Oxford: Oxford University Press, 2007.

Weßels, B. "Whom to Represent? Role Orientations of Legislators in Europe" In *Political Representation and Legitimacy in the European Union*, edited by H. Schmitt and J. Thomassen, 209–34 Oxford: Oxford University Press, 1999.

Willmann, Gerald. "Why Legislators are Protectionists: the Role of Majoritarian Voting in Setting Tariffs." Unpublished manuscript.

Woo, Jaejoon. "Economic, Political, and Institutional Determinants of Public Deficits." *Journal of Public Economics* 87 (2003): 387–426.

Wright, Joseph. "Aid Effectiveness and the Politics of Personalism." *Comparative Political Studies* 43 no. 6 (2010): 735–62.

Appendix A: Interview with Andrew Reynolds

Mala Htun and Betsy Super

In order to get a better picture of the work that political scientists do as "engineers," Mala Htun and Betsy Super sat down with task force member Andrew Reynolds, associate professor of political science at University of North Carolina, Chapel Hill and chair of Global Studies. He has worked for the United Nations, the International Institute for Democracy and Electoral Assistance (IDEA), the UK Department for International Development, the US State Department, the National Democratic Institute, the International Republican Institute, the Organization for Security and Cooperation in Europe (OSCE) and the International Foundation for Election Systems. He has also served as a consultant on issues of electoral and constitutional design for Afghanistan, Angola, Burma, Egypt, Fiji, Guyana, Indonesia, Iraq, Jordan, Kenya, Lebanon, Lesotho, Liberia, Libya, Netherlands, Netherlands Antilles, Northern Ireland, Sierra Leone, South Africa, Sudan, Syria, Tunisia, Yemen, and Zimbabwe; most recently in Libya, Egypt and Burma. Here, Reynolds, Htun, and Super discuss his work, especially on Egypt and Lesotho, and how the role of political scientists in the international sphere has changed over the course of his career.

Betsy Super: Let's talk about your work in the Arab Spring. How did you start working on Egypt?

Andrew Reynolds: The National Endowment for Democracy was running a series of workshops on cases of transition to help the National Security Council with their thinking on some of these issues. And actually, the day of the workshop Mubarak resigned! We watched him resign, and then we went in to closed session. Then the National Security Council asked John Carey and me to write a policy brief on what the election system might look like under any future or transitional arrangement. They wanted the American embassy in Cairo to get it in to the hands that mattered in Cairo.

I ended up going to Egypt in June 2011 to meet with political parties; the election commission; other stakeholders, such as women's groups; and some of the Coptic Christian groups, to think through what they might do.

We wanted the brief to get through to the military: [Mohamed Hussein] Tantawi and whoever was around him. It was a very close situation, and the military weren't listening to international groups, but they weren't really listening to Egyptians either, outside of a very small core group.

We said that: If you use the old Mubarak system, it could be really dangerous for the inclusion of secular parties, new parties, liberal Tahrir Square groups, and women. If you use the old system, you're going to really just either allow the *ancien régime* to come back to power or you're going to allow the Brotherhood—which is the only organized party—to do much better than they should, because they have the organization to exploit the anomalies of the old system.

We just wanted the military to be aware of the fact that the election system mattered quite significantly for the transition and how the constitutional assembly would look. And we weren't clear that the military had a clue about this. There is no reason that Tantawi and the military would have any clue.

When I went to Cairo, an academic who was very close to the military—their elections guy—put on a seminar to explain his views of how the new election system would work. IFES, NDI, Carter Center, and UN and others were invited to the seminar. Everybody understood that these were not merely his views but that this was what was actually going to happen.

He outlined the system the military advocated, emphasizing one specific point: If you didn't win a full quota in a district under the PR side of the system, you wouldn't be eligible to win seats. As you know, under PR systems a lot of the residual seats in districts are given out not on the basis of full quotas but as largest remainders.

Looking at the vote shares in Egypt, we thought that a lot of the new parties would not win anywhere close [to] a full quota. In a five-member district, they weren't going to win 12%, but they would likely pick up enough to get one or two of the seats on the largest remainder.

So this technicality would shut out almost all the new parties, the liberal parties, and the secular parties.

I actually went up to the whiteboard and said: "Do you mean this?" And I gave him an example [of a small party being excluded] and he said, "Yes, that's what we mean."

This response illustrated to us that, either by malfeasance or just by accident, they hadn't a clue what they were doing. It was really dangerous. Whoever was the biggest party would be winning 70% of the seats with 40% of the votes.

At the end of the day, I was told that Robert Gates, the secretary of defense, and Mike Mullen, who was the head of Joint Chiefs of Staff, took five issues to Cairo on five pieces of single, one-page briefing points. One of them dealt with what they needed to do in the elections. I don't know what the causal chain was, but [the Egyptians] did build in a PR side to the election system.

The system was not good, but I think it would have been much worse with what they originally planned. At least the issues were raised so they built in some space for some of the liberals and progressives, though not enough.

When I went back in September, I met with two of the Coptic Christian parties. One of the problems for them was worker/farmer quota. If they won a seat, the person who would have to fill the seat on their list was going to be a worker or a farmer.[1]

They were literally going in the streets trying to find farmers to put on their list. They don't have any farmers—they are doctors and professors! Their leaders were going to be bypassed, and the people filling the seats for the party were going to be the farmers that were lower down the list. That's the way the quota would work: the professional seats would already have been eaten up by the bigger parties earlier on in the seat allocation.

After that, the Egyptians raided NDI and arrested everybody. In November, IFES asked me to come back and do another talk. I said yes. The next day they phoned up and said, "You know, we've just found out you will be detained if you come back." So I didn't.

Mala Htun: Was there discussion about getting rid of this worker/farmer quota?

Reynolds: Oh, constantly. I don't know anybody who thought it was a good idea. John and I went through lots of simulations in papers to show why it was not a good idea. It was Mubarak's thing, and it was manipulated, and it just makes no sense. I don't know why it was retained; I don't know why it was kept. There were lots of discussions, and it is still there.

My guess is that the Egyptian election system is a product of a couple of guys in a room with a little bit of pressure from the Brotherhood at some stage.

I wrote an op-ed in the *New York Times* before the elections that said, "I think this is dangerous because it's going to look like this," and I have to say it's pretty much exactly turned out as I predicted. But everyone predicted that; it wasn't rocket science.

Super: It sounds like the eventual electoral system in Egypt was incremental and even accidental.

Reynolds: A lot of designs have been a combination of accident, political interests, misconceptions, and manipulations. It's very rare that you get a well-thought-out process that produces an election system that people buy into. In nearly 25 years of doing this, I can point to just a few specific examples where I feel like what I did had a specific consequence, and mostly it is just because the space was there for that to happen.

Super: Could you give an example?

Reynolds: I was in Sierra Leone in '96 and when I came back, somebody in Liberia phoned up, I think from the UN, and they asked me how big the Liberian parliament should be.

I had no idea how big it should be. They said, "We need to know today."

There is a model of how big parliaments usually are based on the working-age population and literacy rates (the Taagepera-Shugart model). I'll plug in the numbers for Liberia and tell you what one would expect it to be. I plugged in the numbers. It was 68, and that's how big the Liberian parliament is.

Now, Lesotho. Jørgen Elklit had written an MMP system for Lesotho in around 1998. Lesothoan politics is very fractionalized, and I was brought in by the UN in 2010 to try to negotiate a deal on the election system between the government and opposition to allow the elections to go ahead in 2012.

Previously, they had MMP with a double-vote system. The government would run a proxy party and double dip. They were brilliantly Machiavellian and stayed in power because they worked out this manipulation of the MMP system. The opposition lost out, and it was a nightmare. It brought them to the brink of civil war.

I proposed a single vote: the vote in the single-member district would count for the PR allocation.

It would deny the government the capacity to double dip and manipulate the system and also give the opposition a proportionate share of the parliament. The main thing was persuading both sides they would be served by a single vote.

Htun: How did you convince both sides of that, since the government had clearly been benefiting from the double vote before?

Reynolds: The government realized that if they did it again, there would be war. They were ready to say we won't cheat again; we'll have a single vote. The opposition were the ones who were distrustful of the government. The opposition felt that the government was just trying to hoodwink them again. My biggest job was to persuade the opposition that it was okay.

It was classic shuttle diplomacy, in the sense of telling each side what they want to hear. I was literally going between the deputy prime minister in one room and the leader of the opposition in another room within the UN building and saying, "I'm on your side, it's okay. It's going to work out, trust me. I've been in all these countries, and I know how this will play out. I know how the system works." And then I would go back and emphasize different things to the other side until they were ready to sign on to the deal. They wanted elections to go ahead.

It's interesting because the dynamics of the cases are obviously very different from country to country, but the technical principles, the driving forces, and the challenges are very similar. From country to country, the same issues crop up, whether it's about space for minorities and women in Burma or Serbia or Guyana. The challenges of crafting a system that fulfills all these different requirement is pretty common. I don't think many countries have a very good comparative knowledge of what works in other places. Most of us do who do this work are just bringing experiences from other places.

Htun: Pippa Norris has told us that the bulk of the work political scientists do, and, in fact, our value added, is to speak at big regional and international meetings where we can educate people about global trends, giving them information that they can then take back to their home countries. From listening to you, it seems that people's exposure to your ideas has really happened on the ground in the individual countries where you have worked.

Reynolds: Although I think that's true, I think she is right in the sense that the majority of our influence consists in moving a discussion and changing the agenda. I think the women's gender quotas are the best example of sort of the discussion. The consideration of space for women to contest has permeated international, domestic, UN, all these forums over the last 20, 30 years and has reached a point where, even if you don't do it, you cannot get away with an election system design process without thinking about, discussing it, and choosing deliberately not to do it.

It's become politically correct either to have some space for women or at least consider how you're going to create the space for women to contest everywhere. And I think that is primarily a product of an international discourse that is contributed to dramatically by political scientists like Pippa, you, and others who write about the stuff. It's ammunition for the advocates within the country. If you are a women's group in Libya, you can take some of the material about Latin America or Eastern Europe or Africa and say, "This is how it works; this is how it can work here; this is why it's a good thing." You just have more solid ammunition to do that. I don't think there [are] that many people like me who get to do it on the ground.

Htun: But it also may be the nature of gender quotas, because the issue is called the same thing everywhere and the principle is the same everywhere. By contrast, some more delicate issues that you are working on involve how to get a government to back off controlling the entire electoral outcome. That's more context-specific. Like your brilliant Lesotho story.

Reynolds: Yeah, I think that's true. But there is some capacity to have more hard-and-fast rules of thumb.

All the political scientists we know will say to you: "There is no one-size-fits-all option. Every country needs its own specific election system that suits its own context and history and culture."

Still, I would say that the vast majority of those political scientists, if you actually unpacked what they advise—including myself—pretty much recommend the same thing everywhere. While we may say Congo looks nothing like Sri Lanka, looks nothing like Serbia, at the end of the day we believe that good election systems producing good governments are more uniform than we would own up to.

If you were to say to Arend Lijphart, "Arend, you know that every country is unique, how about Uganda?" He'll say, "PR." "What about Britain?" "Well, actually, PR would be better in Britain." "What about Russia?" "PR." "Papua New Guinea?" "Yeah, pretty much PR." I'm guilty of that too.

Super: Is that because it's what our research keeps on showing, or is it because that you grow to like a particular thing, know how to make it work, and are more familiar with it?

Reynolds: I would like to believe it's the first one. Especially in new democracies that require an inclusive foundation for stability, some form of proportionality, however articulated, is a prerequisite. In established democracies, the evidence shows that there is a lot of normative good in proportionality for other reasons, especially if you build in significant district representation to connect people to their representative.

If the task force and others got together and had to converge on a single system, they would converge on a system that is highly proportional but has significant district representation. Now it may not be Simon [Hix] and John's [Carey] six-to-eight-members list PR. It may be MMP or some version of that, but it's going to do roughly the same thing. I think we would converge on a best-size single system that fits pretty much everywhere. People say national-list PR like Israel is bad. And single-member districts like America are bad. You need some hybrid.

Super: How has the demand for and use of political science research electoral engineering changed since you first started working as opposed to now?

Reynolds: People are more aware both internationally and domestically of the importance of the question. More and more advisers from various places are doing this work, and we have better tools. Not to blow my own trumpet, but I think the IDEA handbook is really widely used and useful. And there is a new generation of scholars, more scholars doing this now than there were 20 years ago. When I did election systems in Africa as a PhD student, there was no one doing it, but now there are quite a lot of people.

Appendix B: Interview with Pippa Norris

Betsy Super and Mala Htun

In a second interview conducted to explore the role of political scientists as electoral "engineers," Betsy Super and Mala Htun spoke with Pippa Norris, McGuire Lecturer in Comparative Politics at the John F. Kennedy School of Government, Harvard University and ARC Laureate Fellow and professor of government and international relations at the University of Sydney. Her research compares elections and public opinion, political communications, and gender politics. She has published more than 40 books on these topics, many for Cambridge University Press. Norris also served as director of the Democratic Governance Group in United Nations Development Programme, New York, and as an expert consultant to many international organizations such as the World Bank, Council of Europe, and OSCE. Here, Norris, Super, and Htun discuss how political scientists work with government agencies and nongovernmental organizations on knowledge production and dissemination, balancing technical support with context-specific considerations.

Betsy Super: You have said that the most valuable contribution of political scientists to electoral systems is technical assistance and policy analysis aimed at capacity building and knowledge sharing. What would be a sort of typical consulting project for you?

Pippa Norris: Let me give an example of how political science has influenced public policy on the issue of gender quotas. I've collaborated with Mona Lena Krook in trying to disseminate awareness about academic research through a variety of practitioner organizations. The initiative started with the OSCE, who were focused on strengthening gender equality in post-Communist Europe, where the word "quotas" is not positive. We developed a six-step plan which distilled academic research into a practical range of policy options that different countries could apply.

Then UNDP Asia-Pacific took up the ideas and said, "Hey, we've got the same problem." UNDP disseminated our report in different places, including at a workshop in Ulan Bator, Mongolia. This event brought in representatives from each of the countries in the region, such as Vietnam, Cambodia, China, and Thailand. Each of the countries faced a different set of problems based on their national context.

Our report presented a comprehensive analytical framework that could apply to strengthening gender equality in any country and a list of six policy options which they could implement. We didn't say, "You should do this, you should do that." Rather, we asked, "Which of these different options would be best for your society, given your own context?

For example, if you are a country debating constitutional reform, like Nepal, it would be important to try and get women's rights strengthened in the new arrangements. Other societies were working on electoral reform, others on party rules, others on capacity development, and so on.

In Mongolia, the June 2012 election was coming along in six months, and the political parties wanted to do something to improve the representation of women. Mongolia has made considerable progress on other Millennium Development Goals, but women members were only 3.9% of the parliament, a dramatic fall since the Communist era. Unfortunately, the key stakeholders in Mongolia were constrained, since they could not amend the electoral law to implement a gender quota in the six-months' run-up to the next election. But political parties could still change their internal party rules. Working with them and learning about their candidate selection processes—how formalized or institutionalized, for example—we were able to present party secretaries with some viable solutions. Following the June 2012 elections, the proportion of women increased to 14.9%—still below the world average but certainly a real improvement on the previous election.

I checked on developments after the June 2012 election, and reports note that the newly elected women formed a caucus which focuses on the lack of maternity hospitals and kindergartens, a major problem in the countryside and informal settlement areas. Despite formidable obstacles, women members of parliament say that there is a greater sense of hope in the political arena. One leader, Luvsan Erdenechimeg, said that 10 years ago, "We were dependent on men. [Now] we are more independent, we can say everything. We can have our own ideas and plans. Before, we were like satellites." Tsedevdamba Oyungerel concurred. "Oh, it's improved a lot. The mentality of the people has improved. Before it was, 'What are you doing in politics?' You were a helper only, but now you are seen as a decision maker, especially in my party." [1]

Our report and meetings did not do this—we simply expanded awareness of some practical steps tried elsewhere, which Mongolians could take to improve gender equality. By presenting options, local actors were empowered to develop national action plans that they could take back to their own country to develop with their own agencies, with their own ministries, with their own departments. UNDP Asia-Pacific has most recently developed an online interactive knowledge network to try and network all the women and other groups working on gender equality in elected office in the region.

Mongolia is not an isolated example; instead, I've participated with Mona Krook, Drude Dahlerup, and many other colleagues in regional meetings and workshops which have been organized by UN Women and local partners to take this work forward in many countries, including in Bangladesh in October 2012, Mexico City in October 2012, Beijing in January 2013, Sydney (for women legislators in the Pacific) in February 2013, and in Hyderabad in April 2013.

In this way, scholars integrate the best political science—and social science, for that matter—in ways that multilateral development organizations and local actors could potentially turn into effective policy mechanisms.

Some people think of our contribution in terms of advising specific governments: "Let's go to Burma and help them reform their electoral system." But I think the regional knowledge products and technical reports published by all the multilateral agencies are the ones where social scientists have a bigger impact, because we're not the most legitimate experts on Burma or experts on Cambodia, for example. The most effective way for us to intervene is by spreading awareness about options to local stakeholders—elected politicians, party leaders, government officials, NGOs, and the media.

Mala Htun: Will you talk about your report on reserved seats for women in Afghanistan?

Norris: In this case, in 2003–2004, Afghanistan was considering constitutional options. NYU commissioned a number of different experts to write briefing reports about electoral systems, party systems, and other constitutional options. I wrote a briefing paper that said that if Afghanistan wanted to strengthen gender equality in the new Wolija Jirga, they should consider adopting PR elections and party-list gender quotas.

Within three weeks representatives from Afghanistan came back and said, "We can't do that. We can't do PR, because we don't have any district boundaries. We don't have any boundaries because we don't know the population, and we don't have a census." They said that they wanted to have some sort of majoritarian system, common in the region due to the British legacy, and they wanted to know the options for strengthening gender equality within that system.

I had to give up some of my priors but still provide important information. Accordingly, I eventually advised them that they could use reserved seats for women, because that's the classic thing to do in majoritarian systems such as Pakistan and Bangladesh.

The briefing report reached many women's groups in Afghanistan, and they later told me that it was very useful and it helped them press for women's representation. The report presented information about Pakistan's law, a case that was culturally resonant. Pakistan, and, indeed, South Asia, have had a long tradition of using reserved seats. I emphasized above all that they should make sure that women were elected for reserved seats—not selected by leadership appointment—because otherwise women legislators would lack an independent power base.

In the constitutional debate, Hamid Karzai agreed to the proposal, in part because gender equality in elected office is now adopted as a global norm—through the MDGs—and it can be regarded as part of modernizing Afghanistan.

Afghanistan's constitution approved the use of reserved seats, but at the time many who participated in the debate didn't realize how many women were actually going to get elected. The constitution specified that two women would be elected per province, but at the time many didn't actually do the math, which would have worked out to about 30% of the entire parliament. When drafters came to design the electoral law, it was quickly realized that they would have had real problems implementing the constitutional principle, because it would have meant that in some smaller provinces with two members, only women could be elected. The electoral commission therefore had to readjust the law on reserved seats to specify an overall target which would vary from place to place.

I don't approve of SNTV for all sorts of other reasons, but at least the 2004 Afghan elections brought in all sorts of women candidates, who faced tremendous challenges and real danger. Some candidates faced real threats of violence, and a few were killed. Overall, around 28% of the new parliament was female. Some were liberal. Some conservative. Nevertheless, women were able to get their voices heard in the very early stages of developing the new Afghan parliament.

Iraq happened fairly shortly after that, and because of my work in Afghanistan I was invited to write another briefing report. I recommended a 25-to-30% gender quota for Iraq, and again I suggested that PR would be best option.

The women who were arguing with the US transitional administration basically said, "No, we want 40%." I thought 25 to 30% was incredibly generous, and it would be very hard to get, but they said, "No, we want to go higher!" This was marvelous, and I was able to give Iraqi women technical information that they could use against the American administration who didn't want to have reserved seats or quotas in any shape or form, because, as you know, it's just not done in America.

Ultimately, what happened in Iraq was the introduction of PR and gender quotas. They adopted a 28% quota for women, which was very successful. Through this process, women in both countries were provided with technical assistance with an academic backing that allowed them to expand their voice and their arguments against other experts.

Htun: Do you think there could be a way that the academic backing could be counterproductive?

Norris: Mainly if I were to say, "This is what you should do." Which I never try to do, instead I always try to say, "Here are three options, here are five options." I provide a schematic analytical framework which local actors can understand and examples from other similar countries in the region. In the Iraq case, I talked about Morocco, not Sweden. If you go in as the American or the Anglo or just a Harvard professor saying, "This is what you should do," it doesn't work.

But when you say to local actors, "Here are some choices, let's think about the pros and cons. There is no one best electoral system; there is no one best quota system, or system of getting women into politics." In this way, you're empowering the national stakeholders to make their own legitimate decisions. And they are the ones who have to live with the consequences of the choices. We are ones who are parachuting in, essentially giving local actors ways of thinking more than anything else.

Htun: How do you see the motivation in Mongolia, Afghanistan, Iraq, and other countries for pursuing greater gender equality in elected office?

Norris: There is a window of opportunity that opens with transitional states. When a new assembly is being created, there is a new opportunity, and for leaders, bringing in women is a costless opportunity. It's not like they have to get rid of incumbents, so they are not faced with challenges from men who are in positions of power. In addition, it's a way of signaling to the world: "We are modern."

It doesn't cost you anything financially, it doesn't cost you that much politically, and you don't have the incumbent problems and the rigidity of, say, an American system or system in Europe, which has already been going for so many years that people just assume that it's the way to do things.

When the right circumstances are there, in Egypt and Libya and so on, you can make a tremendous leap forward just in terms of the numbers of women.

But we often only focus on that first step. The international community is far less effective at building up capacity of the women who are then being elected. We leave that to other agencies instead of doing the hard work of making sure that those women in office have power as well as numbers.

Super: Do you think working on gender quotas is easier because you can see the impact more immediately than if you're trying to analyze empowerment or other issues?

Norris: Yes. And I bring in here the academic idea of norm diffusion, which is a great concept. One stage is "norm advocacy," in which you try to set international standards on a range of different issues. Think about issues like corruption that weren't really mainstream 20 years ago. TI [Transparency International] comes in as the norm advocate, the World Bank climbs aboard, then the prevention of corruption gradually becomes mainstream. The second stage is "norm cascade," and that's where international norms are implemented in different countries, but with some pushback in other places. Then you get "internalization"—the third stage—which is where the countries themselves take on those norms.

In terms of gender equality in politics, there has been a long, long period of norm advocacy. It then became the international standard. And what a lot of us are now doing is documenting how that norm cascade can be implemented in different regions. It's also become internalized in some countries, particularly those like Mongolia and China, which always thought that gender equality was important.

I'm now engaged with my Electoral Integrity Project. This is part of norm advocacy, trying to improve standards in certain areas of failed elections, but also looking at implementation.

The end stage is the easiest part for academics, because it's essentially a technical fix. A country says, "We want to do X": we want to have better elections, we want to have more women in parliament, we want to have human rights or human rights institutions. You're working with them as a technician to say, "Here is what you could do to achieve this goal." The stage of norm advocacy is far more complicated, however, especially for a scholar, because you're dealing with essentially contested values.

Htun: Could you tell us a little bit about origins of the Electoral Integrity Project?[2] How did you become convinced that this was something important?

Norris: It struck me that electoral integrity was a cutting-edge issue involving a tremendous range of institutions, multilateral organizations, scholars, and so on. Nobody had really conceptualized and measured the notion of electoral integrity before, and we lacked an umbrella organization that could bring all the different parts together. The generous funding of the Australian Research Council and other sources has launched the new six-year research project, with a team of researchers based at the University of Sydney and Harvard University.

The new concept of electoral integrity brings together four different subfields in political science that haven't always talked with each other.

One is public administration, where scholars focus on the sort of problems of election management, voter registration, and ballot design exemplified by Florida in *Bush v. Gore*.

You also have many scholars who work on problems of electoral violence, such as in Africa and Asia, who emphasize that peace is at risk if you don't get elections right, exemplified by the aftermath of the 2007 contests in Kenya.

It also brings together political scientists working on classifying authoritarian regimes, like Steven Levitsky and others, who say if elections fail, then the regime itself often fails to transition towards democracy. Manipulated elections can be used to consolidate autocratic rulers and stabilize regimes.

Finally, electoral integrity also brings together a range of researchers who work on electoral systems and voting behavior, who want to know about the institutions and how people behave in each context.

Each of these different silos has been expanding tremendously during the last decade. The Electoral Integrity Project—www.electoralintegrityproject.com—is trying to bring each of them together and also bring practitioners into contact with scholars.

Htun: What is the project focused on?

Norris: We have three basic questions. The first is: Why does electoral integrity matter, and what are the consequences? If people don't believe elections are fair, what are the consequences for political participation, confidence in government, political representation, violence, and protest?

For this question, electoral integrity is my independent variable. Why and how does it shape a variety of dependent variables, including types of regimes? That's something a lot of scholars are working upon, although at present they are not necessarily conceptualizing the problem as one of "electoral integrity."

The second issue focuses on what causes problems of electoral integrity as a dependent variable. Is it democratization or other processes—such as the quality of the electoral management body, the competitiveness of the election, the institutionalization of the party system, and so on—that produce electoral integrity?

The last question is focused on what we do to improve electoral integrity, such as changes to the legal framework, technology, monitoring, transparency, legal process of adjudication, international pressures, opposition boycotts, etc. A range of different policy options will be tested through some natural field experiments in conjunction with agencies like the Carter Center, UNDP, and IFES.

Many of these are classic issues, but they are not conventional issues about electoral systems or rules. They have been treated as much more detailed aspects of the processes of electoral administration and electoral procedures.

In many elections around the world, however, electoral integrity has emerged as a basic problem. In Canada, the United States, the UK, and France, I can give you examples of recent problems which have occurred. Most of the new democracies like Ghana or Mali are problematic, and in the worst authoritarian regimes, the election is stolen or manipulated or otherwise fraudulent.

In Mexico, for example, people were given credit cards to vote—though worth $3, apparently. Think about the fact that there were reports of robo-calls during the last Canadian elections telling people to go to the wrong polling places. If this happened in Canada, what hope is there for Azerbaijan?

The political science profession hasn't yet woken up to this issue yet. We still interpret elections that fail in terms of types of regimes and democratization. But we don't really understand what's happening during the election itself.

If we analyze only electoral systems, we're missing 99% of what is actually of interest nowadays. The new project brings together a wide range of scholars, through workshops, seminars, conferences, visiting fellows, and so on, and develops new data sets to examine these sorts of issues.

Appendix C: Case Studies:
Political Scientists as Electoral Engineers

Compiled by Andrew Reynolds

I. Jordan 2011 — John Carey

In April of 2011, I was recruited by the International Foundation for Electoral Systems (IFES) to conduct a series of workshops for Jordanian members of parliament on options for electoral reform in the Hashemite Kingdom. The government's motivation for reform had been spurred by the events of the Arab Spring, and by a series of Friday-afternoon protests in Amman against the democratic deficit in Jordan's representative institutions. King Abdullah II may have some genuine commitment to reform, but the immediate impetus was anxiety at the events sweeping the region, and at the fates of neighboring regimes. Early in 2011, the king had appointed a National Dialogue Committee with a broad mandate to make recommendations for reform in Jordan's political institutions, including elections to parliament.

Jordanian elections in the 1990s and early 2000s had relied on the single nontransferable vote (SNTV) method, with districts electing between one and seven members. The two key characteristics of this system were the disincentives for the formation of alliances inherent in SNTV, and the severe malapportionment by which the more rural, east Jordanian regions enjoyed vastly greater representation by population than did Amman and the western part of the country. That the east is solidly monarchist, whereas the west has a far greater population of Palestinian Jordanians, and a greater level of support for the Islamic Action Front (IAF), the political party affiliated with the Muslim Brotherhood, was widely recognized. The monarchy has traditionally counted on support among parliamentary independents and distrusted political parties in general. Although the palace had acknowledged demands that the development of viable parties is necessary for representation of popular political sentiment, it was clearly nervous about any reform that would advantage the IAF, the largest and best organized political party in Jordan.

For parliamentary elections in 2010, the government had imposed a variant of the SNTV system, in which individual candidates were randomly assigned to "virtual subdistricts" within the existing SNTV districts—each of which amounted to a single-member district plurality contest against other candidates slotted into the same virtual subdistrict. The experiment had proven immensely confusing, to candidates as well as to voters, and everyone with whom I met, including incumbent legislators who had prevailed the 2010 contest, expressed a commitment to reform the system.

Over the course of a week in Amman, I met for day-long sessions with different blocs of parliamentarians, as well as having separate meetings with some government ministry officials and representatives of civil society organizations. My job was not to advocate for a specific reform, but to provide them with a broad understanding of the various electoral system design options—that is, what the potential menu looks like—and to discuss the experiences of other countries with various methods of election. The legislators expected to receive a proposal for electoral reform from the NDC later in the spring, so my goal was to get them better equipped to evaluate the proposal, and possibly to amend it.

I was initially struck by the near-universal commitment to the idea of a "mixed system." Nearly every Jordanian with whom I met started with that phrase. But equally striking was the lack of detail or coherence when I pushed just slightly further to ask what, specifically, a mixed system should entail. Some (but not all) legislators had a general idea that candidate-oriented contests would be combined with party-list elections. Almost none had a clear sense for how many of each type seat there ought to be; whether the candidate-oriented elections should take place in single- or multimember districts; whether partisans ought to be allowed to contest those seats; whether party-list seats should be contested at the national or governorate level; what sort of proportional formula should be used; how reserved seats for women or other designated ethnic or religious minorities ought to be incorporated into a mixed system; or whether the allocation of PR seats ought to operate independently of the outcome of the candidate-centered contests. Our day-long sessions focused more than anything else on the many devils lurking in the details of mixed electoral systems.

Whatever my week in Amman provided for the legislators, it offered me a crash course in Jordanian politics. With the support of IFES staff, I produced a report that analyzed Jordanian elections up to the present, summarizing the reservations about the present system gleaned from the Jordanians with whom I met and offering ideas for various reforms that could combine some of the priorities they had expressed with the general goals articulated as the motivation behind the formation of the NDC. These reform options included both open-list and closed-list PR systems at the governorate level, and a plan for a mixed SMD-PR system. All included reapportionment to mitigate the severe underrepresentation of urban voters, as well as methods to preserve, and augment, the representation of women in the Jordanian parliament.

The NDC's proposal, when it was released in June 2011, was for a system that would combine SNTV contests within governorates with a national-level upper tier contested by open-list PR. Although I was unable to return to Jordan for further meetings, I collaborated with an IFES staff member in August 2011 on a review and analysis of the NDC's proposal. That proposal, however, was eventually dropped by the Jordanian government, and the NDC disbanded.

In the space of the next year, two more Jordanian prime ministers came and went, and along with them a raft of electoral reform proposals. In late June 2012, parliament approved an electoral reform that increased the size of parliament, retaining all 108 of the old SNTV seats while adding 17 national-level PR seats and increasing the number of reserved seats for women from 12 to 15. Critics in the opposition dismissed the reform as cosmetic—preserving SNTV for the overwhelming majority of seats, adding far too few for parties, and leaving the gross malapportionment across districts in place. Elections held in January 2013 were boycotted by the IAF, and loyalists to the king won some 75% of the seats.[1]

II. Lesotho: The First MMP Elections in Africa • Jørgen Elklit

Lesotho—a small, landlocked country within the borders of South Africa—has a fascinating electoral history. At independence in the mid-1960s, Lesotho got an FPTP electoral system with 65 SMDs, a number later increased to 80. Lesotho's political history during the first three decades was complicated and dramatic, but is not the topic here.

The May 1998 National Assembly elections resulted in the Lesotho Congress for Democracy (LCD) taking 79 of the 80 seats with only 61% of the vote. This surprised many—in particular many activists in the 11 opposition parties—and it did not take long before the losers cried foul. Serious public unrest arose, and the Southern African Development Community (SADC) sent in a military contingent to restore order (and secure that the water supply to South Africa was not interrupted).

In the aftermath of this a new political institution—the Interim Political Authority (IPA)—was established, based on suggestions from the international community. The IPA had two members from each party contesting the elections, so the election's losers suddenly had a 22:2 lead over the winning LCD. The IPA was given a broad mandate to prepare for an early election and suggest improvements to the electoral process, electoral systems, etc., but all in conjunction with the ordinary legislative and executive structures. It was no surprise that this arrangement could not work.

A presentation by German political scientist Michael Krennerich convinced the IPA that introduction of an MMP electoral system was the best solution to the seat allocation problems at hand, so the IPA opted for MMP. However, the LCD was opposed to this, and when I was invited in December 1999 to give a presentation to the IPA, it became obvious that IPA members had a very opaque picture of what MMP actually meant and what the procedural and political consequences of that decision were.

There was also no agreement over the actual format. Because of the 65 constituencies in "the good old days," the IPA majority argued for 80 constituency seats and 50 compensatory seats, as that would give a national assembly of 2 x 65 seats, without distorting the 80 newly established SMDs. The LCD/government position was that 40 compensatory seats were more than enough, but they also claimed that a parallel system was much better, so that was their preferred option. This position reflected the hope that the party would again sweep the 80 SMDs and even get a further 60% of the compensatory seats.

I got involved with the process as an international adviser; it was easy enough to see that a possible compromise would be to take the IPA's MMP suggestion and apply that to the LCD/government 80 + 40 format. This idea was developed in conversations with two colleague advisers (Dr Afari-Gyan of Nigeria and Danish professor Palle Svensson). The IPA was happy to accept the proposal, but the LCD/government only entered the compromise after private conversations with key LCD stalwarts, who eventually understood that it was most likely that the party would still be able to win a majority of the assembly's seats.

I was then invited to present the package both to the national assembly and to the senate so that both houses would vote in favor. The introduction of a new electoral model had to be in the form of a constitutional amendment, which would either require a referendum, which was not possible because of the miserable condition of the voters' roll, or a two-third majority in both houses. The latter was the only feasible option, and in late 2001 the fourth constitutional amendment on the introduction of MMP was eventually passed.

The May 2002 elections went well, the MMP system worked as expected, and the LCD won a comfortable victory with 77 SMD seats (but no compensatory seats), while the opposition parties shared the remaining constituency and compensatory seats according to their vote shares. Mission completed, I thought.

However, when I was invited back to Lesotho in February 2007 as a resource person to follow the vote count and the seat allocation in the national assembly elections, I realized that a major problem had been allowed to develop: The electoral commission, and/or its key staff had not realized that a proposal by the LCD and the small National Independent Party (NIP) was actually a circumvention of the constitution as it was with the amendment. The proposal was to form an electoral union between the two parties so that LCD would only run in the 80 constituencies, while NIP only ran for compensatory seats—but with leading LCD figures, including the prime minister, on its party list. Voters for both parties were then advised to cast the constituency vote for the LCD candidate and the party vote for the NIP.

The electoral legislation did not explicitly disallow that candidates run for more than one party—an oversight by the legal drafters—and formal electoral alliances were not explicitly prohibited, even when consciously created to circumvent the constitution. So seat allocation had to follow the letter of the law, and in the end LCD won 61 constituency seats and NIP 21 compensatory seats, of which LCD candidates got 11. The 82 seats for the alliance could be compared to the 62 seats the alliance would have won under "normal" circumstances according to a hypothetical seat distribution based on conservative assumptions.

The other parties all lost on this, and one of them took the case to court. The high court of Lesotho did not treat the case with the urgency one would have expected, and in the meantime, parliamentary activities came to an almost standstill because the opposition felt cheated by the incumbent.

SADC attempts of mediation did not succeed for a variety of reasons, and the high court's final decision did not solve any problems, as the court in reality shied away from taking a position on the issues before it, so the national assembly was more or less left in a limbo.

In the end, a solution had to be found, and American-British political scientist Andrew Reynolds suggested that MMP had to be conducted with only one ballot for each voter, that is, a variation of MMP, which does not allow vote splitting, but which still contains an element of proportionality and which is also not a parallel system. This variant is rare (only Denmark in 1918 comes to mind), but it provided a much-needed way forward, so the case of Lesotho can be described as two steps forward, but only one step back. The 2012 elections conducted according to this system took place recently without major problems.

Conclusion: The oversight in the drafting of the 2002 electoral law—in combination with Basotho politicians' willingness to circumvent the country's constitution and the fact that high court did not want to stand up to defend it—had dramatic effects. The case also demonstrates that experiences with party behavior and norms in one setting cannot necessarily be used as a predictor of how parties will behave in other settings. Both lessons are useful and certainly valid elsewhere.

I was deeply involved in the discussions concerning a democratic and peaceful solution to the apartheid problem in South Africa in the 1970s and 1980s, and I visited the country in order to participate in conferences and talk with the various stakeholders eight times between 1971 and 1991. Another crucial meeting took place in Titisee, Germany, in 1978, especially important because it was attended by African National Congress (ANC) representatives, who were unable to participate in meetings in South Africa until the late 1980s; during my last visit to South Africa in 1991, however, I did have a second opportunity to personally meet with ANC members.

On the basis of my research on divided societies starting in the mid-1960s, I became convinced that a power-sharing (consociational) system offered the optimal opportunity for democratic government in divided countries in general—and for the deeply divided South African society specifically. I tried to encourage South Africans to start thinking of power-sharing as a realistic possibility for their country, and I tried to formulate the optimal form of power-sharing for the country on the basis of my interpretation of its needs and my discussions with the people. One of the four basic elements of power-sharing is proportionality, and, ideally, power-sharing democracies use some form of proportional representation (PR). I therefore consistently advocated PR for South Africa, but this was not my exclusive focus—and not even my main focus.

There were two other limitations with regard to my involvement in South Africa's selection of PR for its first democratic election in 1994 and its subsequent elections. One was that, with one exception, all of my recommendations consisted of informal advice; I was never a formal member of a committee or council proposing or drafting electoral laws. The one exception was my formal membership to the Buthelezi Commission, which discussed alternative electoral systems and which, in its final report published in 1982, proposed a list-PR system for the KwaZulu-Natal area. The second limitation was that I never participated in any discussions or negotiations about detailed provisions of the electoral law.

Having stated the above provisos, I can also say that I consistently advocated—in my writings, in formal statements at conferences, and in informal discussions with individuals—a particular form of PR. I advocated list-PR, rather than STV, mainly because STV requires relatively small districts, which tends to reduce proportionality; relatively large districts or a nationwide district to allow representation by small minorities; and no or a very low electoral threshold, again in order not to bar small minorities from being represented. I tried to make the case for PR—and for this kind of highly proportional PR—as strongly as I could during my last visit in 1991, because Donald Horowitz's book *A Democratic South Africa?* had just been published. Horowitz advocated the highly disproportional alternative-vote method, which I believed would be disastrous for South Africa. Because of Horowitz's stature in the field and the book's publication by the prestigious University of California Press, I was afraid that his recommendation would influence the South African negotiators. Fortunately, this turned out not to be the case.

In the end, the negotiators agreed on one of the most thoroughly proportional PR systems ever used in the world: list PR in what is effectively a large 400-member nationwide district without a legal electoral threshold. This was exactly in line with my recommendations—but obviously not as a direct result of any advice that I gave: I was not formally involved in the drafting of the electoral law, and I was not the only academic or nonacademic advocate of a thoroughly proportional PR system. Perhaps somewhat immodestly, however, I do think that my consistent advice over many years did have a bit of indirect positive influence.

IV. Israel 2006–12 ■ Simon Hix

In March 2006, I was invited to Israel as part of a team led by Itai Sened of Washington University in St Louis to analyze and make a proposal on electoral reform to Kadima, one of the main center parties in Israel, which had been formed in 2005 and was at that time in government. The other members of the team were John Carey of Dartmouth College and Burt Monroe of Penn State. Itai invited me to join the team, as he felt that our proposals would be more credible if the team included someone from outside the United States.

Itai had been invited to make a reform proposal by some senior figures in Kadima. One of these figures, Prof. Uriel Reichman, had been a proponent of a directly elected prime minister in the 1990s. That experiment had led to further fragmentation of the party system and was quickly reversed. Reichmann and his colleagues now believed that electoral reform might be the way to reduce the number of parties and so make coalition negotiations less complex.

For the first few days, we were based at the Interdisciplinary Center (IDC) in Herzliya, where we met with several constitutional lawyers and political scientists, including professors Reichman, Amnon Rubenstein, and David Nachmias, to discuss the issues at stake in electoral reform in Israel. It was clear from these discussions that for a reform to pass the Knesset, it could not compromise on the principle that the Knesset should represent all groups in Israeli society. In other words, a new system would have to maintain the high level of proportionality between votes cast and seats won for each political party in the existing system of closed-list PR in a single national district of 120 seats and a national threshold of only 2%. Everyone we spoke to, however, also wanted to strengthen the representation of the larger parties at the expense of the smaller parties. As Professor Reichman put it: "We are fed up with being held to ransom by the small parties!"

We scratched our heads and tried to explain that the classic view in political science was that there is a tradeoff between these two goals. On the one hand, if the main aim is a highly representative parliament, then a proportional electoral system is best. On the other hand, if the main aim is accountable/stable government, then a majoritarian electoral system is best. However, the reformers in Israel would have none of it: "You guys are smart; go figure it out."

We hence got to work trying to design an electoral system that might be a reasonable tradeoff between a highly representative parliament and a government with fewer parties than was the norm in Israel. Building on some of our existing theoretical knowledge and anecdotal evidence from Latin America and Europe, we proposed a mixed-member parallel system, with 30 seats elected in single-member districts and 90 seats allocated proportionally in a single national district, with a 3% national threshold. We argued that such a system would lead to more seats for the larger parties, and so reduce coalition complexity; maintain representation for minority parties, above 3% or with geographically concentrated support; and introduce some individual accountability of politicians, with the SMD seats.

We also proposed that a single vote should be used rather than two separate votes. We argued that two votes would lead to a high incidence of split-ticket voting, as had occurred during the experience of the directly elected prime minister, which would lead to further fragmentation of the party system.

We presented our proposals in Jerusalem to Foreign and Justice Minister Tzipi Livni and her team. It was clear in the discussion that followed the presentation that different members of the team preferred different aspects of the proposal, with some liking single-member districts and others opposing them.

It was hoped that a reform plan could be agreed upon between the three largest parties—Kadima and Labor in government and Likud in opposition—and so be adopted by the Knesset. However, Likud refused to consider any agreement at that time.

I was invited back to Israel in December 2008 to continue the discussions. Inspired by our visit in 2006, between then and 2008 John Carey and I conducted research into the tradeoff between a highly representative parliament and an accountable government. We looked at more than 600 elections in more than 80 countries and concluded that relatively small multimember districts (e.g., in the 4 to 8 range) do, in fact, maximize these two supposedly competing objectives.[2]

I revised the proposal from 2006 and this time proposed a system of PR in multimember districts of between four and 11 seats, based on Israel's local government units. I also presented a simulation of the March 2006 elections under this system, to demonstrate how the system would boost the larger parties and would probably have led to a two-party coalition between Kadima and Labor rather than the four-party coalition between Kadima, Labor, Shas, and Gil.

This proposal seemed to gain more traction with policy makers than our earlier proposal. This was probably because several other scholars were making similar proposals at that time, such as Matthew Shugart of the University of California, San Diego, who also visited Israel around that time, and Moaz Rosenthal and several other scholars in Israel.

The smaller parties and Likud continued to block progress on reform. Nevertheless, in May 2012 the issue arose again, this time under a "unity government" of Kadima, Likud, Labour, and several other parties. A Knesset committee discussed a proposal for electoral reform that combined aspects of the proposals we had made in April 2006 and December 2008. The reform under consideration was a two-tier system, in which 60 members would be elected by PR in small multimember districts, and 60 would be elected by PR in a single national constituency. In an e-mail exchange with several people at IDC and a phone conversation with Professor Reichman, John Carey and I questioned the wisdom of a two-tier system and reiterated our support for a single-tier system of small multimember districts.

Kadima then pulled out the government in July 2012, which suggests that electoral reform has been put on hold. Given the continued problems of government formation, electoral reform is likely to remain a key policy concern in Israel.

V. Fiji * Donald Horowitz

I consulted with the Reeves Commission, whose chair and legal counsel were from New Zealand, when I was in that country in late 1995 or 1996. I met once with the chair and several times with the legal counsel. She was looking for an electoral system with conciliatory properties.

As we talked, it occurred to me that Fiji might have good conditions for AV: more than one party per ethnic group; a fair amount of intergroup territorial intermixture that might produce a significant number of ethnically heterogeneous constituencies; and willingness to borrow from Australia, the original home of AV (Australia was and is a close trading and political partner). It also had major obstacles, especially ethnic reserved seats elected on communal rolls—that is, seats reserved for group A or B, in which the voters are only members of group A or B, respectively. I then gave one briefing to the whole commission on why AV might be suitable. Apart from a paper I gave at a conference in Australia on the subject after the commission's report was in, which supported the commission's recommendation of AV but suggested that its tallying method be fixed, that was it.

The inspiration for AV was definitely mine, but once the commission got the idea and I had left the region, it consulted Australian experts on the particulars, including the strange way of tallying ballots that it recommended. The commission also reduced the number of reserved seats, but a parliamentary select committee then dramatically increased them. So, if I recall correctly, only 25 of 71 seats were, in the end, open seats, that is, elected by members of all groups, rather than on a communal roll, and of these only 15 were significantly heterogeneous. Even so, two multiethnic coalitions were formed, and the winning one exchanged a great many second and subsequent preferences across ethnic group lines. The winning coalition consisted of an Indian party and three Fijian parties. The Indian party was the largest, and its leader became prime minister, with two Fijian deputy prime ministers.

So, I gave them the idea for AV but did not play a role in the specifics of the design. The specific design was devised by the commission and its consultants, particularly, I believe, Australian trade unionists (who used an odd version of AV in their union elections) and then modified by the parliamentary select committee. The outcome was far more favorable than its principal detractor has suggested. A multiethnic coalition came to power after the 1999 election. The fact that it was overthrown a year later in a putsch led by a former official whom the sitting PM had dismissed for alleged corruption scarcely bears on evaluation of the system or the election that took place under it.

Appendix D: Glossary of Electoral Systems Terminology

Taken from Electoral System Design: the New International IDEA Handbook
© International Institute for Democracy and Electoral Assistance 2005–06.

Absentee voting – Another term for *remote voting.*

Additional Member System – Another term for a *Mixed Member Proportional system.*

Alternative Vote (AV) – *A candidate-centred, preferential plurality/majority* system used in *single-member districts* in which voters use numbers to mark their preferences on the ballot paper. A candidate who receives an absolute majority (50 per cent plus 1) of valid first-preference votes is declared elected. If no candidate achieves an absolute majority of first preferences, the least successful candidates are eliminated and their votes reallocated until one candidate has an absolute majority of valid votes remaining.

Apparentement – A term of French origin for a provision which can be included in *List Proportional Representation (List PR)* systems which enables two or more parties or groupings which fight separate campaigns to reach agreement that their votes will be combined for the purpose of seat allocation. See also *Lema* and *Stembusaccoord.*

Average district magnitude – For a country, local authority or supranational institution, the number of representatives to be elected divided by the number of *electoral districts.* See also *District magnitude.*

Ballotage – Another term for a *two-round system*, used primarily in Latin America.

Ballot structure – The way in which electoral choices are presented on the ballot paper, in particular whether the ballot is *candidate-centred* or *party-centred.*

Bicameral legislature – A legislature made up of two houses, usually known as an *upper house* and a *lower house.*

Block Vote (BV) – A *plurality/majority* system used in *multi-member districts* in which electors have as many votes as there are candidates to be elected. Voting is *candidate-centred.* The candidates with the highest vote totals win the seats.

Borda Count (BC) – A *candidate-centred preferential* system used in either *single-* or *multi-member districts* in which voters use numbers to mark their preferences on the ballot paper and each preference marked is then assigned a value using equal steps. For example, in a ten-candidate field a first preference is worth one, a second preference is worth 0.9 and so on, with a tenth preference worth 0.1. These are summed and the candidate(s) with the highest total(s) is/are declared elected. See also *Modified Borda Count.*

Boundary delimitation – The process by which a country, local authority area or area of a *supranational institution* is divided into *electoral districts.*

Candidate-centred ballot – A form of ballot in which an elector chooses between candidates rather than between parties and political groupings.

Circonscription – The term most frequently used for *electoral* district in francophone countries. See Electoral *district.*

Closed list – A form of List PR in which electors are restricted to voting only for a party or political grouping, and cannot express a preference for any candidate within a party list. See also *Open list* and *Free list.*

Communal roll – A register of electors for which the qualification for registration is a determinable criterion such as religion, ethnicity, language or gender. All electors who meet the criterion may be entered in the communal roll automatically, or each such elector may be able to choose whether or not to be entered. This register is used for the election of representatives of the group defined by the criterion from *electoral districts* specified for that purpose.

Compensatory seats – The *List PR* seats in a *Mixed Member Proportional* system which are awarded to parties or groupings to correct disproportionality in their representation in the results of the elections held under the first part of the *MMP* system, normally under a *plurality/majority* system.

Constituency – A synonym for *electoral district* used predominantly in some anglophone countries. See *Electoral district.*

Contiguous district – An *electoral district* that can be enclosed in a single continuous boundary line.

Cross-cutting cleavages – Political allegiances of voters which cut across ethnic, religious and class divisions in a society.

Cumulation – The capacity within some *electoral systems* for voters to cast more than one vote for a favoured candidate.

Democratic consolidation – The process by which a country's political institutions and democratic procedures become legitimized, stable and broadly accepted by both political actors and the wider population.

D'Hondt Formula – One of the options for the series of divisors used to distribute seats in List *PR* systems which adopt the *Highest Average Method.* The votes of a party or grouping are divided successively by 1, 2, 3... as seats are allocated to it. Of the available formulas, D'Hondt tends to be the most favourable to larger parties. See also *Sainte- Laguë Formula.*

Distribution requirements – The requirement that to win election a candidate must win not merely a specified proportion of the vote nationally but also a specified degree of support in a number of different states or regions.

District – Used in this Handbook to mean *electoral district.*

District magnitude – For an *electoral district,* the number of representatives to be elected from it. See also *Average district magnitude.*

Droop Quota – A variant of *quota* used in *proportional representation systems* which use the *Largest Remainder Method,* defined as the total valid vote divided by the number of seats to be filled in the *electoral district* plus one. Also known as *Hagenbach-Bischoff Quota.* See *Quota (a).* See also *Hare Quota* and *Imperiali Quota.*

Elector – A person who is both qualified and registered to vote at an election.

Electoral district – One of the geographic areas into which a country, local authority or *supranational institution* may be divided for electoral purposes. See also *Circonscription, Constituency, Electorate (b)* and *Riding*. An electoral district may elect one or more representatives to an elected body. See *Single-member district* and *Multi-member district*.

Electoral formula – That part of the *electoral system* dealing specifically with the translation of votes into seats.

Electoral law – One or more pieces of legislation governing all aspects of the process for electing the political institutions defined in a country's constitution or institutional framework.

Electoral management body (EMB) – The organization tasked under *electoral law* with the responsibility for the conduct of elections. The EMB in most countries consists either of an independent commission appointed for the purpose or of part of a specified government department.

Electoral regulations – Rules subsidiary to legislation made, often by the *electoral management body*, under powers contained in the *electoral law* which govern aspects of the organization and administration of an election.

Electoral system – That part of the electoral law and regulations which determines how parties and candidates are elected to a body as representatives. Its three most significant components are the *electoral formula*, the *ballot structure* and the *district magnitude*.

Electorate – May have one of two distinct meanings:

a. The total number of *electors* registered to vote in an *electoral district*.

b. A synonym for *electoral district* used predominantly in some anglophone countries. See *Electoral district*.

External voting – A mechanism by which voters who are permanently or temporarily absent from a country are enabled to cast a vote, also called *out-of-country voting*.

First Past The Post (FPTP) – The simplest form of *plurality/majority electoral system*, using *single-member districts* and *candidate-centred* voting. The winning candidate is the one who gains more votes than any other candidate, even if this is not an absolute majority of valid votes.

Free list – A form of *List PR* in which voters may vote for a party or grouping and in addition for one or more candidates, whether or not those candidates are nominated by that party or grouping. Also known as *panachage*. See also *Closed list* and *Open list*.

Gerrymandering – The deliberate manipulation of *electoral district* boundaries so as to advantage or disadvantage a particular political interest.

Hagenbach-Bischoff Quota – Another term for the *Droop Quota*.

Hare Quota – A variant of *quota* used in *proportional representation systems* which use the *Largest Remainder Method*, defined as the total valid vote divided by the number of seats to be filled in the *electoral district*. See *Quota (a)*. Also known as Hare-Niemeyer. See also *Droop Quota* and *Imperiali Quota*.

Heterogeneous district – An *electoral district* in which, either by design or as a result of the operation of other criteria for *boundary delimitation*, the *electorate* manifests social, ethnic, religious or linguistic diversity.

Highest Average Method – A principle for converting votes into seats in *List PR* systems. One seat is allocated in a *district* at each of a series of counts to the party or grouping with the highest vote total. When a seat is allocated, the original vote of the party that wins it is reduced by division. The most common series of divisors used are *D'Hondt* and *Sainte-Laguë*. The Highest Average Method tends to be more favourable to larger parties than its alternative, the *Largest Remainder Method*.

Homogeneous district – An *electoral district* in which, either by design or as a result of the operation of other criteria for *boundary delimitation*, the *electorate* manifests substantial social, ethnic, religious or linguistic uniformity.

Hybrid System – The result of dividing a country into two or more non-overlapping areas, in each of which a different *electoral system* is used.

Imperiali Quota – A variant of *quota* used in *proportional representation systems* which use the *Largest Remainder Method*, defined as the total valid vote divided by the number of seats to be filled in the *electoral district* plus two. See also *Droop Quota* and *Hare Quota*.

Index of disproportionality – A figure which is designed to measure the degree of deviation from proportionality in the allocation of seats to parties or groupings which participated in an election. It is most commonly defined as the square root of the sum of the squares of the differences for each party or grouping between the percentage of votes received and the percentage of seats gained.

Invalid votes – Votes which cannot be counted in favour of any participant in an election due to accidental or deliberate errors of marking by the voter.

Largest Remainder Method – A principle for converting votes into seats in *List PR* systems. After parties and groupings have been allocated seats in an *electoral district* because they have received full *quotas (a)* of votes, some seats will be unfilled, and some votes remain—for each party, less than a full *quota (a)*. The remaining seats are then awarded to parties and groupings in order of the number of left-over votes they possess. The Largest Remainder Method tends to be more favourable to smaller parties than the alternative approach, the *Highest Average Method*.

Lema – A term used in Latin America for an umbrella list including two or more sub-lists which receive votes separately but whose votes are counted together for the purposes of seat allocation in some *List PR* systems. See also *Apparentement* and *Stembusaccoord*.

Limited Vote (LV) – An *electoral system* used in *multi-member districts* in which electors have more than one vote, but fewer votes than there are candidates to be elected. The candidates with the highest vote totals win the seats, in the same way as in a *Block Vote* system and in *SNTV*.

List Proportional Representation (List PR) – A system in which each participant party or grouping presents a list of candidates for an *electoral district*, voters vote for a party, and parties receive seats in proportion to their overall share of the vote. Winning candidates are taken from the lists. See *Closed list, Open list* and *Free list*.

Lower house – One of the two chambers in a *bicameral legislature*, usually seen as comprising 'the representatives of the people'. It is the more powerful chamber when the powers of the two chambers are unequal.

Majoritarian – Designed to produce an absolute majority (50 per cent plus 1) of votes.

Malapportionment – The uneven distribution of voters between *electoral districts*.

Manufactured majority – An election result, more commonly found where a *plurality/majority* system is used, in which a single party or coalition wins less than 50 per cent of the valid votes but an absolute majority of the seats in an elected body.

Member state – A country which is a member of a *supranational institution*, for example the European Union.

Mixed Member Proportional (MMP) – A *mixed system* in which all the voters use the first *electoral system,* usually a *plurality/majority system,* to elect some of the representatives to an elected body. The remaining seats are then allocated to parties and groupings using the second *electoral system,* normally *List PR*, so as to compensate for disproportionality in their representation in the results from the first *electoral system.*

Mixed system – A system in which the choices expressed by voters are used to elect representatives through two different systems, one *proportional representation* system and one *plurality/majority* system. There are two kinds of mixed system: *Parallel systems* and *Mixed Member Proportional systems.*

Modified Borda Count – A *candidate-centred, preferential* system used in either *single-* or *multi-member districts* in which voters use numbers to mark their preferences on the ballot paper and each preference marked is then assigned a value calculated by using the series of divisors 1, 2, 3 ... . For example, in a ten-candidate field a first preference is worth one, a second preference is worth 0.5, a third preference 0.3333, and so on. These are summed and the candidate(s) with the highest total(s) is/are declared elected. See also *Borda Count.*

Multi-member district – A *district* from which more than one representative is elected to a legislature or elected body. See also *Single-member district.*

Multiple-tier system – An *electoral system* in which two or more sets of representatives are elected to the same chamber by the entire electorate of a country. The multiple tiers may be *electoral districts* defined at different levels within a country, for example, *single- member districts* and regions, or regions and the country as a whole. Systems in which two distinct sets of representatives are elected from the same level are also multiple-tier systems. All *mixed systems* are multiple-tier systems.

One Person One Vote One Value (OPOVOV) – A principle of representation in which each elected representative represents the same number of electors, and under which *malapportionment* is minimized.

Open list – A form of *List PR* in which voters can express a preference both for a party or grouping and for one, or sometimes more, candidates within that party or grouping. See also *Closed list* and *Free list.*

Out-of-country voting – A mechanism by which voters who are permanently or temporarily absent from a country are enabled to cast a vote. See *External voting*. See also *Remote voting.*

Overhang mandate – See *Überhangsmandat*.

Panachage – The term used in francophone countries for the version of *List PR* in which voters may vote for a party or grouping and in addition for one or more candidates, whether or not those candidates are nominated by that party or grouping. See also *Free list*.

Parallel System – A *mixed system* in which the choices expressed by the voters are used to elect representatives through two different systems, usually one *plurality/majority* system and one *proportional representation* system, but where no account is taken of the seats allocated under the first system in calculating the results in the second system. See also *Mixed-Member Proportional*.

Party Block Vote (PBV) – A *plurality/majority* system using *multi-member districts* in which voters cast a single *party-centred* vote for a party of choice, and do not choose between candidates. The party with most votes will win every seat in the *electoral district*.

Party-centred ballot – A form of ballot in which a voter chooses between parties or groupings, rather than individual candidates.

Party magnitude – For an *electoral district*, the average number of representatives elected by each party and grouping. For a country, the average of the party magnitudes for all electoral districts.

Personation – The fraudulent casting of the vote of a registered *elector* by another person.

Plurality/majority systems – Plurality/majority systems are based on the principle that a candidate(s) or party with a plurality of votes (i.e. more than any other) or a majority of votes (i.e. 50 per cent plus one—an absolute majority) is/are declared the winner(s). Such a system may use *single-member districts*—for example, *First Past The Post, Alternative Vote* or the *Two-Round System*—or *multi-member districts*—for example, the *Block Vote* and *Party Block Vote*.

Preferential voting systems – Electoral systems in which voters rank parties or candidates on the ballot paper in order of their choice. The *Alternative Vote*, the *Borda Count*, the *Single Transferable Vote* and the *Supplementary Vote* are all examples of preferential voting systems.

Proportional Representation (PR) – An *electoral system* family based on the principle of the conscious translation of the overall votes of a party or grouping into a corresponding proportion of seats in an elected body. For example, a party which wins 30 per cent of the votes will receive approximately 30 per cent of the seats. All PR systems require the use of *multi-member districts*. There are two major types of PR system, *List PR* and the *Single Transferable Vote (STV)*.

Quota – May have one of two distinct meanings:
  a. The number of votes which guarantees a party or candidate to win one seat in a particular *electoral district* in a *proportional representation* system. There are three variants in common use, the *Hare, Droop* (or *Hagenbach-Bischoff*) and *Imperiali* quotas.

  b. A number of seats in an elected body or a proportion of candidates nominated by a party or grouping which are required by law to be filled by representatives of a particular kind; most commonly used to ensure the nomination and election of a minimum number of women.

Regional fiefdom – A situation in which one party wins all, or nearly all, of the seats in a particular geographic region of a country.

Remote voting – A mechanism by which voters are enabled to cast a vote which does not involve their attendance at a polling station on the day or days fixed for voting. See also *Out-of-country voting*.

Reserved seats – Seats in which a determinable criterion such as religion, ethnicity, language or gender is a requirement for nomination or election.

Riding – A synonym for electoral district used in some countries. See *Electoral district*.

Sainte-Laguë Formula – one of the options for the series of divisors used to distribute seats in *List PR* systems which adopt the *Highest Average Method*. The votes of a party or grouping are divided successively by 1, 3, 5... as seats are allocated to it. See also *D'Hondt Formula*.

Single-member district – An electoral district from which only one member is elected to a legislature or elected body. See also *Multi-member district*.

Single Non-Transferable Vote (SNTV) – An *electoral system* in which voters cast a single *candidate-centred* vote for one candidate in a *multi-member district*. The candidates with the highest vote totals are declared elected.

Single Transferable Vote (STV) – A *preferential candidate-centred proportional representation system* used in *multi-member districts*. Candidates that surpass a specified *quota* (see *Quota (a)*) of first-preference votes are immediately elected. In successive counts, votes are redistributed from least successful candidates, who are eliminated, and votes surplus to the *quota* are redistributed from successful candidates, until sufficient candidates are declared elected.

Spoilt votes – See *Invalid votes*.

State – Used in this Handbook to denote a sub-national unit of a country, often in the context of a federal constitution.

Stembusaccoord – A term of Dutch origin for a provision which can be included in *List PR* systems which enables two or more parties or groupings which are fighting separate campaigns to reach agreement that their votes will be combined for the purpose of seat allocation. See also *Apparentement* and *Lema*.

Supplementary Vote – A *candidate-centred, preferential plurality/majority* system, similar to the *Alternative Vote*. If no candidate achieves an absolute majority of first preferences, all candidates except the two leading candidates are eliminated and their votes reallocated according to the second, third and so on preferences expressed. The candidate with the highest number of votes is declared elected.

Supranational institution – an organization created by a number of countries by treaty where power is held by independent appointed officials or by representatives elected by the legislatures or people of the member states.

Threshold – The minimum level of support which a party needs to gain representation in the legislature. A threshold may be a formal threshold, which is a figure laid down in the constitution or the law, usually in the form of a percentage of the valid votes cast, or an effective or natural threshold, which is a mathematical property of the electoral system in use.

Two-Round System (TRS) – A *plurality/majority* system in which a second election is held if no candidate achieves a given level of votes, most commonly an absolute majority (50 per cent plus one), in the first election round.

A *Two-Round System* may take a majority-plurality form, in which it is possible for more than two candidates to contest the second round. An example is the French system, in which any candidate who has received the votes of over 12.5 per cent of the registered electorate in the first round can stand in the second round. The candidate who wins the highest number of votes in the second round is then declared elected, regardless of whether they have won an absolute majority. Alternatively, a *Two-Round System* may take a majority run-off form, in which only the top two candidates in the first round contest the second round.

Überhangsmandat – An additional seat in a legislature which results in an *MMP* system when a party or grouping wins more seats in a region under the first, usually *plurality/majority*, electoral system than the number to which it would be entitled in total on the basis of its proportion of the vote. Also known as *excess mandate* or *overhang mandate*.

Upper house – One of the two chambers in a *bicameral legislature,* often seen either as containing 'the representatives of regions/federal states' or as 'a chamber of review'. The less powerful chamber when the powers of the two chambers are unequal.

Wasted votes – Valid votes which do not ultimately count towards the election of any candidate or party.

Appendix E: APSA-Wide Survey

Start Page

Welcome to the survey to assess political scientists' opinions about rules for electing national legislatures. It is being conducted by the APSA's Presidential Task Force on Electoral Rules and Democratic Governance. All survey responses will be anonymous. A full report on the results of the survey will be made available to all APSA members and will be publicly available online.

The survey should take between 2 and 5 minutes to complete.

(Continued, next page)

Page 2: Electoral System Goals

(the order of Pages 2 and 3 will be randomized)

Question 1.

What goals do you think an electoral system for a national parliament or congress should try to achieve?

Please indicate the importance you place on each of the goals:

	Not at all Important	Marginally Important	Important	Very Important	Top Priority	No Opinion
A proportional parliament (where each party's share of seats is proportional to its share of votes)	○	○	○	○	○	○
Cohesive political parties	○	○	○	○	○	○
Accountable individual politicians	○	○	○	○	○	○
An equal representation of men and women	○	○	○	○	○	○
Representation of minority racial, ethnic, religious, and linguistic groups in accord with their share of the population	○	○	○	○	○	○
A stable government	○	○	○	○	○	○
A single-party government	○	○	○	○	○	○
Governments that produce policies preferred by the median voter	○	○	○	○	○	○
A decisive election outcome (where there is a clear winner)	○	○	○	○	○	○
Another goal. Please specify: _____ _____	○	○	○	○	○	○

(the order of these choices, except "Other," will be randomized)

Page 3: Electoral System Preferences

(the order of Pages 2 and 3 will be randomized)

Question 2.

Please indicate your opinion of the following electoral systems for electing a national parliament or congress:

	Very Bad System	Bad System	Neutral	Good System	Very Good System	No Opinion
Single-member district - simple-plurality (first-past-the-post) (e.g., UK, USA)	○	○	○	○	○	○
Single-member district - two-round system (e.g., France, Mali)	○	○	○	○	○	○
Single-member district - alternative vote (instant run-off) (e.g., Australia, Fiji)	○	○	○	○	○	○
Multi-member district - closed-list proportional representation (e.g., South Africa, Spain)	○	○	○	○	○	○
Representation of minority racial, ethnic, religious, and linguistic groups in accord with their share of the population	○	○	○	○	○	○
Multi-member district - open-list proportional representation (e.g., Brazil, Sweden)	○	○	○	○	○	○
Multi-member district - single-transferable-vote (e.g., Ireland, Malta)	○	○	○	○	○	○
Mixed-member proportional (compensatory) system (e.g., Germany, New Zealand)	○	○	○	○	○	○
Mixed-member majoritarian (parallel) system (e.g., Japan, Mexico)	○	○	○	○	○	○
Another system. Please specify: _____ _____	○	○	○	○	○	○

(the order of these choices, except "Other," will be randomized)

Question 3. Of which country are you a citizen?	Country: (drop-down country choices)
Question 4. In which country do you normally live?	Country: (drop-down country choices)
Question 5. How old are you?	Age (in years): _____
Question 6. What is your sex?	Female ○ Male ○
Question 7. Are you a member of a racial, ethnic, religious or linguistic minority group?	No ○ Yes ○
Question 8. What do you consider to be your level of expertise on electoral systems and their consequences?	None ○ Modest ○ Moderate ○ High ○ Very high ○

Appendix F: Invitation Letter to Consultants' Survey

The APSA Task Force on **Electoral Rules and Democratic Governance**, established by APSA President G. Bingham Powell, Jr. is engaged in an examination of the role of political scientists in the configuring and refashioning of electoral rules in aspiring and established democracies. Led by Professor Mala Htun, the task force consists of APSA members who have spent their careers studying and advising on election system design in a broad array of cases and contexts.

As part of its work, the task force seeks to collect information on the advising experiences of academics. We have crafted a short web-based survey of twenty multiple choice questions which should not take more than a few minutes to complete. The survey and its resulting data are anonymous. Each form asks for your experiences working in a specific case. If you have worked in more than one country, and you have the time or inclination, please fill out a form for each case you have been involved in.

We value greatly your time in assisting us with this project and look forward to disseminating the knowledge which the task force produces next year.

With great thanks

Bing Powell (APSA President)

Mala Htun (Task Force Chair)

John Carey, Andrew Reynolds, Shaheen Mozaffar
(Group 5: Political Scientists and
Electoral Reform)

(Continued, next page)

Text of the Consultants' Survey

What is the name of the country in which you were involved in advising on electoral system design?

What was the year of this mission?

What organization contracted you and connected you to political actors in that country?

- · 1 = National Democratic Institute
- · 2 = European Union
- · 3 = United Nations
- · 4 = International Foundation for Electoral Systems
- · 5 = US Agency for International Development
- · 6 = Others
  - o African Union
  - o Center for the Study of Islam and Democracy
  - o Creative Associates
  - o International Republican Institute
  - o Management Systems International
  - o Open Society Institute
  - o Organization of American States
  - o Organisation of Economic Cooperation and Development
  - o Other (name: _____)
  - o US Department of State
  - o Westminster Foundation
  - o World Bank

How much time did you spend in country, in total, consulting and advising?

- · 1 = Did not visit country
- · 2 = Less than 1 week
- · 3 = 1–2 weeks
- · 4 = 2–4 weeks
- · 5 = 1–3 months
- · 6 = More than 3 months

How would you describe your knowledge of politics in the country prior to your involvement advising on electoral system design?

- · 1 = Minimal—I had no deep knowledge of politics in that country.
- · 2 = Substantial—I was not a 'country specialist,' but had solid background knowledge of its politics, and of the prominent actors and their interests and agendas.

- 3 = Extensive—I had conducted extensive academic research on the country prior to advising on an electoral system and/or had spend substantial time in the country studying or doing research.
- 4 = Native—I was born in the country, or lived there for much of my life.

With what sorts of actors did you interact in the course of your advising work? [Check all that apply]?
- High government officials (e.g., cabinet ministers, electoral commission members, members of parliament)
- Mid-level government officials (e.g., vice-ministers, electoral commission staff and technical officers)
- Party officials
- Representatives of civil society groups
- Representatives of opposition protest (or rebel/insurgent) groups
- Representatives/staff of international aid agencies or INGOs
- Labor and trade union representatives
- Academics
- Journalists
- Other (name: _____)

Which of the following best describes the content of the advice you (or the team with which you worked) provided?
- 1 = We presented technical information and analysis, but offered no negative or positive assessments with respect to the case at hand.
- 2 = We presented technical information and analysis on electoral system design, and we offered negative assessments of some design alternatives, but we did not explicitly endorse any specific design (or reform) alternative.
- 3 = We offered and explicitly endorsed specific recommendations for electoral system design (or reform).
- 4 = Other (Explain: _____)

If you chose either of the first two options in the previous question, then which of the following best describes your sense of the extent to which your advice affected the outcome of electoral system design (or reform) in the country?
- 1 = None of the recommendations I (or my team) offered were incorporated into the design (or reform) outcome.
- 2 = Some elements of the advice I (or my team) provided were incorporated in the electoral system design (or reform) outcome.
- 3 = The advice I (or my team) provided was accepted and implemented.
- 8 = The electoral reform process on which I advised has not yet been resolved, so it's too soon to tell.

- 9 = The episode on which I advised ended with no agreement on reform (or electoral system design).

Of the following types of electoral system design issues, which were on the agenda during your advising work (check all that apply)?

- Single-winner vs. PR vs. mixed-member system
- Size and structure of electoral districts
- Election formulas and/or thresholds
- Ballot structure (e.g., closed lists vs. personal preference voting)
- Process of nominating candidates and securing ballot access
- Voter registration and identification
- Poll watching and election monitoring
- Voting and vote-counting technologies
- Election dispute arbitration mechanisms
- Anti-fraud and anti-vote-buying measures
- Other (Explain: _____)

Which of the following describes the disposition toward the advice and analysis you offered among the political actors in the host country with whom you interacted?

- 1 = Lack of interest or engagement.
- 2 = Incapacity to understand the results from academic analysis of electoral systems, or its relevance to the questions of electoral system design (or reform) on the table.
- 3 = A reasoned reluctance, based on deep local knowledge, to accept the relevance of academic analysis to the matters of electoral system design (or reform) at stake in the country at that time.
- 4 = Interest motivated by partisan (or personal, sectarian, movement) concerns, and proclivity to select results from academic research that could be used to bolster positions motivated by other factors.
- 5 = Sincere interest and desire to use the results from academic research to improve the quality of representation through elections.
- 6 = Other (Explain: _____)

Please indicate the degree to which political representation more inclusive of women was explicitly considered (whether ultimately realized or not) as a goal of the electoral reforms on which you consulted?

- 1 = Not considered
- 2 = A consideration, but not a priority
- 3 = A priority, to be balanced against others
- 4 = The central goal

Please indicate the degree to which political representation inclusive of marginalized groups (e.g., racial, ethnic, linguistic, religious, etc.) other than women was explicitly considered (whether ultimately realized or not) as a goal of the electoral systems reforms on which you consulted?

- · The central goal
- · A priority, to be balanced against others
- · A consideration, but not a priority
- · Not considered

Please indicate the degree to which fostering stable governments was explicitly considered (whether ultimately realized or not) as a goal of the electoral systems reforms on which you consulted?

- · The central goal
- · A priority, to be balanced against others
- · A consideration, but not a priority
- · Not considered

Please indicate the degree to which increasing or decreasing the number of parties was explicitly considered (whether ultimately realized or not) as a goal of the electoral systems reforms on which you consulted?

- · The central goal
- · A priority, to be balanced against others
- · A consideration, but not a priority
- · Not considered

Please indicate the degree to which ensuring that each citizen's vote carries equal weight in determining election outcomes (e.g., questions of malapportionment and/or disproportionality) was explicitly considered (whether ultimately realized or not) as a goal of the electoral systems reforms on which you consulted?

- · The central goal
- · A priority, to be balanced against others
- · A consideration, but not a priority
- · Not considered

Please indicate the degree to which improving the accountability of representatives to voters was explicitly considered (whether ultimately realized or not) as a goal of the electoral systems reforms on which you consulted?

- · The central goal
- · A priority, to be balanced against others
- · A consideration, but not a priority
- · Not considered

Please indicate the degree to which fostering more cohesive political parties was explicitly considered (whether ultimately realized or not) as a goal of the electoral systems reforms on which you consulted

- · The central goal
- · A priority, to be balanced against others
- · A consideration, but not a priority
- · Not considered

Please rank order your own approach to your advising mission.

- · Raise awareness of election system options generally
- · Advocate for a specific system choice to be adopted
- · Advocate for a constrained range of choices
- · Focus on one or more specific technical issues
- · Focus on gender or minority issues of representation

What is your primary professional occupation:

- · Private consultant
- · Professional staff in a consulting firm (e.g., MSI, Creative Associates, IFES)
- · Professional staff in an NGO (e.g., IRI, NDI)
- · Professional staff in government agency (e.g., USAID, DFID, DOS, EU)
- · Academic
- · Other (please specify_____)

Please use the space below to offer any additional comments or reflections on your experience.

Notes

Chapter 1

1   See, for example, the Electoral Integrity Project, http://www.electoralintegrityproject.com/.

2   Lehoucq, "Electoral Fraud;" Birch, *Electoral Malpractice;* Norris, "The Concept of Electoral Integrity."

3   Drometer and Rincke, "The Impact of Ballot Access Restrictions." In addition, violations of electoral integrity produce racialized and gendered exclusion from politics. The discretionary use of poll taxes, literacy and residency requirements, and other policies by Southern states to disenfranchise African Americans is well known. (Keyssar 2000; Key 1949.) At the same time, supposedly neutral requirements to improve electoral integrity can have disparate effects: voter identification policies in New Mexico, for example, are far more likely to be applied to Hispanic men than to non-Hispanics and women. Civil rights groups have claimed that the growing adoption of voter ID laws in the United States disenfranchises minority voters and depresses turnout. On poll taxes, see Keyssar, *The Right to Vote,* Key, *Southern Politics in the State and Nation*; on effects of voter ID policies, see Atkeson et al., "A New Barrier to Participation," Ethan Bronner, "Legal Battles Erupt Over Tough Voter ID Laws," Silver, "Measuring the Effects of Voter ID Laws."

4   Birch, for example, explains why electoral malpractice occurs more often under SMD electoral rules than under PR in post-Communist countries. Others show how patterns of electoral fraud and malpractice reflect calculations about the relative benefits of such strategies as voter monitoring and the costs of getting to the polls, the presence of election observers, politicians' desire to deter supporters of their opponents from voting, and the intensity of political competition. Birch, "Electoral Systems and Electoral Misconduct." See also Ferree and Long, "Violating the Secret Ballot," on voter monitoring; Hyde, "The Observer Effect in International Politics," *The Pseudo-Democrats Dilemma,* Ichino and Schuendeln, "Deterring or Displacing Electoral Irregularities?" on observers; Collier and Vicente, "Violence, Bribery and Fraud," on politicians' desires; and Lehoucq, "Electoral Fraud," on political competition.

5   Powell, *Elections as Instruments of Democracy*.

6   A large group of scholars maintains, however, that it is often impossible for institutions to translate individual preferences into a collective outcome in a rational way, see for example, Riker, *Liberalism Against Populism*.

7   Quoted in Przeworski, Stokes, and Manin, "Elections and Representation," 46.

8   We thank Pippa Norris for making this point.

9   International IDEA, *International Electoral Standards*. Available at http://www.idea.int/publications/ies/.

10 For more analysis of electoral system goals, see, for example, Powell, *Contemporary Democracies* and *Elections as Instruments of Democracy*; Lijphart and Grofman, *Choosing an Electoral System*; Taagepera and Shugart, *Seats and Votes*; Horowitz, "Electoral Systems"; Norris, *Electoral Engineering*.

11 See, for example, Lijphart, *Patterns of Democracy*; Powell, *Elections as Instruments of Democracy*; Diamond, "Three Paradoxes of Democracy."

12 More recently, Carey and Hix have argued for an electoral "sweet spot" that combines the advantages of both SMD and PR systems: PR in small, multimember districts of 4–8 representatives. Carey and Hix, "The Electoral Sweet Spot."

13 Powell, *Elections as Instruments of Democracy*; Lijphart, *Patterns of Democracy*.

14 See, for example, Iversen and Soskice, "Electoral Institutions." On the other hand, these countries have regulatory policies that yield higher real prices for consumers while increasing the income of business and labor groups (see, for example, Chang et al., "Electoral Systems and Real Prices"; Chang et al., *Electoral Systems and the Balance of Consumer-Producer Power*). The net redistributive effects of PR versus SMD systems, therefore, are somewhat in doubt. See the essay by Carey and Hix in this report.

15 Our second survey shows that policy makers and actors on the ground similarly placed the highest value on the goals of government stability and the accountability of individual representatives. Survey respondents tended to consider other goals such as proportionality, the number of parties, the equal weighting of all votes, party cohesiveness, minority inclusion, and women's representation, but did not deem these a priority. Note that the survey reports political scientists' views of the goals of policy makers and other actors. It does not survey the policy makers directly. See essay by Carey and Hix.

16 Mill, *Consideration*.

17 Riker, "The Two-party System and Duverger's Law."

18 Duverger, *Political Parties*.

19 "Mechanical" refers to the strictly numerical processes that ideally execute electoral rules, whereas "behavioral" refers to the choices of individuals.

20 Rae, *The Political Consequences of Election Laws*.

21 Shugart, "Comparative Electoral Systems Research," 31.

22 By the macro-dimension, Shugart means the studies of the aggregate outcomes associated with various election rules, whereas the micro-dimension refers to the motivations and consequences of individual choices.

23 Cox, *Making Votes Count*.

24 Shugart, "Comparative Electoral Systems Research," 29–30. See also Riker, "The Two-party System and Duverger's Law," and Powell, "Political Representation in Comparative Politics."

25 Cox, *Making Votes Count*.

26 Moser and Scheiner, *Electoral Systems and Political Context*.

27 Matland and Studlar, "The Contagion of Women Candidates."

28 Ibid.

29 Moser and Scheiner, *Electoral Systems and Political Context*.

30 Htun and Jones, "Engendering the right to participate"; Jones, "Gender Quotas"; Matland, "Electoral Quotas: Frequency and Effectiveness."

31 Alesina et al., "Why Doesn't the US Have a European-Style Welfare System?"

32 This report refers primarily to the activities and experiences of US-based political scientists, with some exceptions.

33 Reynolds et al., *Electoral Systems Design*.

34 Norris, "Implementing Women's Representation."

35 Htun, "Intersectional Disadvantage and Political Inclusion."

36 See interview with Pippa Norris, Appendix B.

37 See the Case Studies in Appendix C.

38 Scott, "French Universalism in the Nineties."

39 See the interview with Andrew Reynolds, Appendix A.

40 Personal communication, September 1, 2012.

41 See the Case Studies in Appendix C.

42 Przeworski, "Institutions Matter?"

43 Benoit, "Electoral Laws as Political Consequences."

Chapter 2

1 See also Reynolds et al., *Electoral System Design*, 7ff.

2 Schedler, "The Menu of Manipulation."

3 Rae, *The Political Consequences of Election Laws*; Scheiner, "Does Electoral System Reform Work?"

4 Our behavioral mechanism has its roots in the psychological effect described by Duverger, *Political Parties*.

5 See, for example, Cox, *Making Votes Count*; Duverger, *Political Parties*; Lijphart, *Electoral Systems and Party Systems*; Taagepera and Shugart, *Seats and Votes*.

6 Taagepera and Shugart, *Seats and Votes*; Powell and Vanberg, "Election Laws."

7 To highlight the mechanical side of disproportionality, we emphasize here that our discussion is conditional on a given distribution of votes. See Moser and Scheiner (2012, Chapter 3) for a discussion of ways that strategic behavior may shape vote shares, and, in turn, disproportionality.

8 Shugart, "Comparative Electoral Systems Research"; Taagepera, *Predicting Party Sizes*.

9 To avoid attributing too much significance to parties that receive few votes or seats, political scientists typically measure the number of parties by means of the effective number of parties (ENP) index, which gives little weight to parties with few votes or seats.

10 Duverger, *Political Parties*.

11 In proportional representation systems, there is more than one seat, and parties are allocated a share of seats roughly identical to the share of votes they win.

12 By elites, we refer here to actors who play an influential role in elections through their allocation of resources such as campaign financing, endorsements, access to media, etc.

13 Cox, *Making Votes Count.*

14 Norris, *Electoral Engineering.*

15 Reed, "Structure and Behavior."

16 Ferree, *Framing the Race in South Africa.*

17 Cox, *Making Votes Count*, 76–80.

18 Horowitz, *Ethnic Groups in Conflict.*

19 Ferree et al., "Social Diversity"; Moser and Scheiner, *Electoral Systems and Political Context*; Moser et al., "Social Diversity."

20 Cox, *Making Votes Count*, 78.

21 Moser, "Electoral Systems"; Moser and Scheiner, *Electoral Systems and Political Context.*

22 Filippov et al., "Party Fragmentation"; Grofman et al., "Introduction: Evidence for Duverger's Law"; Moser and Scheiner, *Electoral Systems and Political Context.*

23 Horowitz and Long, "Does Ethnicity Reduce Strategic Voting?"

24 Hicken and Stoll, "Presidents and Parties."

25 Norris, *Electoral Engineering*; Rae, *The Political Consequences of Election Laws*; Riker, "The Two-party System and Duverger's Law."

26 Moser and Scheiner, *Electoral Systems and Political Context*, Chapter 4.

27 See, for example, Chhibber and Kollman, *The Formation of National Party Systems*; Cox, *Making Votes Count*; Hicken, *Building Party Systems in Developing Nations*. The flow of Figure 2.3 creates the impression that the district-level behavioral effect occurs prior to the coordination between voters and elites in different districts. However, political actors at the district level may choose to concentrate their support on particular parties based on the strength of those parties at the national level. We therefore include a feedback arrow from the national level back to the district level in Figure 2.3.

28 In reality, there are additional steps that we leave out of the figure, but which play a part in government formation: the mechanical translation of district votes into district seats, which, in turn, mechanically becomes aggregated into the number of parties in the national legislature. By and large, the number of parties winning seats is simply a mechanical extension of the number of parties winning votes. As we have highlighted, contextual factors shape the distribution of votes in each district and the extent to which all districts share the same parties, but only mechanical effects transform these distributions of votes into seats. In short, as we move beyond the number of electoral parties to the formation of the national legislature, there are no other behavioral links in the causal chain, thus providing little opportunity for additional contextual factors to shape that formation.

29 Formally, the head of state designates the potential prime minister (formateur), who chooses a cabinet. In some parliamentary systems, the new PM and cabinet face a formal investiture vote. In others, they may not have to do so unless required by parliament (Gallagher et al., *Representative Government in Modern Europe*).

30 Strøm, *Minority Government.*

31 Mitchell and Nyblade, "Government Formation and Cabinet Type."

32 Martin and Stevenson, "Government Formation in Parliamentary Democracies."

33 This is also the case in legislative elections with a single national district like Israel, South Africa, and the Netherlands.

34 We are taking government formation to mean, simply, the selection of the president. The executive branch involves more than the president, however—the vice president, the cabinet, etc. The selection of these individuals is not a mechanical function of the executive election, but rather is at the discretion of elite-level decision makers and is therefore behavioral.

35 King et al., "A Unified Model of Cabinet Dissolution"; Warwick, *Government Survival in Parliamentary Democracies*; Laver, "Government Termination."

36 However, a growing literature analyzes the substantial number of Latin American presidents since the mid-1980s whose terms were shortened by the use of impeachment and "presidential disability" within the rules and without changing the regime (Helmke, *Institutions on the Edge*; Perez-Linan, *Presidential Impeachment*; Valenzuela, "Latin American Presidencies"). To the extent that these kinds of actions increase, we would have to amend our classification of stability in presidential regimes as mechanical.

37 Powell, *Elections as Instruments of Democracy.*

38 Ibid.

39 Similarly, divided government, whereby a different party controls each branch of a bicameral legislature, can permit the government to blame the party controlling the opposing branch for many failures.

40 Strøm, *Minority Government.*

41 See Duch and Stevenson, *The Economic Vote.*

42 Carey, *Legislative Voting and Accountability.*

43 Huber and Powell, "Congruence"; Cox, *Making Votes Count*, Chapter 12; Powell, *Elections as Instruments of Democracy.*

44 Downs, *An Economic Theory of Democracy*.

45 Laver and Schofield, *Multiparty Government*; Mitchell and Nyblade, "Government Formation."

46 Powell, *Elections as Instruments of Democracy*; McDonald et al., "What Are Elections For?"

47 Blais and Bodet, "Does Proportional Representation"; Powell, "The Ideological Congruence Controversy."

48 Powell, "Party Polarization."

49 McGillivray, *Privileging Industry*.

50 Downs, *An Economic Theory of Democracy*.

51 A separate dimension of geographic representational advantage may emerge from deliberate manipulation of the patterns of representation mechanically following from the election rules, especially in malapportioned or gerrymandered smaller districts. Whereas in most of our discussion we have taken the nature of the election rules as given, the phenomena of malapportionment and gerrymandering remind us that the rules themselves may be behaviorally manipulated to generate their mechanical consequences.

Chapter 3

1 Reynolds, "Reserved Seats in National Legislatures"; Schwindt-Bayer and Mishler, "An Integrated Model of Women's Representation."

2 Beckwith and Cowell-Meyers, "Sheer Numbers"; Cameron et al., "Do Majority-Minority Districts"; Celis et al., "Rethinking Women's Substantive Representation."

3 Reynolds, *Designing Democracy in a Dangerous World*, 89.

4 Matland and Studlar, "The Contagion of Women Candidates," 709.

5 Iversen and Rosenbluth, "Work and Power," and *Women, Work, and Politics*.

6 See also Bjarnegård, *Gender, Informal Institutions*.

7 Matland and Studlar, "The Contagion of Women Candidates."

8 Lovenduski and Norris, *Gender and Party Politics*; Meier, "The Mutual Contagion Effect."

9 Jones, "Gender Quotas"; Schwindt-Bayer, "Making Quotas Work."

10 Lijphart, "Constitutional Choices for New Democracies"; Norris, *Electoral Engineering*.

11 Matland, "Women's Legislative Representation."

12 Moser and Scheiner, *Electoral Systems and Political Context*.

13 Moser, "The Effects of Electoral Systems."

14 Reynolds, "Electoral Democratization in Nepal."

15 Matland, "Institutional Variables."

16 Schwindt-Bayer et al., "Candidate Gender."

17 Moser and Scheiner, *Electoral Systems and Political Context*.

18 Barkan, "Elections in Agrarian Societies"; Moser 2008.

19 Moser, "Electoral Systems."

20 Reynolds, *Designing Democracy in a Dangerous World*.

21 Krook, *Quotas for Women in Politics*.

22 Celis et al., "The Rise of Gender Quota Laws."

23 Freidenvall et al., "The Nordic Countries."

24 Htun and Jones, "Engendering the Right to Participate"; Krook et al., "Military Invasion and Women's Political Representation"; Longman, "Rwanda."

25 Bauer and Britton, "Women in African Parliaments"; Waylen, *Engendering Transitions*.

26 Kolinsky, "Political Participation and Parliamentary Careers"; Lovenduski and Norris, *Gender and Party Politics*; Matland and Studlar, "The Contagion of Women Candidates"; Meier, "The Mutual Contagion Effect."

27 Baldez, "Elected Bodies"; Fréchette et al., "Incumbents' Interests"; Krook, "Gender and Political Institutions."

28 Hughes et al., "Transnational Women's Activism."

29 Bauer and Britton, "Women in African Parliaments"; Bush, "International Politics"; Dahlerup, *Women, Quotas, and Politics*; Towns, *Women and States*.

30 Brownlee et al., *The Arab Spring*.

31 Krook and O'Brien, "The Politics of Group Representation."

32 Reynolds, "Reserved Seats in National Legislatures"; Van Cott, "Building Inclusive Democracies."

33 Bird, "The Political Representation"; Htun, "Is Gender like Ethnicity?"

34 Alionescu, "Parliamentary Representation"; Geddis, "A Dual Track Democracy?"; Reynolds, "Reserved Seats in National Legislatures."

35 Reynolds, "Reserved Seats in National Legislatures"; Van Cott, "Building Inclusive Democracies".

36 Bird, "The Political Representation."

37 Geddis, "A Dual Track Democracy?"; Htun, "Is Gender like Ethnicity?"

38 Rigby, "Lebanon"; Hartzell and Hoddie, "Institutionalizing Peace."

39 Htun "Is Gender like Ethnicity?"

40 Holmsten et al., "Do Ethnic Parties Exclude Women?"

41 Jones, "Gender Quotas"; Krook, *Quotas for Women in Politics*.

42 Krook and O'Brien, "The Politics of Group Representation."

43 Krook, "Minorities in Electoral Politics."

44 Strolovitch, "Do Interest Groups Represent the Disadvantaged?"

45 Hughes, "Intersectionality"; see also Htun and Ossa, "Political Inclusion of Marginalized Groups."

46 Paxton and Hughes, *Women, Politics and Power*.

Chapter 4

1 Some US states offer exceptions: the recently adopted rules in California and those formerly used in Louisiana are two-round systems in which a party may have more than one candidate in the first round. Despite terminology used in both states, this round is not a "primary," because it is possible for the second round (the "general") also to have two candidates from the same party. Hence these systems allow for a ballot structure that offers intraparty choice in a decisive round of voting, despite single-seat districts.

2 On candidate selection rules, see Hazan and Rahat, *Democracy without Parties*; on promotion and discipline within the ranks of a parliamentary party, see Benedetto and Hix, "The Rejected, the Ejected, and the Dejected."

3 Samuels and Shugart, *Presidents, Parties, and Prime Ministers*.

4 Simplifying from Carey and Shugart "Incentives to Cultivate a Personal Vote."

5 Ibid.

6 Ibid.

7 See also Shugart, "Comparative Electoral Systems Research."

8 Grofman et al., *Elections in Japan, Korea and Taiwan under the Single Non-Transferable Vote*.

9 See the chapters in Grofman et al., *Elections in Japan, Korea and Taiwan*, as well as the references to the literature contained therein.

10 The most important distinctions come from the incentives of parties, as collective actors, to manage their internal competition under STV and especially SNTV. Under open lists, by contrast, parties can tolerate laissez faire competition among their candidates See Bergman, Shugart and Watt, "Patterns of Intra-Party Competition in Open-List and SNTV Systems" 2013; similar points are also made by Johnson and Hoyo, "Beyond Personal Vote Incentives," and Swindle, "The Supply and Demand of the Personal Vote." That is, there is a greater alignment of individual and collective incentives under open lists than under the other two systems, because any candidate preference vote accrues to the party as a whole. On the other hand, precisely because of the more free-for-all competition in open lists, parties may face greater challenges disciplining their rank and file. These possible effects remain under-explored in the literature.

11 This section draws substantially on Audrey André, Sam Depauw, and Matthew S. Shugart, "The Effect of Electoral Institutions on Legislative Behavior." Shugart is grateful to André and Depauw for agreeing to have some of this material reproduced here.

12 Cain et al., *The Personal Vote*.

13 Carey, *Legislative Voting and Accountability*.

14 Mitchell, "Voters and their Representatives."

15 Curtice and Shively, "Who Represents Us Best?"

16 Carey, *Legislative Voting and Accountability*; Samuels, "Incentives to Cultivate a Party Vote"; Shugart et al., "Looking for Locals."

17 Samuels, "Incentives to Cultivate a Party Vote"; Shugart et al., "Looking for Locals"; Weßels, "Whom to Represent?"

18 Norris, "Ballot Structures and Legislative Behavior."

19 Strøm, "Rules, Reasons and Routines," 162.

20 André and Depauw, "District Magnitude."

21 Morgenstern and Vázquez-D'Elía, "Electoral Laws."

22 Carey and Shugart, "Incentives to Cultivate a Personal Vote," 430; Mitchell, "Voters and their Representatives"; André and Depauw, "District Magnitude."

23 Examples include involvement in casework or other contact with constituents. See Bowler and Farrell, "Legislator Shirking and Voter Monitoring;" Farrell and Scully, *Representing Europe's Citizens?* On frequent travel to the district see Ingall and Crisp, "Determinants of Home Style;" on sponsoring bills of local or other particularistic interest, see Crisp et al., "Vote-Seeking Incentives and Legislative Representation in Six Presidential Democracies;" on dissenting on legislative voting, see, for example, Carey, "Competing Principles, Political Institutions, and Party Unity in Legislative Voting."

24 Crisp, "Incentives in Mixed-Member Electoral Systems."

25 Swindle, "The Supply and Demand of the Personal Vote."

26 See Bowler, "Parties in Legislature."

27 Johnson and Hoyo, "Beyond Personal Vote Incentives"; Bergman et al., "Patterns of Intra-Party Competition "

28 Ramseyer and Rosenbluth, *Japan's Political Marketplace*; Carey and Shugart, "Incentives to Cultivate a Personal Vote"; Ames, "Electoral Rules," and "Electoral Strategy"; Samuels, "Incentives to Cultivate a Party Vote."

29 Reed, "Democracy and the Personal Vote"; Golden and Chang, "Competitive Corruption"; Chang and Golden, "Electoral Systems."

30 Bawn and Thies, "A Comparative Theory of Electoral Incentives"; Kunicova and Rose-Ackerman, "Electoral Rules."

Chapter 5

1   Iversen and Soskice, "Electoral Institutions," "Distribution and Redistribution," and "Real Exchange Rates and Competitiveness"; Cusack et al., "Economic Interests," and "Coevolution"; Rogowski and Kayser, "Majoritarian Electoral Systems"; Chang et al., "Electoral Systems and Real Prices"; Linzer and Rogowski, "Lower Prices"; Chang et al., *Electoral Systems and the Balance of Consumer-Producer Power*; Persson and Tabellini, "The Size and Scope of Government," and *The Economic Effects of Constitutions*; Persson et al., "Electoral Rules." See also Vernby, "Strikes Are More Common in Countries with Majoritarian Electoral Systems," which relies on vote-elasticity, a la Rogowski et al. to explain different motivations for union behavior under SMD versus PR.

2   The contrast is particularly stark between Iversen and Soskice's 2006 analysis of reduction in Gini coefficients (income inequality) from before to after taxes and government transfers, and Chang, Kayser, and Rogowski's 2008 analysis of price and exchange rate ratios. Iverson and Soskice, "Electoral Institutions and the Politics of Coalitions," Chang, Kayser, and Rogowski, "Electoral Systems and Real Prices." In subsequent work, Iverson and Soskice broaden their analysis of redistribution to include regulatory policies on wage compression, education, and vocational training—all of which can be expected to affect relative price levels within an economy. Iverson and Soskice, "Distribution and Redistribution."

3   Rogowski and Kayser, "Majoritarian Electoral Systems and Consumer Power."

4   Cf. Chang et al., *Electoral Systems and the Balance of Consumer-Producer Power*.

5   Rogowski et al. divide citizens into producers and consumers. Producers are those who derive their livelihoods from industries in which production costs and market positions, including the labor market, are shaped by government regulatory policies. Consumers are all others. This model holds that producers influence politicians with both votes and money, whereas consumers wield only votes. Producers, therefore, may always exercise leverage above their population share of the electorate, but the *relative* influence of consumers to producers corresponds to the relative influence of each marginal vote on partisan fortunes. Higher vote-seat elasticity, therefore, increases the influence of consumers' preferences on policy. This argument hinges on the proposition that vote-seat elasticity is systematically higher in SMD than in PR systems. See Chang et al., *Electoral Systems and the Balance of Consumer-Producer Power*, 31.

6   Chang et al., "Electoral Systems and Real Prices"; Chang et al., *Electoral Systems and the Balance of Consumer-Producer Power*.

7   Persson and Tabellini, "The Size and Scope of Government," and *The Economic Effects of Constitutions*.

8   Cf. Blume et al., "The Economic Effects of Constitutions."

9   Persson et al., "Electoral Rules."

10 Iversen and Soskice, "Electoral Institutions."

11 Persson et al., "Electoral Rules."

12 Ibid.

13 Huber and Powell, "Congruence"; Powell and Vanberg "Election Laws, Disproportionality, and Median Correspondence."

14 Iversen and Soskice, "Real Exchange Rates and Competitiveness."

15 For example, Birchfield and Crepaz, "The Impact of Constitutional Structures"; Crepaz, "Inclusion versus Exclusion"; Verardi, "Electoral Systems and Income Inequalities"; Kang and Powell, "Representation and Policy Responsiveness."

16 Alesina et al., "Why Doesn't the US Have a European-Style Welfare System?"

17 Amat and Wibbels, "Electoral Incentives."

18   Cusack et al., "Electoral Incentives," and "Coevolution of Capitalism."

19   Chang, "Electoral Incentives and Budgetary Spending"; Evans, "A Protectionist Bias in Majoritarian Politics"; Kono, "Market Structure"; Kim, "Making or Breaking a Deal"; Rickard, "Democratic Differences."

20   Funk and Gathmann, "How Do Electoral Systems Affect Fiscal Policy?"

21   Gagliarducci et al., "Electoral Rules."

22   For example, Evans, "A Protectionist Bias in Majoritarian Politics"; Roelfsema, "Political Institutions and Trade Protection"; Willmann, "Why Legislators Are Protectionists." Kono suggests an interaction effect, in that small geographical constituencies (for instance, SMDs) produce more protectionism when intraindustry trade is high; Kono, "Market Structure, Electoral Institutions, and Trade Policy."

23   Kim, "Making or Breaking a Deal."

24   Vernby, "Strikes Are More Common."

25   Rickard, "A Non-Tariff Protectionist Bias," and "Electoral Systems."

26   Rickard, "Democratic Differences."

27   McGillivray, "Party Discipline as a Determinant."

28   Neugart, "Unemployment Insurance."

29   Dickson, "Seat-Vote Curves."

30   Park and Jensen, "Electoral Competition."

31   McGillivray, "Redistributive Politics." She also finds that stock price dispersion responds more quickly to electoral shifts, and to exogenous economic shocks, under SMD than PR systems.

32   Rickard, "Strategic Targeting."

33   Carey and Shugart, "Incentives to Cultivate a Personal Vote."

34   Crisp et al., "Vote-Seeking Incentives"; Hankla, "Party Strength and International Trade."

35   Bagashka, "The Personal Vote and Economic Reform."

36   Naoi and Krauss, "Who Lobbies Whom?"

37   Ehrlich, "Access to Protection."

38   Franchino and Mainenti, "Electoral Institutions."

39   Golden and Picci, "Pork-Barrel Politics in Postwar Italy, 1953–94."

40   Chang and Golden, "Electoral Systems."

41   For example, Grilli et al., "Political and Monetary Institutions"; Stein et al., "Institutional Arrangements and Fiscal Performance"; Persson and Tabellini, "The Size and Scope of Government"; Persson, "Do Political Institutions Shape Economic Policy?"; Scartascini and Crain, "The Size and Composition of Government Spending"; Woo, "Economic, Political, and Institutional Determinants"; Bawn and Rosenbluth, "Short versus Long Coalitions"; Fabrizio and Mody, "Can Budget Institutions Counteract Political Indiscipline?"; Persson et al., "Electoral Rules"; Blume et al., "The Economic Effects of Constitutions."

42   Milesi-Ferretti et al., "Electoral Systems and Public Spending."

43   Akitoby and Stratmann, "Fiscal Policy and Financial Markets."

44   Ames, "Electoral Rules."

45   Hallerberg and Marier, "Executive Authority."

46   Edwards and Thames, "District Magnitude."

47   Thames and Edwards, "Differentiating Mixed Member Electoral Systems."

48   Knutsen, "Which Democracies Prosper?"

49   Béjar and Mukherjee, "Electoral Institutions."

50   Bortolotti and Pinotti, "Delayed Privatization."

51   Bernhard and Leblang, "Democratic Institutions"; Eichengreen and Leblang, "Exchange Rates and Cohesion."

52   Wright, "Aid Effectiveness and the Politics of Personalism."

Chapter 6

1   Dahl, *Polyarchy*, 1.

2   Beitz, *Political Equality*.

3   Lublin, *The Paradox of Representation*.

4   Pettit, *Republicanism*.

5   Pogge, "Self-constituting Constituencies."

6   Rehfeld, *The Concept of Constituency*.

7   Przeworski et al., *Democracy, Accountability, and Representation*; Mansbridge, "A 'Selection Model' of Political Representation."

8   Green, *The Eyes of the People*, 13.

9   McCormick, *Machiavellian Democracy*.

10 Hansen, *The Athenian Democracy in the Age of Demosthenes*, 223.

Chapter 7

1   The survey of electoral reform consultants was conducted in December 2011; the APSA-wide survey was conducted in May 2012.

2   Definitions of all technical terms may be found in the Glossary.

3   Of APSA's 13,630 registered members as of April 2012, 3,000 were randomly selected and invited to take part in the online survey. Four follow-up messages were sent to non-respondents. Of the 3,000, 703 (23%) took at least part of the survey and 611 (20%) completed it.

4   For example, Rae, *The Political Consequences of Election Laws*; Taagepera and Shugart, *Seats and Votes*; Lijphart, *Electoral Systems and Party Systems*; Powell, *Elections as Instruments of Democracy*; Shugart and Wattenberg, *Mixed-Member Systems*.

5   C. Lijphart, *Electoral Systems and Party Systems*.

6   Taagepera and Shugart, *Seats and Votes*; Gallagher, "Proportionality"; Lijphart, *Electoral Systems and Party Systems*; Powell, *Elections as Instruments of Democracy*.

7   For example, Persson and Tabelini, *The Economic Effects of Constitutions*; Shugart and Wattenberg, *Mixed-Member Systems*.

8   Banducci and Karp, "Perceptions of Fairness"; Htun, "Is Gender like Ethnicity?"

9   Htun and Jones, "Engendering"; Jones, "Gender Quotas."

10 Htun, "Women, Political Parties and Electoral Systems in Latin America"; Krook and Moser, this report; Schmidt, "The Implementation of Gender Quotas in Peru"; Rule and Shugart, "The Preference Vote"; Schwindt-Bayer, "Making quotas work"; Matland, "Electoral Quotas: frequency and effectiveness"; Ellis Valdini, "Electoral institutions and the manifestation of bias."

11 Mommsen, *Max Weber and German Politics, 1890–1920*. It bears noting that the electoral system for the Reichstag was a result of compromise, as are almost all matters of institutional design in practice, and that the highly proportional list-PR system was neither Preuss's nor Weber's sole handiwork.

12 By way of full disclosure, some members of this task force, including the authors of this report, have been active in this area.

13 Bear in mind, our survey only asked academics who served as consultants for their assessments of reformers' goals. It is entirely possible that the assessments are affected by the academics' own priorities.

14 Political scientists' self-assessments of audience interest and comprehension should, of course, be subject to a standard deflator, as any first-year comparative politics student can attest—and as many can demonstrate.

15 Shugart and Wattenberg, *Mixed-Member Systems*.

Appendix A

1   According to the IFES report on Egypt's 2011 elections, "The list with the smallest Coefficient must elevate a worker/farmer from its list to ensure that the occupational quota is upheld. Because the lists no longer have to start with a worker/farmer candidate at the top, the worker/farmer seats are likely to be filled by the last (smallest) parties winning seats in the PR districts." Page 9.

Appendix B

1   Michelle Tolson, "Mongolian Women's Hard-Won Victory."

2   See http://www.electoralintegrityproject.com.

Appendix C

1   http://themonkeycage.org/2013/01/25/2013-jordan-post-election-report-and-the-winner-isthe-king/.

2   See John M. Carey and Simon Hix, "The Electoral Sweet Spot."